DUTCH NEW YORK

BOOKS BY MISS SINGLETON

TURRETS, TOWERS, AND TEMPLES. Great Buildings of the World Described by Great Writers.

GREAT PICTURES. Described by Great Writers.

WONDERS OF NATURE. Described by Great Writers.

ROMANTIC CASTLES AND PALACES. Described by Great Writers.

FAMOUS PAINTINGS. Described by Great Writers.

HISTORIC BUILDINGS. Described by Great Writers.

FAMOUS WOMEN. Described by Great Writers.

GREAT PORTRAITS. Described by Great Writers.

HISTORIC BUILDINGS OF AMERICA. Described by Great Writers.

HISTORIC LANDMARKS OF AMERICA. Described by Great Writers.

HOLLAND. Described by Great Writers.

PARIS. Described by Great Writers.

LONDON. Described by Great Writers.

RUSSIA. Described by Great Writers.

JAPAN. Described by Great Writers.

VENICE. Described by Great Writers.

ROME. Described by Great Writers.

A GUIDE TO THE OPERA.

LOVE IN LITERATURE AND ART.

THE GOLDEN ROD FAIRY BOOK.

THE WILD FLOWER FAIRY BOOK.

GERMANY. Described by Great Writers.

SWITZERLAND. Described by Great Writers.

GREAT RIVERS OF THE WORLD. Described by Great Writers.

DUTCH NEW YORK. Manners and Customs of New Amsterdam in the Seventeenth Century.

CORNELIS STEENWYCK

Mayor of New York, with view of New Amsterdam, painted by Jan van Goosen about 1668. Owned by the New York Historical Society.

DUTCH NEW YORK

BY

ESTHER SINGLETON

AUTHOR OF "DUTCH AND FLEMISH FURNITURE"
"HOLLAND," "SOCIAL NEW YORK UNDER
THE GEORGES," ETC.

WITH NUMEROUS ILLUSTRATIONS

NEW YORK
DODD, MEAD AND COMPANY
1909

> ## *Notice*
>
> In many older books, foxing (or discoloration) occurs and, in some instances, print lightens with wear and age. Reprinted books, such as this, often duplicate these flaws, notwithstanding efforts to reduce or eliminate them. The pages of this reprint have been digitally enhanced and, where possible, the flaws eliminated in order to provide clarity of content and a pleasant reading experience.

Dutch New York

Copyright © 1909, by Dodd, Mead and Company

Originally published:
The University Press
Cambridge, U.S.A.
1909

Reprinted by:

Janaway Publishing, Inc.
732 Kelsey Ct.
Santa Maria, California 93454
(805) 925-1038
www.JanawayGenealogy.com

2016

ISBN: 978-1-59641-385-6

Made in the United States of America

PREFACE

NUMEROUS as are the books that have been written about this Metropolis of the Western Hemisphere, I venture to hope that there is room for one more, especially one that deals with the life, hardships, struggles, manners, customs, joys, sorrows, beliefs, superstitions, and worldly possessions of the first white settlers in New Netherland. In the following pages I have tried to reproduce the daily life of the Dutch burgher in New Amsterdam, rising with him in the morning; describing his house and garden or farm, his furniture, and his costume; accompanying him through the day to his morning prayers, his breakfast, his counting-house, his midday meal, his afternoon recreation, his evening meal and devotions; accompanying him also to church and to the tavern; describing his family — christenings, courtships, weddings, and funerals, as well as the great festivals of the year — Saint Nicholas' Eve, New Year's Day, Twelfth Night, Shrovetide, May Day, Whitsuntide, Saint Martin's Eve, the *Kermis,* and other merry-making. I have also described his wife's activities in the household, her cleaning, marketing, and cooking. I have also fully depicted the condition of domestic servitude and schooling in the colony. I have not devoted much space to identifying old landmarks, or describing the courses of the original streets and canals, or the sites of many of the homes mentioned in the text. This has been done more or less exhaustively by others who are well versed in such antiquarian lore. For my purpose it is sufficient that the reader should know that during the period that I treat of Dutch life here was concentrated in a small area on Manhattan Island below Trinity Church, the principal points of interest of which were the Fort, including the Church and windmill, the Strand, and the City Tavern at the Ferry.

The writer who tries to reconstitute the life of the original Dutch settlers in New York is seriously handicapped by the almost ineradicable impression left in the mind of the casual reader by the brilliant author of *Knickerbocker's History of New York*, who belabored the Dutch Governors and their charges with a bludgeon of ridicule. The effect of that entertaining work is that it is hard to convince anyone but a student of the old days that the Dutchman is worthy of anything more than derision, or a half-contemptuous and languid interest at most. Even some of those who claim descent from the Dutch of the Seventeenth Century speak of the manners and customs of their forefathers half apologetically. I hope that a perusal of the following pages will satisfy the candid reader that so far from the average Dutchman in New Amsterdam being an uncivilized boor, he compared very favorably, in all that civilization means, with the contemporary middle classes of England, France, or any other European country. The Dutchman here was a transplanted Dutchman, pure and simple. He did not come into a foreign community like an immigrant of the present day and have to adjust himself to alien speech and customs; he was transplanted with his family to a tract of land on the edge of a big waterway where he could dig his canals and live under physical conditions which did not differ materially from those he had left. He spoke no language but his own, and he was ruled in accordance with the laws of the States-General, occasionally slightly modified to suit the convenience of a monopolistic trading-company. His bodily and spiritual needs were ministered to by Dutch professional men who had received their diplomas in Holland and were authorized to practice here by the Directors of the West India Company. He brought with him Dutch furniture, and the Company's stores supplied him with Dutch manufactures of clothing, implements, and utensils. His houses and barns were built and his table was supplied by Dutch masons, bricklayers, carpenters, glaziers, millers, brewers, and bakers. Not satisfied with mere comfort, his rooms were adorned with the productions of the contemporary Dutch Great and Little Masters. His gardens were as bright with tulips and other flowers as those of his brother in Amsterdam; his table was more plentifully supplied with game, fish, poultry, fruits, and vegetables; and he very soon could afford the porcelains and lacquers that were pouring into Holland by way of the Spice Islands, and he soon found a way to help himself direct to the products of Oriental looms and lathes by piratical measures. Silver plate adorned his sideboard, and Delft and porcelain brightened the shelves and tops of his cabinets, brackets, and cornices.

When fully dressed in his silks, satins, velvets, and rich cloths, an idea of his appearance may be best obtained from contemporary Dutch portraits by Hals, Bol, Van der Helst, Ravesteyn, and Rembrandt. His wife and daughters at christenings, betrothals, weddings, and other festivities were resplendent in jeweled headgear (of their native fashions), ear-rings, brooches, necklaces, *châtelaines,* breast-hooks, buttons, chains, watches, rings, laces, furs, silks, satins, fans, and fine linen.

The burghers lived well at home and entertained one another royally in the taverns. There is a record of at least one dinner shared among cronies at the City Tavern at $80 a cover. We have records of other dinners of which the cost is not given. Fortunately for us, the bill of this one was disputed and so the landlord went to court. Tavern revelry in the town called forth many a reproving ordinance, and many a riotous gang of night-hawks was haled into court by the *Schout*. Personal violence and bloodshed in consequence of excessive indulgence was not infrequent among the upper classes and was very common among the lower orders. Drunkenness was scarcely a reproach. On one occasion it was at least a blessing in disguise, namely, when at the Governor's instigation a collection was taken up from half-seas-over wedding-guests which was sufficient to start the building of the church of the Fort. We must conclude that New Amsterdam was indeed a thirsty town, when in 1646 we learn that one in every four of its inhabitants was engaged in the business of selling strong liquor!

It is noticeable that a number of the fair sex in New Amsterdam were tavern-keepers and tapsters.

Valiant as the Dutch were as toss-pots, they were probably matched by the English rake-hells, one of whom appears as early as 1672. Of him it is chronicled:

Another disaster about 12 dayes since befell a young man in this towne, by name one Mr. Wright, a one-eyed man and a muff-maker by trade, who drinking hard upon rum one evening, with some friends, begann a health of a whole pint at a draught, which he had noe sooner done but downe hee fell and never rose more, which prodigy may teach us all to have a care how wee drink, in imitation of that good old lesson, *Fœlix quem faciunt*, etc.

Shrovetide seems to have been a week in which the license of the Italian Carnival was matched here. Excise privileges were largely extended during this festival, to the great scandal of the sober-minded. Thus, in 1655:

Fiscal makes known to the Court that apparently some of the Company's soldiers and servants will ask the Court for permission to tap, and as they will thereby be led into debauchery and many irregularities will occur, he requests the Court will be pleased not to grant their application.

Shrovetide was the Saturnalia of the lower classes, during which they indulged in such gentle and joyous pastimes as all kinds of racing, and ball-games in the streets, Pulling the Goose, etc., even in defiance of stringent ordinances. The youth of the town were sadly led astray by their turbulent elders, and some of their choice indulgences consisted of cutting *koeckies*, or stakes, out of the fences for bonfires and "halloing after Indians in Pearl Street," which pleasures were strictly prohibited in 1660.

The chief pleasures of the women seem to have consisted in gossip and slander. The good wives of the day, like their English sisters, abused one another in the purest Billingsgate. Innumerable are the cases that come into court in which one woman complains of defamation of character by another. In nine cases out of ten the affair is settled by the offender declaring that she knows nothing of the complainant but what is virtuous and honorable, and begging pardon of God, the complainant, and the honorable Court.

In the following pages considerations of space have deterred me from describing the military establishment here and its regulation; or the civic guards, the watch, and the police; or the courts and the administration of justice. The question of crimes and punishment, however, must not be entirely ignored.

It would seem that the most serious misdemeanor of which a man could be guilty was speaking ill of those in authority. The penalties inflicted for this were far more severe than those for felonious assault; for instance, in 1642, the penalty for drawing a knife and wounding was fifty florins or three months' labor in chains with the negroes. Five years later the penalty was raised to three hundred guilders. This was small in comparison with the punishment inflicted for *lèse-majesté* in 1660, when Walewyn van der Veen said in Allard Anthony's hearing that the magistrates were only fools and simpletons. He was condemned to repair the injury honorably and profitably, — honorably, by praying with uncovered head pardon of God and Justice; profitably, with a fine of twelve hundred guilders. Walewyn preferred imprisonment.

In 1638, it was ordered that court should be held every Thursday, and that persons guilty of adultery, perjury, calumny, theft, and other immoralities should be punished. In 1643, the burgher guard was regulated and fines were provided for taking the name of God in vain, for traducing a comrade, for being drunk on guard, for discharging a gun without orders after daybreak, and for being absent without leave.

Various punishments were inflicted for various crimes. Sometimes different punishments were inflicted for the same crime. For example, for drawing a knife in 1638, Gysbert van Beyerland was sentenced to be ducked three times from the yard-arm of the *Hope,* and receive three blows from each of the crew. The soldiers at the Fort were very frequently unruly and turbulent. Desertion was common. Insubordination, absence from duty, drunkenness on parade, fighting in barracks, street brawling, and wounding inoffensive citizens were also frequent offenses that were severely dealt with by the authorities. "Riding the Wooden Horse" was the usual punishment for minor offenses. Running the Gauntlet was a punishment sometimes inflicted for a serious crime. The old *lex talionis* seems to have been recognized here to some extent. For example, in 1665, Jan Smedes's horse ran over and killed Frans van Hooghten's child. The Schout demanded that the horse be forfeited, and the parent be satisfied. A few days later Van Hooghten made the strange request that Jan be ordered "to keep out of his sight, and not to resort to the Manhathans so as to prevent mischief." The order was issued.

It would appear that "the terrible avengers of the majesty of law" did not themselves always lead blameless lives, judging from a letter written at the Fort in 1673:

Lastly for our city news, lett this satisfy: that t' other day wee had like to have lost our hangman, Ben Johnson, for hee being taken in diverse thefts and robberyes convicted and found guilty, scap'd his neck through want of another hangman to truss him up, soe that all the punishment that hee receiv'd for his 3 yeares roguery in thieving and stealing (which was never found out till now) was only thirty-nine stripes at the whipping-post, loss of an ear and banishment.

Torture was resorted to on more than one occasion in the case of accused persons who refused to confess. On one occasion a sailor whose crime consisted in stealing a table-cloth from a tavern was put on the rack before he confessed.

Capital crimes were variously punished. In 1638, Jan Gysbertsen for the murder of Gerrit Jansen was sentenced to be punished by the sword until he is dead, his property and wages confiscated for the benefit of the widow (one half), the Company (one quarter), and the public prosecutor (one fourth). In 1666, Engel Hendricx, " having turned out al motherly affection, buried [her child] with sods uppon the boddy in a open field to the mercy of al wild beasts, by which it evidently appeares she intended throw those means to murther the same." She was hanged.

After a careful study of the public and private life of the Seventeenth Century Dutchman, we must come to the conclusion that he was by no means a character to be dismissed with a jest or a sneer. He was a faithful husband and an affectionate father. He was generally devout, jovial, industrious, thrifty, but luxurious in his tastes. He was brave; but in his dealings with the aborigines and rival settlers he was oppressive, treacherous, and cruel. Although the term "honest Dutchman" has passed into a proverb, his business rectitude must remain a debatable question. It is not too much to say that every householder in New Amsterdam was a merchant, or a shop-keeper. Even the clergy, doctors, and schoolmasters engaged in trade. It is evident from the Court Records that sharp practices of all kinds were indulged in almost universally in the constant barter of which the great mass of the local trade consisted. The collection of petty accounts and the settlement of trade disputes took up by far the greatest amount of the time of the lower court. The Dutchmen in Fatherland had a bad reputation in the writings of their fellow-countrymen, particularly on account of their readiness to go bankrupt, offering their creditors as little as three or

PREFACE

four per cent, till "he lies like a broker" became a proverb.

The drama of the day teems with biting passages bearing on the faithlessness, covetousness, meanness, and dishonesty of the merchant of the day. The thunder of pulpit oratory was also directed against the sins of the mercantile class. We must allow, however, for the exaggerations of both church and stage, and conclude that the average Dutchman was at least as scrupulous in his dealings as the merchants of other nations. That he was able to drive a close bargain, however, and was up to all the tricks of the trade, we gather from the following. Miller (1695) says:

As to their wealth and disposition thereto, the Dutch are rich and sparing; the English neither very rich, nor too great husbands; the French are poor, and therefore forced to be penurious. As to their way of trade and dealing, they are all generally cunning and crafty, but many of them not so just to their words as they should be.

Madam Knight (1707) writes:

They have Vendues very frequently and make their Earnings very well by them, for they treat with good Liquor Liberally, and the Customers Drink as Liberally and Generally pay for't as well, by paying for that which they Bidd up Briskly for, after the sack has gone plentifully about, tho' sometimes good penny worths are got there.

The sources from which I have drawn the material for this work are the old wills, inventories, Court Records, diaries, letters, and documentary colonial history. For the details of contemporary Dutch life I am largely indebted to the works of Dr. G. D. J. Schotel, *Het Maatschappelijk Leven onzer Vaderen in de Zeventiende Eeuw* and *Het Oud-Hollandsch Huisgezin*

PREFACE

der Zeventiende Eeuw. The miniature house and its rooms and specimens of porcelain, glass, and watches in the Rijks Museum, Amsterdam, were photographed especially for this book. My best thanks are due to Miss Anne van Cortlandt, who kindly permitted me to have photographs taken of the Van Cortlandt house and some of the family heirlooms; also to the New York Historical Society for permission to reproduce the portrait of Cornelis Steenwyck, Mayor of the city; and to the Albany Institute and Historical and Art Society for permission to have photographs taken of their relics. I also have to thank Mr. Arthur Shadwell Martin for valuable assistance.

E. S.

NEW YORK,
November, 1908.

CONTENTS

CHAPTER I

PAGE

SETTLEMENT AND EARLY CONDITIONS OF NEW NETHERLAND 1

Early Voyagers—Block, Hudson, and Christiaenss van Cleef; Arrival of the *New Netherland;* the *Sea-Mew* brings Peter Minuit; Arrival of the *Arms of Amsterdam;* Cornelis Hoorn and Willem Van Hulst; Minuit's Purchase of the Island of Manhattan; Early Conditions; Letter of Jonas Michaëlius; Wouter Van Twiller, Willem Kieft, and Growth of Colony; Impressions of Father Jogues; Montanus's Description of New Amsterdam; Adriaen Van der Donck's Description of the Scenery—Beautiful Woods and "Bush Burning"; Farms and Farmers; City Lots and Bouweries; Native Birds; Cattle and Pasture Lands; Goats, Dogs, and Pigs; Ordinances Regarding Cleanliness in the Streets.

CHAPTER II

ORCHARDS AND GARDENS, HOUSES AND STREETS OF NEW AMSTERDAM 27

The Dutch Love of Gardens and Flowers; the Tulip Mania; Flowers in New Netherland; the Company's Garden; Early Gardeners; Fruit in New Netherland; Vegetables and Orchards; the Town and Fort; the Tavern and Church; the First Houses; Native Brick; Stuyvesant's Whitehall and Bouwery; Glass and Leaden Window Frames; Contract to build an Inn; a Typical Dwelling; the Van Cortlandt and Philipse Houses; Surveyors of Streets and Buildings; the City Wall; the Palisades; Primitive Streets; Danger from Fire; the Burgher Watch and Rattle Watch; Lighting the Street; Descriptions of New Amsterdam by Governor Andros, William Byrd, and Madam Knight.

CONTENTS

CHAPTER III

COSTUME 56

Sumptuous Apparel of the Period; New Amsterdam Shop Goods; the Petticoat; the Rain Dress; Samars and Night-rails; Aprons, Sleeves, Ruffs, and Stomachers; Headdresses; *Châtelaines* and Gold Head Ornaments; Jewels of Steenwyck, Cristina Cappoens, Margarita Van Varick, Asser Levy, Peter Marius, and Others; the Dress of Children; Costume of Farmers' Wives and Daughters; Coats, Waistcoats, and Breeches; the Burgomaster's Suit; Wardrobes of Cornelis Steenwyck, Dr. Jacob de Lange, Asser Levy, and Others; Shirts and Neckwear; Stockings and Shoes; Gloves, Hats, Wigs, and Cloaks; Swords, Belts, and Canes; a Melancholy Wardrobe.

CHAPTER IV

ROOMS AND FURNITURE 81

Tastes of the Prosperous New Netherlander; Ebony, Ivory, and Other Oriental Goods; the Chimney-piece, Bed, *Kas*, Cabinet, and Other Furniture; the *Voorhuis*, or Fore Room; Homes of Dr. de Lange, Steenwyck, and Marius; Typical English Homes; Furniture of Rombouts and De Milt.

CHAPTER V

PICTURES, SILVER, CHINA, GLASS, AND CURIOS 102

Dutch Painters of Interiors; Pictures in New Amsterdam; Silver of the Period; Collections of Mrs. Van Varick, Peter Marius, and Others; Thefts of Silver; Great Use of Pewter; Porcelain and Earthenware; Glass; Miniature Houses and Curios.

CHAPTER VI

NEW AMSTERDAM HOUSEKEEPING 120

Breakfast; Going to Market; Fish in New Amsterdam; Breads, Pasties, Cakes, and Bakers; Setting the Table; Table Furniture; the Noonday Meal; Favorite Dishes; Tea,

CONTENTS

Coffee, and Chocolate; Winter Evenings; Supper; Household Pets; Foot-warmers and Church Seats; the Dutch Housewife's Passion for Cleaning; Love of Fine Linen.

CHAPTER VII

SERVANTS AND SLAVES 143

Indentured Servants; Masters and Servants; Parental Rights; Employer's Liability; Cruelty and Abuse; Parental Solicitude; Disposal of Children and Servants by Bequest; Troubles of the Lone Widow and of the Fatherless Children; Runaway Servants; Pauper Children from Amsterdam—not all Desirable Citizens; Negro Slaves; Humane Treatment; Manumission; the Chain Gang; Slave Trade; Prices of Slaves.

CHAPTER VIII

EDUCATION 158

Education in Holland; Provision made for Education by the West India Company; Adam Roelantsen, the First Schoolmaster of New Amsterdam; Deplorable Condition of Schools; Early Schoolmasters; Grades of Schools; Lessons and Punishments; Penmanship; Importance of Languages; General Illiteracy; Provision by Parents for the Education of their Children; Latin Schools; Ægidius Luyck; Routine of School Life; Dancing and Dancing-schools; Libraries and Books.

CHAPTER IX

RELIGION, PERSECUTION, AND SUPERSTITION 182

Consolers and Visitors of the Sick; Dominies Michaëlius and Bogardus; the Church in the Fort; Feud between Kieft and Bogardus; the Company's Rules; Dominies Megapolensis and Drisius; an Indian Convert; State of Religion in New Amsterdam and Long Island; Persecution of the Lutherans; the Troublesome Quakers; Church Service; Blom ministers to Long Island; Henricus Selyns; Rudolphus Van Varick; Governor Andros, Governor Dongan, William Byrd, Miller and Madam Knight on the Religions in New Amsterdam; Sabbath-breaking; Days of Fasting and Prayer; Superstition and Witchcraft; Stuyvesant's Relative held for a Witch.

CONTENTS

CHAPTER X

COURTSHIP AND MARRIAGE 207

Infant Betrothal; Courtship; Breaches of Promise; Story of Maria Verleth; Separation and Divorce; Ceremonies of Betrothal; Play-youths and Play-maidens; the Bride's Basket; Publishing the Banns; Receptions and Congratulations; the Bride's Costume; Jewels in New Amsterdam; Parents' Gifts to Bridegrooms; the Bridal Escort; the Nuptial Banquet; the Bride's Crown; Wedding Outfits; Weddings in New Amsterdam.

CHAPTER XI

PHYSICIANS AND SURGEONS, BIRTHS AND DEATHS . . . 235

Dignity of the Physician; the Quack Doctor; Barber-surgeons; Ships Doctors and Barbers; First Surgeons of New Netherland; Various Activities of the Early Physicians; Bill for Nursing; No Cure, No Pay; Doctors' Suits; Plenty of Employment for Doctors; the First Hospital on Manhattan Island; Native Medicinal Plants; Preparations for a New Member of the Family; the Christening; the Baby's Costume; the Christening Dinner; Christening Presents; the Consoler of the Sick; Burial Customs; Mourning and Funerals; Interments; Pomp and Splendor at Funerals; Burial of Suicides; Funerals in New Amsterdam.

CHAPTER XII

TAVERNS AND EXCISE LAWS 264

The Drink Evil; Importance of the Tavern in Civic Life; Dutch Taverns Beverages; Drinking Vessels, Dinners, and Drinking Customs; Feasts in the New Amsterdam City Tavern; Roistering, Revelling, and Tavern Brawls; Excise Laws and Court Cases; Sunday Liquor Laws.

CHAPTER XIII

SPORTS, FESTIVALS, AND PASTIMES 290

Favorite Games — *Kaetsen*, Golf, Bowls, Skittles, Ninepins, and Disc-throwing, Clubbing the Cat; Pulling the Goose; Bird-cutting; Archery; Racing; Cards, Billiards, and Back-

CONTENTS

gammon; the Indian Game of *Senneca*; Saint Nicholas, the Patron Saint of New Amsterdam; Saint Nicholas Eve; Christmas, New Year's, and Twelfth Night; Masquerade of the Three Kings; Shrove Tuesday and its Pastimes; May-day and Whitsuntide; Saint Martin's Day and Saint Martin's Goose; Excursions and Picnics; the Game of Sea-carrying; Kissing; the "Kissing-bridge"; Skating and Sleighing; Indoor Diversions; the Sausage-making Evening; Cattle and Other Livestock; the *Kermis*.

CHAPTER XIV

MERCHANTS AND TRADE 321

The Atlantic Passage; Transport Expenses; Names of Ships; Ship-building in New Amsterdam; Shipping Regulations; Bill of Lading; Volume of Trade; Indian Trade; Wampum and Sewan; Currency Regulations; Treatment of Indians; Laws against Selling Liquor and Ammunition to the Natives; Private Trade; Smuggling; Great and Small Burghers; Piracy; Opposition to its Suppression; Bellomont's Difficulties; Oriental Wares; a Merchant's Office; New Netherland Industries; Trade Profits; Shops and Shop Goods; Confused Currency; Barter; Women Traders and Merchants; Jews; Intolerance; Disabilities; Establishment.

INDEX 351

ILLUSTRATIONS

Portrait of Cornelis Steenwyck. Owned by the New York Historical Society. (In Photogravure) . . .	*Frontispiece*
	Facing page
New Amsterdam (earliest known view)	8
New Amsterdam about 1670	16
Old Hopper House, Second Avenue and 83d Street, New York	24
Kip House, Kip's Bay, New York	24
Old Stone House, 152d Street, Kingsbridge Road, New York	24
Gardens of the Van Cortlandt Manor House, Croton-on-Hudson	32
Van Cortlandt Manor House (1681), Croton-on-Hudson . .	40
Wall of the Van Cortlandt Manor House, showing Loopholes	48
Entrance Door of the Van Cortlandt Manor House, Croton-on-Hudson	54
Hall and Stairway, Van Cortlandt Manor House	62
Old Dutch Watches. Rijks Museum, Amsterdam	70
Mahogany Table brought from Holland in 1668	82
Dutch China Cabinet with Porcelain. Owned by Mr. Frans Middelkoop, New York	90
Dutch China Cabinet and Porcelain. Owned by Mr. Frans Middelkoop, New York	98
Miniature Silver Articles and Silver Toys. Rijks Museum, Amsterdam	108
Dutch Silver from the Van Cortlandt Manor House . . .	112

ILLUSTRATIONS

	Facing page
Silver Tankard. Owned by Sara de Rapelje	116
A Family Meal (seventeenth century)	120
Dutch Kitchen. Jan Steen	126
Old Church Bench or Stool. Albany Institute and Historical and Art Society	132
Napkin Press (seventeenth century). Owned by Mr. Frans Middelkoop, New York	138
Voorhuis in the Doll's House. Rijks Museum, Amsterdam	144
Bedroom, Doll's House. Rijks Museum, Amsterdam	150
Show Room, Doll's House. Rijks Museum, Amsterdam	156
Kitchen, Doll's House. Rijks Museum, Amsterdam	162
Old Dutch School Scenes	166
General View of Doll's House. Rijks Museum, Amsterdam	172
Porcelain and Earthenware. Rijks Museum, Amsterdam	178
Drinking-Glasses. Rijks Museum, Amsterdam	184
Porcelain, Earthenware Ornament and Glass Tumbler in the Van Cortlandt Manor House	190
Flowers. Jan Van Huysam	196
The Parrot Cage. Jan Steen	202
Country House. Pieter de Hooch	208
Glass Drinking Vessels. Rijks Museum, Amsterdam	216
A Dutch Bride in State (seventeenth century)	224
Porcelain and Earthenware. Rijks Museum, Amsterdam	232
Dutch Clock in the Van Cortlandt Manor House	240
Old Chest, Linen Press, and Two Warming-Pans. Owned by Mr. Frans Middelkoop, New York	246
Dutch Cradle and Child's Chair. Albany Institute and Historical and Art Society	254
Silver Spoons. Rijks Museum, Amsterdam	262
Tavern Scene. Teniers	266
Clover Leaf Drinking Cup	272
Old Dutch Tankard	272

ILLUSTRATIONS

Facing page

A Tavern Brawl. Adriaen Brouwer	288
Pulling the Goose	296
St. Nicholas Eve. Jan Steen	300
Three Kings' Evening (Twelfth Night)	304
Sports on the Ice	308
Kermis. Teniers	316
Winter Scene. Ostade	330
Old Dutch House in Broad Street, New Amsterdam (1698)	344

CHAPTER I

SETTLEMENT AND EARLY CONDITIONS OF NEW NETHERLAND

THE history of the early voyages and settlements of the Dutch is told by a writer during Minuit's directorship of the new colony. He says:

This country, or the river, Montagne, called by our's Mauritius, was first sailed to by the worthy Hendrick Christiaensen van Cleef. It so happened that he and the worthy Adriaen Block chartered a ship with the skipper, Ryser, and accomplished his voyage thither, bringing back with him two sons of the principal sachems there.

Hudson, the famous English pilot, had been there also, to reach the South Sea, but found no passage.

This aforesaid Hendrick Christiaensz, after he had dissolved partnership with Adriaen Block, made ten voyages thither, in virtue of a grant from the Lords States who gave him that privilege for the first establishment of the place. On the expiration of that privilege, this country was granted to the West India Company, to draw their profits thence.

The West India Company being chartered to navigate these Rivers did not neglect to do so, but equipped in the spring [of 1623] a vessel of 130 lasts, called the *New Netherland*, with thirty families, mostly Walloons, to plant a colony there. They sailed in the beginning of

DUTCH NEW YORK

March, and directing their course by the Canary Islands, steered towards the Wild Coast, and gained the westwind which luckily [took] them in the beginning of May into the River called, first *Rio de Montagnes,* now the River Mauritius, lying in 40½ degrees.

The ship sailed up to the Maykans, 44 miles, near which they built and completed a Fort named Orange, with 4 bastions, on an Island by them called Castle Island. They forthwith put the spade in the ground and began to plant, and before the *Mackerel* sailed, the grain was nearly as high as a man, so that they are bravely advanced. They also placed a Fort named Wilhelmus on Prince's Island, heretofore called Murderer's Island; it is open in front, and has a curtain in the rear and is garrisoned by sixteen men for the defence of the River below. On leaving there, the course lies for the west wind, and having got it, to the Bermudas and so along the channel in a short time towards Patria. The Yacht, the *Mackerel,* sailed out last year on the 16th June and arrived yonder on the 12th of December. . . .

The fur and other trade belongs to the West India Company, others being forbidden to trade there. Rich beavers, otters, martins and foxes are found there. This cargo consists of five hundred otter skins, and fifteen hundred beavers and a few other things, which were in four parcels of twenty-eight thousand some hundred guilders.[1]

On Jan. 9, 1626, Peter Minuit sailed in the *Sea-Mew,* Captain Adriaen Joris, and arrived at Manhattan on May 4. The next ship sent out by the West India Company was the *Arms of Amsterdam,* which arrived on July 27, 1626, and started on her return voyage on Sept. 23, 1626, with a valuable cargo of furs and wood under charge of Peter Barentsen, the Indian trader. She arrived in Amsterdam on November 4; and on

[1] The cargo of the *New Netherland* was sold in Amsterdam, Dec. 20, 1624.

SETTLEMENT AND EARLY CONDITIONS

the following day the Secretary thus informed the States-General:

There arrived here yesterday the ship called the *Arms of Amsterdam*, which sailed from the river Mauritius [the Hudson], in New Netherland, on the 23d of September. Report is brought that our people there are diligent and live peaceably; their wives have also borne them children. They have purchased the Island of Manhattes from the Indians for the sum of sixty guilders; it contains 11,000 morgens of land. They have sown all kinds of grain in the middle of May, and reaped in the middle of August. I send you some samples of the summer grains, as wheat, rye, barley, oats, buckwheat, canary seed, beans and flax.

The cargo of the ship consists of 7246 skins of beaver, 853 otter, 81 mink, 36 cat lynx, 34 small rat, together with a considerable quantity of oak timber and nutwood.

Our historian continues:

The Company there administers Justice in criminal matters as far as imposing fines (*boet-straffe*), but not as far as capital punishment. Should it happen that any one deserves that, he must be sent to Holland with his sentence. Cornelis Hoorn was, in the year 1624, the first Director there; Willem Van Hulst was the second in the year 1625. He returns now. . . .

Respecting these Colonies they have already a prosperous beginning; and the hope is that they will not fall through provided they be zealously sustained, not only in that place but in the South River. For their increase and prosperous advancement, it is highly necessary that those sent out be first of all well provided with means both of support and defence, and that being Freemen, they be settled there on a free tenure; that all they work for and gain be their's to dispose of and to sell according to their pleasure; that whoever is placed over them as Commander act as their Father, not as their Executioner, leading them with a gentle hand. . . .

In the year 1628, there already resided on the Island of the Manhates, two hundred and seventy souls, men, women and children, under Governor Minuit, Verhulst's successor, living there in peace with the Natives. But as the land, in many places being full of weeds and wild productions, could not be properly cultivated in consequence of the scantiness of the population, the said Lords Directors of the West India Company, the better to people their lands, and to bring the country to produce more abundantly, resolved to grant divers Privileges, Freedoms and Exemptions to all Patroons, Masters or Individuals who should plant any Colonies or Cattle in New Netherland.

After Minuit purchased the island of Manhattan, no time was lost in providing for the security of the settlement. The engineer, Krijn Frederijcke, staked out a fort on the southern point of the island to which the name Fort Amsterdam was given. The Company's counting-house was a stone building with a thatched roof, but the other houses were of wood. Director Minuit and the Opper Koopman, De Rasieres, lived together; and there were about thirty houses on the east side of the river. Frances Moelmacker began to build a horse mill with a large room above to be used as a meeting-place for religious services; for although there was as yet no regular clergyman, two Comforters of the Sick (*Kranck-besoeckers*), Sebastiaen Jansen Krol and Jan Huych, read the Bible and held meetings on Sundays. Another officer of the colony was Jan Lempo, the *schout,* or sheriff.

Each colonist had his own farm on the Company's land, and was supplied with cows; but the milk was for his own profit. These temporary homes were outside the Fort; but as soon as that should be completed the people intended to reside within its walls, for the sake of greater security. Two years later, when the

SETTLEMENT AND EARLY CONDITIONS

Three Kings, Captain Jan Jacobsen, and the *Arms of Amsterdam,* Captain Adriaen Joris, were sent by Director Minuit to the West India Company, arriving in Amsterdam in October, 1628, with furs and timber, they brought the good news that Fort Amsterdam was completed with four bastions, and faced with stone; that the colony numbered two hundred and seventy souls, including men, women, and children; that the cattle throve well, and that everything seemed prosperous. At this period the colonists supported themselves chiefly by farming, and any deficiencies were supplied by the West India Company.

During Minuit's administration Staten Island was also purchased.

The letter of Jonas Michaëlius (1628) gives a good picture of the infant colony, and the difficulties the early settlers had to face:

As to what concerns myself and my household: I find myself by the loss of my good and helping partner very much hindered and distressed, — for my two little daughters are yet small; maidservants are not here to be had, at least none whom they advise me to take; and the Angola slaves are thievish, lazy and useless trash. The young man whom I took with me, I discharged after Whitsuntide, for the reason that I could not employ him out of doors at any working of the land, and, in doors, he was a burden to me instead of an assistance. He is now elsewhere at service with the boers.

The promise which the Lords Masters of the Company had made me to make myself a home, instead of a free table which otherwise belonged to me, is wholly of no avail. For their Honours well know that there are no houses, cows nor laborers to be obtained here for money.

The country yields many good things for the support of life, but they are all to be gathered in an uncultivated and wild state. It is necessary that there should be better regulations established, and people who have the knowledge and the implements for gathering things in their season, should collect them together, as undoubtedly will gradually be the case. In the meanwhile I wish the Lords Managers to be courteously inquired of, how I can have the opportunity to possess a portion of land, and at my own expense to support myself upon it. For as long as there is no more accommodation to be obtained here from the country people, I would be compelled to order everything from Fatherland at great expense, and with much risk and trouble, or else live here upon these poor and hard rations alone, which would badly suit me and my children. We want ten or twelve farmers with horses, cows and labourers in proportion, to furnish us with bread and fresh butter, milk and cheese.

Having been recalled, Minuit left in the *Union* in 1632, and was succeeded by Wouter Van Twiller, of Nieuwkerke, a clerk in the employ of the West India Company and a relative of the Patroon Van Rensselaer. He arrived at Fort Amsterdam in the Company's ship, *De Zoutberg* (the *Salt Mountain*), of two hundred and eighty tons, manned by fifty-two men and which carried twenty guns and one hundred and four soldiers, — the first military force sent to New Netherland.

During his administration Dominie Everardus Bogardus arrived, and also the first schoolmaster, Adam Roelantsen; a church was built on Pearl Street, and the block-house was succeeded by a fort that was finished in 1635. Van Twiller also bought Pagganck, or Nut Island (now Governor's Island), and two islands in Hell Gate.

Director Van Twiller was succeeded by Willem Kieft, who arrived on March 28, 1638, in the *Herring* (two hundred and eighty tons and twenty guns). The new Director's administration was not at first prosperous, for the West India Company gave up the

SETTLEMENT AND EARLY CONDITIONS 7

privileged trade with the Indians, opening this commerce to all the inhabitants of the Dutch provinces; and many colonists were thus drawn to New Netherland.

On the other hand the English came both from Virginia and N. England, on account of the good opportunity to plant tobacco here, first divers servants, whose time had expired; afterwards families, and finally, entire colonies, having been forced to quit that place, in order to enjoy freedom of conscience, and to escape from the insupportable government of N. England, and because many more commodities were to be obtained here than there, so that in place of seven bouweries and two or three plantations which were here, thirty bouweries were to be seen as well cultivated and stocked as in Europe [and] one hundred plantations which in two or three [years] would become regular bouweries, for after the tobacco was out of the ground, corn was planted there without ploughing, and the winter was employed preparing new lands. The English colonies had settled under us by patent on equal terms with the others. Each of these was in appearance not less than one hundred families strong, exclusive of the Colonie of Rensselaerswyck, which is prospering, with that of Mynders, Meyndertsz and Cornelius Melyn, who began first. Also the village of N. Amsterdam around the fort, one hundred families, so that there was appearance of producing supplies in a year for fourteen thousand souls without straitening the country, and had there not been a want of labourers or farm servants, twice as much could be raised.

During Kieft's administration a new stone church was built within the Fort, building lots were granted, citizens were allowed a vote in public affairs, and a body of " Eight men " was selected to advise the governor in the Indian trouble. The Indian war made Kieft unpopular, and he was recalled. He set sail in the *Princess* in July, 1647. The boat suffered shipwreck, and he and the other passengers, including Dominie Bogardus, were drowned.

Father Jogues, 1643, says:

For the garrison of the said Fort, and of another which they had built still further up against the incursions of the Indians, their enemies, there were sixty soldiers. They were beginning to face the gates and bastions with stone. Within the fort there was a stone church, which was quite large, the house of the Governor, whom they call Director-General, quite neatly built of brick, the storehouses and barracks.

On this Island of Manhate and in its environs, there may well be four or five hundred men of different sects and nations: the Director General told me that there were men of eighteen kinds of languages; they are scattered here and there on the river, above and below, as the beauty and convenience of the spot invited each to settle: some mechanics, however, who ply their trade, are ranged under the fort; all the others being exposed to the incursions of the Indians, who, in the year 1643, while I was there, had actually killed some two score Hollanders, and burnt many houses and barns full of wheat.

There is no religious exercise except the Calvinist, and orders are to admit none but Calvinists, however this is not observed; there being in the Colony besides the Calvinists, Catholics, English Puritans, Lutherans, Anabaptists, whom they call Mnites, etc., etc.

When any one first comes to settle in the country, they lend him horses, cows, etc.; they give him provisions, all which he returns as soon as he is at ease; and as to the land, after ten years he pays to the West India Company the tenth of the produce which he raises. . . .

The first comers found lands quite fit for use formerly cleared by the savages who had fields there. Those who came later have cleared in the woods which are mostly oak. The soil is good. Deer hunting is abundant in the

NEW AMSTERDAM
(EARLIEST KNOWN VIEW)

SETTLEMENT AND EARLY CONDITIONS 9

fall. There are some houses built of stone: lime they make of oyster shells, of which there are great heaps, made formerly by the savages, who subsist in part by that fishery. . . .

Ascending the river to the 43d degree, you meet the second Dutch settlement, which the tide reaches but does not pass.

There are two things in this settlement (which is called Renselaerswick, as if to say, settlement of Renselaers, who is a rich Amsterdam merchant) 1st, a miserable little fort called Fort Orange, built of logs, with four or five pieces of Breteuil cannon, and as many swivels. This has been reserved, and is maintained by the West India Company. This fort was formerly on an island which the river makes; it is now on the main land towards the Hiroquois, a little above the said island. Secondly, a colony sent here by this Renselaers, who is the patroon. This colony is composed of about a hundred persons who reside in some twenty-five or thirty houses built along the river, as each found convenient. In the principal house lives the patroon's agent; the Minister has his apart, in which service is performed. There is also a kind of Baliff here, whom they call the Seneschal, who administers justice. Their houses are all merely of boards and thatched. There is as yet no mason work except in the chimneys. The forests, furnishing many large pines, they make boards by means of their mills, which they have for the purpose.

Montanus (1671) thus describes what would be the first view obtained by the settlers of their future home:

On the Manhattan's island stands New Amsterdam, five miles from the ocean: ships run up to the harbour there from the sea with one tide. The city hath an earthen fort. Within the fort, and on the outermost bastion towards the river, stand a wind mill and a very high staff, on which a flag is hoisted whenever any vessels are seen in Godyn's bay. The church rises with a double roof between which a square tower looms aloft. On one side is the prison, on the other side of the church the Governor's house. Without the walls are the houses mostly built by the Amsterdamers. On the river side stand the gallows and whipping-post. A handsome public tavern adorns the farthest point. Between the fort and this tavern is a row of suitable dwelling-houses: among which stand out the warehouses of the West India Company.

A view of New Amsterdam at this period faces page 16, and an earlier view, page 8.

The beautiful scenery and the vast natural resources of the country, as well as its attractions for the farmer, formed the theme of many an enthusiastic letter and treatise by early travelers. A charming description of the landscape, climate, physical features, productions, etc., is afforded by Adriaen Van der Donck in 1654. He says:

The whole country has a waving surface, and in some places high hills and protruding mountains, particularly those named the Highlands, which is a place of high, connected mountain land, about three miles broad, extending in curved forms throughout the country; separated in some places and then again connected. There also is much fine level land, intersected with brooks, affording pasturage of great length and breadth, but mostly along the rivers and near the salt side. Inland, most of the country is waving, with hills which generally are not steep, but ascend gradually. We sometimes in travelling imperceptibly find ourselves on high elevated situations, from which we overlook large portions of the country. The neighbouring eminence, the surrounding valleys and the highest trees are overlooked, and again lost in the distant space. Here our attention is arrested in the beautiful landscape around us, here the painter can find rare and beautiful subjects for the employment of his brush; and here also the huntsman is animated when he

SETTLEMENT AND EARLY CONDITIONS

views the enchanting prospects presented to the eyes; on the hills, at the brooks and in the valleys, where the game abounds, and where the deer are feeding or gamboling or resting in the shades in full view. . . .

Near the rivers and watersides there are large extensive plains containing several hundred *morgens;* in one place more and in another less, which are very convenient for plantations, villages and towns. There also are brooklands and fresh and salt meadows; some so extensive that the eye cannot oversee the same. Those are good for pasturage and hay, although the same are overflowed by the spring tides, particularly near the seaboard. These meadows resemble the low and outlands of the Netherlands. Most of them could be dyked and cultivated. We also find meadow grounds far inland, which are all fresh and make good hayland. Where the meadows are boggy and wet, such failings are easily remedied by cutting and breaking the bogs in winter and letting off the water in the spring. There also would be much more meadow ground, but as the soil is natural for wood, and as the birds and the winds carry the seeds in every direction; hence, those moist, low grounds are covered with timber and underwoods which we call cripple bushes.

Montanus also writes in 1671:

New Netherland hath, moreover, divers remarkable waterfalls tumbling down from lofty rocks, broad creeks and hills, fresh lakes and rivulets and pleasant springs and fountains, which smoke in winter, are right cold in summer, and, nevertheless, are much drank. Meanwhile the inhabitants are at no time much incommoded by floods, nor by the sea, inasmuch as at spring tide the water scarcely ever rises a foot higher; nor by freshets which cover only some low lands for a short while, and enrich them by their alluvium. The sea-coast rises hilly out of sand and clay wherefore it produces abundantly all sorts of herbs and trees.

The oak usually grows sixty to seventy feet high, for

the most part free of knots, for which reason it is well adapted to ship-building. The Hickory trees furnish a hot and lasting fire and a curious appearance whenever the bush is cut away either for the purpose of more open hunting, or for clearing the ground for a bouwery.

Van der Donck also tells us that the country was so thickly wooded that those who cultivated the land cut down the trees ruthlessly, collected the wood into great heaps and burned it to get it out of the way. The Indians and the Dutch were also careless regarding the chestnuts. The Indians destroyed the trees by stripping off the bark for thatching their huts, and they frequently cut off the limbs to gather the nuts, — a practice followed by the Dutch. Pine trees grew so large inland that they were heavy and tall enough to be used for masts and spars of ships; the wild ash was plentiful, and there were also maples, linden, birch, yew, poplar, fir, alder, willow, thorn, sassafras, persimmon, mulberry, wild cherry, crab, and oak trees. The white-wood, also known as canoe-wood because the Indians made canoes of it, was used by the settlers for flooring, because it was bright and free of knots.

Amongst the other trees, the water-beeches grow very large along the brooks, heavier and larger than most of the trees of the country. When those trees begin to bud then the dark becomes a beautiful white, resembling the handsomest satin. This tree retains the leaves later than any other tree of the woods. Trees of this kind are considered more ornamental and handsomer than the linden-trees for the purpose of planting near dwelling-houses.

The Indians have a yearly custom (which some of our Christians have also adopted) of burning the woods, plains and meadows in the fall of the year, when the leaves have fallen, and when the grass and vegetable substances are dry. Those places which are then passed over are fired in the spring in April. This practice is named by us and the Indians "bush burning," which is done for several reasons; first, to render hunting easier, as the bush and vegetable growth renders the walking difficult for the hunter, and the crackling of the dry substances betrays him and frightens away the game. Secondly to thin out and clear the woods of all dead substances and grass, which grow better the ensuing spring. Thirdly, to circumscribe and enclose the game within the lines of the fire, when it is more easily taken, and also, because the game is more easily tracked over the burned parts of the woods.

The bush burning presents a grand and sublime appearance. On seeing it from without, we would imagine that not only the dry leaves, vegetables and limbs would be burnt, but that the whole woods would be consumed where the fire passes, for it frequently spreads and rages with such violence that it is awful to behold; and when the fire approaches houses, gardens and wooden enclosures, then great care and vigilance are necessary for their preservation; for I have seen several houses which have recently been destroyed before the owners were apprized of their danger.

Notwithstanding the apparent danger of the entire destruction of the woodlands by the burning, still the green trees do not suffer. The outside bark is scorched three or four feet high, which does them no injury for the trees are not killed. It, however, sometimes happens that in the thick pine woods, wherein the fallen trees lie across each other and have become dry that the blaze ascends and strikes the tops of the trees, setting the same on fire, which is immediately increased by the resinous knots and leaves which promote the blaze, and is passed by the wind from tree to tree, by which the entire tops of the trees are sometimes burnt off, while the bodies remain standing. Frequently great injuries are done by such fires, but the burning down of entire woods never happens. I have seen many instances of wood-burning in the colony of Rensselaerwyck, where there is much pine wood. Those fires appear grand at night from the passing vessels in the river, when the woods are burning on both sides of the same. Then we can see a great distance by the light of the blazing trees, the flames being driven by the wind, and fed by the tops of the trees. But the dead and dying trees remain burning in their standing positions, which appear sublime and beautiful when seen at a distance.

In 1650, the Secretary of the Province, Tienhoven, gives the following "Information relative to taking up land in New Netherland":

Those who have no means to build farm-houses at first according to their wishes, dig a square pit in the ground, cellar fashion, six or seven feet deep, as long and as broad as they think proper, case the earth inside all round the wall with timber, which they line with the bark of trees or something else to prevent the caving in of the earth; floor this cellar with plank and wainscot it overhead for a ceiling, raise a roof of spars clear up, and cover the spars with bark or green sods, so that they can live dry and warm in these houses with their entire families for two, three and four years, it being understood that partitions are run through these cellars which are adapted to the size of the family.

After the houses are built in the above-described manner, or otherwise according to each person's means and fancy, gardens are made and planted in season with all sorts of pot-herbs, principally parsnips, carrots and cabbage, which bring great plenty into the husbandman's dwelling. The maize can serve as bread for men and food for cattle.

A good idea of a farm of the early period is shown in the inventory of the effects and goods at Achtervelt, upon Long Island, belonging to Andries Hudde and Wolfert Gerritsen, July 9, 1638. He had five cows,

SETTLEMENT AND EARLY CONDITIONS 15

three oxen, and a calf; five horses; a new wagon and appurtenances; a wheelplow and appurtenances, an iron harrow, and some farm tools; a house twenty-six feet long, twenty-two feet wide, and forty feet deep, with the roof covered above and all around with planks, two garrets, one above the other, and a small chamber on the side with an outlet on the side. The house, moreover, was surrounded by long round palisades. The barn was forty feet long, eighteen wide and twenty-four high, with the roof; a *bergh* (a sort of open shed with a roof to shelter hay or grain) with five posts, forty feet long; about six *morgens* of land sown with summer and winter grain; a garden planted with a number of fruit trees; and a yawl with appurtenances.

The West India Company leased land on "advantageous terms," as we should say to-day, to the settlers, and stocked the farms with cattle, horses, etc., the rent usually being paid by a stipulated share of the crops and the increase of the cattle. The following early leases may be taken as examples.

Governor Kieft leased two lots near the Fort to Jan Damen in 1638,

the larger one of which has heretofore been cultivated by the negroes and is situate on the east side of the road, to the north of the said Jan Damens, south of the esplanade of the Fort and east of Philipp de Truy, and the smaller situate to the north of the Company's garden, extending from the road to the river. John Damen shall plant the land for six years, also be bound to convey twice all his manure on said land at his own cost, for which the Director shall receive as rent half the produce . . . said Director shall maintain and keep tight the fences now put up around it and furnish to Jan Damen two laborers, 14 days during the harvest to be paid by the Company and fed by Jan Damen; likewise if the Company think proper to plant a vineyard or gardens in the low place, the lessee shall be bound to allow it and have nothing to say.

When J. E. Bout in 1638 leased the Company's farm at Pavonia, he was to have the use of the house and lands for six years, keeping everything in good repair at his own expense. He was to " deliver yearly to Mr. Kieft or his successor one fourth part of the crop, whether of corn or other produce, with which God shall favor the soil, also every year two tuns of strong beer and twelve capons, free of expense."

In 1640, a farm was let for one hundred and fifty pounds of good, cured tobacco yearly. " The said Smith shall clear as much land as is neccessary for 2000 pallisades."

Wouter van Twiller leased the Company's Bouwery No. 1 on Manhattan Island from May, 1638, for three years " for the sum of 250 Carolus guilders to be paid yearly, to-gether with a sixth part of the produce with which God shall bless the field."

In May, 1639, Bouwery No. 5 on Manhattan Island was leased to Hendrick Harmensen for six years. He was to " cultivate the land with all diligence and industry and not attend exclusively to the increase of the cattle, but diligently till the ground, which is the Company's principal object herein." For this he was to receive fifty guilders per annum for servant's wages; and the Company delivered to him five head of cattle and two mares for his use for six years. He was to pay thirty pounds of good butter yearly for every cow. " At the expiration of six years the Company's agent shall first take away the number of cattle in such condition as now delivered; and then the remaining cattle which will be procreated shall be divided half and half."

NEW AMSTERDAM ABOUT 1670

SETTLEMENT AND EARLY CONDITIONS 17

Bouwery No. 6 was let by Kieft with two mares, one stallion, three cows, one heifer, and one calf for twenty years to Abraham Pietersen, who was to pay yearly forty-five *schepels* of rye and ninety pounds of butter, and the increase of cattle was to be divided with the Company every four years.

In 1642, a tract of land was let for "the tenth part of the produce of the fields, whether cultivated with the plough, the hoe or otherwise (orchards and gardens not exceeding one acre Holland measure excepted)."

On June 24, 1638, an order was issued granting freemen patents for the lands they were cultivating, on condition that at the end of ten years they pay yearly the tenth part of all their crops, and also a couple of capons yearly for house and garden.

A lease of a somewhat unusual character, dated May 17, 1639, shows that Rev. Everardus Bogardus leased to

Richard Brudenell a tobacco house and plantation with a water dog, gun and powder at a certain rent payable in tobacco, and one third of all the game he shall kill, as long as the powder and ball last.

The woods were full of game. An old traveler remarks:

There are all sorts of fowls, both in the water and in the air. Swans, geese, ducks, bitterns abound. The men scarcely ever labour, except to provide some game, either fowl or other description, for cooking, and then they have provided everything. The women must attend to the remainder, tilling the soil, etc.

Wassenaer speaks of the innumerable waterfowl, — cranes, swans, bitterns, geese, ducks, widgeons, — and remarked that birds fill also the woods so that men can scarcely go through them for the whistling, the noise and the chattering. Whoever is not lazy can catch them with little difficulty. Turkey beans is a very common crop, pigeons fly wild, they are chased by the foxes like fowl. . . . 'T is surprising that storks have not been found there if it be a marshy country. Spoonbills, ravens, eagles, sparrow-hawks, vultures are numerous and are actually shot or knocked down by the natives.

John Miller, 1695, also speaks of

much wild fowl, as swans, geese, ducks, turkies, a kind of pheasants and partridges, pigeons, etc., and no less store of good venison, so that you may sometimes buy at your door a quarter for nine pence or a shilling.

There were marshes on Manhattan Island in which cattle occasionally got bogged. In November, 1643,

Claes van Elslant and Cosyn Gerritsen declare that they saw a herd of cattle which were driven into the swamp near Old John's plantation on the Manhattans, sink over their backs in the marsh.

Unoccupied land was used for common pasturage; and goats, sheep, hogs, and cattle needed protection against their natural enemies as well as against Indians and dishonest white men. In April, 1640, Claes Groen and Pieter Lieresen contracted to herd daily the goats of Philip de Truy and others in the woods on Manhattan Island at one guilder a year for each goat. In 1648, it was ordered that goats beyond the Fresh Water be attended by a herdsman, or be forfeited to the Fiscal. In 1644, it was resolved to make a clearing extending "from the Great Bouwery to Emanuel's plantation"; and that all who wished to pasture their cattle within this clearing, to save them from the Indians, should appear on the following Monday to build a fence around the same.

In 1660, Gabriel Carpsey demands 6.15 florins and one pound of butter for taking care of a cow. Defendant's son appears and says that Carpsey let the cow stray in the bush, and he and his brother-in-law, Dirck Siecken, were two days in search of her. Plaintiff says that defendant did not deliver his cow, like others, on the blowing of the horn to be led to pasture. The court gave judgment for the cowherd.

On March 10, 1648,

Goats beyond the *Fresh Water* shall not be pastured without a Herdsman and Keeper, on pain of having the Goats found at large on this side of the *Fresh Water*, or without a Herdsman or Keeper beyond it, taken up by the Fiscal and declared forfeit.

In 1673, on account of " the great ravages committed by wolves on the small cattle, therefore whoever shall produce a wolf that has been shot on this Island on this side of Haarlem shall be promptly paid therefor. For a wolf fl. 20 and for a she-wolf, fl. 30, seawant or the value thereof, which Under Schout and Schepens shall by their Messenger levy off those who keep cattle, great or small, within their district."

Again, on Aug. 1, 1685, was published a " licence to the inhabitants of the island of Manhattan to hunt and destroy wolves thereon, on Thursday next."

Dogs were also a danger to live-stock. In the records we find more than one lawsuit over sheep-biting. On April 9, 1642, Peter van der Linde, Barent Dircksen, and Tennis Cray complain against Nicholaes Sloper's dog, which roves the woods and kills their goats. Dogs were highly valued, doubtless because of their fetching and carrying qualities. For some reason not specified,

Dirck Cornelissen, in his hasty wrath, enables posterity to compute the worth of a hound in 1638. He was condemned to pay twenty-five guilders for the dog he killed, also a fine of twenty-five guilders and costs. How the animal met its fate we are not informed, — not by stoning, however, in all probability, for a New Amsterdam dog was able to dodge missiles, as is attested by the following moving entry dated Nov. 22, 1644:

Gerrit Hendricksen, a lad, throwing a piece of an earthen pot at a dog, accidentally struck Jacob Melyn in the eye.

From two other entries we gather that butter was an emollient for dog-bites; that a dog might chew on a stranger during the hours of darkness, but not in the daytime; and that it was just as well to be a general's dog in case of trouble.

In 1653, Roelof Jansen complained that Philip Geraerdy's dog had bitten him " in the daytime, as may be seen by the wound and he claims for loss of time and surgeon's fees 12 fl. Defendant says plaintiff may kill said dog, and that plaintiff has not lost any time or work on that account; he has already sent plaintiff by his wife 4 lbs. of butter, and is still willing to give him as a charity 4 fl. more." The case was dismissed. In 1665, Thomas Francen said that John Cocx's dog bit his horse standing under the cart and demanded satisfaction. Defendant replied that it was not his, but the General's dog. The Mayor therefore undertook to speak to the General on the subject.

Another case involving the misdemeanor of a dog was that of Marretie Pietersen, plaintiff, *versus* Jacob Eldertsen, defendant.

The plaintiff complains that defendant shot her dog; requests indemnification for the same to the amount of

SETTLEMENT AND EARLY CONDITIONS

fl. 16 as it was a good water dog. Defendant acknowledges having shot the dog, for the dog attempted to attack him in the street; and in catching a stone to drive him away, he bit him in the finger, so that he was obliged to have it dressed by the surgeon. Maintains therefore that he is not liable to pay a stiver for it.

The plaintiff denied that the dog bit the defendant and the court deferred judgment.

The householders of New Amsterdam gave their municipal authorities great trouble by neglecting properly to fence their own grounds and prevent their cattle and other animals from straying into their neighbors' fields, gardens, and orchards, — neighbors, of course, whose fences must also have been out of repair. Goats and pigs were the worst offenders, and were often the cause of serious quarrels in the community. Many actions for trespass and even cases of battery and assault occasioned by stray animals appear in the Court Records. For example, on Oct. 5, 1654:

Wolfert Webber was summoned to Court by the Worshipful Magistrates on the complaint of some Neighbours in consequence of damages he inflicted attacking with dogs and beating certain pigs which went on his land. Wolfert Webber demands the name of Complainant. William Beekman states it to be on the complaint handed to him of Mde. Verleth and Stillen's wife, because their hogs were unwarrantably attacked and injured by Webber and his dogs, so that he considered it proper to acquaint the Court. Webber said he was so annoyed by the hogs on his land, whereby all his seed was destroyed that he divers times drove them home, but not being able to keep them off he hunted them with dogs, but he did not injure them in the least; on the contrary, he was at various times insulted and threatened with a beating by Mde. Verleth. The Worshipful Court admonished Webber to keep himself clear of complaint, and to institute his action should he suffer wrong.

Peace, however, was not patched up, for on June 28, 1655,

Wolfert Webber plaintiff v/s Judith Verleth appeared in Court, complaining of violence force and abuse committed against him by defendant and her sister, Sarah, last week in his house; striking him in his own house and flinging stones at him; requesting that said defendant be ordered to let him remain in peace in his own house.

Judith Verleth denied that she

ever gave plaintiff any trouble; complains that he berated her for a whore and strumpet, and threatened in his own house to strike her with the whip, as he daily does his wife; that he assaulted her, bruising and dragging her arm, and kicked her sister so that her hip is blue. Parties were ordered to prove their complaints and statements on both sides by the next Court day, and further to leave each other unmolested. Webber was fined 12 stivers on account of fulminating lies, etc., in presence of the Court.

In 1647,

All inhabitants of New Netherland are commanded well to fence their lands, that the cattle may not do any damage. The cattle, be it horses or cows or especially goats and pigs must be taken care of or otherwise disposed of, that they can do no damage, for which purpose Fiscal van Dyck shall build a pound and keep the animals until the damage is repaired and the fine paid.

On Jan. 16, 1657, an ordinance was issued permitting firewood and other timber to be cut gratis on uninclosed lots.

SETTLEMENT AND EARLY CONDITIONS 23

Pigs were incorrigible in New Amsterdam, notwithstanding frequent official fulminations. They did not even respect the sacred ground of the Fort, and seemed to care no more for the autocratic Director Stuyvesant than they had for his predecessors, judging from several ordinances covering his entire administration. In 1650, on account of the damage done to the walls of this decayed fortress, fines were imposed on those who allowed their pigs, goats, sheep, or cattle to stray on the walls. On July 11, 1654, an ordinance was published for impounding sheep and goats found injuring the fortifications.

Pigs and goats were not the sole offenders. Boys were as mischievous and destructive then as now, and often a cause of trouble to their parents. A court case of 1656 exemplifies this.

Jan Vinje exhibits the decision of the arbitrators, commissioned by the Court, on the damage committed by the defendant's son and schoolmates among his peas, requesting that defendant be condemned to pay the same according to valuation; and since his hens and pigs still daily run among his corn that he be ordered to keep the same out, or that the plaintiff be authorized to kill them. Defendant maintains that he is not bound to make good any of the damage claimed by plaintiff, since the children have not taken or injured anything to the value of a pea's-pod, and his son has already been beaten therefor by plaintiff, so that he came home black and blue, and has been punished, saying that many other children when they came out of school were in there. Plaintiff being heard thereupon acknowledges to have struck defendant's son at the time: he could not catch any other but him. Both being heard, the Court decides, since defendant acknowledges to have beaten and punished defendant's son, that he has destroyed his right. Therefore, his demand is dismissed in this instance; and the Court further orders that defendant shall keep his hens and pigs out of the corn, or otherwise disposition shall be made therein.

New Amsterdam was laid out in streets and lots, and the Company made great efforts to induce the colonists to take up the land and build good houses. Great difficulty was met, however, in fostering agriculture, and even dairy-farming was neglected for trade, — particularly illicit trade with the Indians, and smuggling. The authorities were greatly disturbed over the neglect in improving the city; and, when Stuyvesant took charge, he found he had a hard task in enforcing the old laws and that new measures were necessary. Consequently, in 1647 the following ordinance was issued:

Whereas we see and remark by experience the irregularity heretofore and still daily observed in building and erecting of Houses; in extending of Lots far beyond the survey line; in setting up Hog pens and Privies on the highways and streets; in neglecting and omitting duly to build on granted and conceded lots; we have resolved to appoint three Street Surveyors (Roymeesters) to condemn and stop all irregular and unsightly buildings, fences, palisades, posts, Rails, etc. Therefore we Order and warn all and every of our Subjects, who from now henceforth are inclined to build on, or inclose any Gardens or Lots within or near the City New Amsterdam, not to proceed in the erection or construction thereof without the previous knowledge of speaking to and survey by the aforesaid appointed Street Surveyors, under a fine of 25 Carolus guilders and the abatement of what they have built or set up. In like manner, we will have all and every who have heretofore received any lots, warned and notified to build within Nine months from this date, regular, good and decent houses on their lots, according to law, or in default thereof, such unimproved Lots shall be forfeit to the Patroon or Lord Proprietor, or shall be conveyed to whomsoever he pleases.

From old prints

OLD HOPPER HOUSE
Second Avenue and 83d Street, New York

KIP HOUSE
Kip's Bay, New York

OLD STONE HOUSE
152d Street, Kingsbridge Road, New York

SETTLEMENT AND EARLY CONDITIONS

The Dutch have always been famed for extreme cleanliness, but this applied only to the interior of their dwellings. More than one ordinance proves that the streets were quagmires of filth, and worse. As an example, we may quote from that of 1657:

> Many burghers and inhabitants throw their rubbish, filth, dead animals and such like things into the public streets to the great inconvenience of the community and dangers arising from it. Therefore the Burgomasters and Schepens ordain and direct that henceforth no one shall be allowed to throw into the streets or into the graft any rubbish, filth, ashes, oyster-shells, dead animal or anything like it, but they shall bring all such things to the to them most convenient of the following places, to wit the Strand, near the City Hall, near the gallows near Hendrick the baker, near Daniel Litsco, where tokens to that effect shall be displayed, but not on public streets under a penalty of 3 fl. for the first offence, 6 fl. for the second and arbitrary punishment for the third.

It was also ordered that every one should keep his house or lot cleaned.

Sometimes people maliciously annoyed their neighbors by breaking these laws. In 1671,

> Martin Simson and Richard Watts having been accessory to the disturbance of the peace in throwing of dirt before the doors of several of the inhabitants of this city came this day before the Court, acknowledged their fault and that they were sorry for it, whereupon the court did pardon them the said fault.

On Aug. 19, 1658, it was enacted:

> As the roads and streets of this City are by the constant rooting of the hogs made unfit for driving over in wagons and carts, the Burgomasters and Schepens direct and order, that every owner of hogs in or about the City

shall put a ring through the noses of their hogs to prevent them from rooting within 8 days under a penalty of 2 fl. for each time.

In 1644, Officer Peter Tonneman wishes to know, whereas some dead hogs lie here and there on the street, where he shall have them conveyed and by whom, to prevent the stench, which proceeds therefrom.

He was notified to send the City's negroes, whom he shall order to collect and bury the same.

CHAPTER II

ORCHARDS AND GARDENS — HOUSES AND STREETS

AT the time that the West India Company was sending its first ships across the Atlantic, the Dutch had already attained distinction in the cultivation of fruits, vegetables, and flowers. Not only did they produce splendid examples of familiar favorites, but their ships constantly brought home exotics of all kinds. The Orient supplied many rare seeds, roots, bulbs, and spices; and from the Western Hemisphere also came such novelties as the pineapple, sweet potato, maize, and many plants useful for the table or for medicine.

The Dutch loved the open air. As soon as business was over people sat outside on the stoop, in the street, in the gardens, or in the courtyard. Rich families spent the entire summer in their country-places on the rivers and seashore. The meanest dwelling had a little back garden, if only a few yards square, with a couple of flower-beds and a bench. At the beginning of the Seventeenth Century the gardens were not yet adorned with statuary, nor were they inclosed with hedges; but they had summer-houses and arbors, furnished with benches and tables where a light meal could be served. The majority of the town gardens consisted of four regular square beds planted with flowers, fruit trees, and kitchen stuff, and contained a wooden summer-house with a thatched roof. The garden was enjoyed especially in the afternoon. Gardens, however, were costly things to keep. The Dutch flowers had a world-wide reputation, and were, for the most part, all grown around Haarlem and sent from there through Europe and to New Netherland. The tulips between 1634 and 1637 made many a man poor and rich — tulips that were considered more costly than gold, pearls, and diamonds. In the second half of the Seventeenth Century the courts and gardens underwent a great change, especially after Europe was filled with pupils of Le Nôtre, the famous architect and landscape gardener of Versailles, which cost two hundred million francs. Under their supervision new gardens and courts were laid out, and a new style was introduced. The square fences disappeared and were replaced by evergreen hedges cut in various shapes and fabulous forms and ornaments. The various plots and flower-beds were made alike with symmetrical precision. Long straight paths or lanes separated them, and sometimes they looked like a chess or checker board. In short, everything about the country-houses was choice, neat, and costly.

The taste for flowers began to show itself in Holland at the end of the Sixteenth Century. Beautiful flowers were introduced from Persia and Constantinople, the East and West Indies. In his flower garden Hondius had lilies of all kinds, tulips and hyacinths "all pure of smell and clear of colour," many kinds of larkspur, narcissus, wild saffron, and tea roses. Also the *apocinum canadense*, wind-flowers, pinks, gillyflowers, sweet peas, violets, anemones, and feathergrass. D'Outrein adorned his flower-plots at Rozendaal with palms and flowers arranged so beautifully that they resembled embroidery on a costly robe. Here he had lilies, red, white, and damask roses, gillyflowers, the fragrant lupin, and innumerable flowers like stars in the Milky Way. Westerbaen was proud of his fine roses, crocuses, anemones, and summer sots. At Sorgvliet "a pointed emperor's crown" was in bloom, although Cats was not a flower fiend. Huygens was fonder of his pine forest than of his flowers; but Beverninck should be mentioned next to Clusius and Paludanus. At Lockhorst he had one of the finest collections of foreign plants, which had been sent to him from all parts of the world; indeed, few ships entered the Dutch ports without bringing him seeds, roots, bulbs, or twigs. In addition to rare exotics, he had lilies, tuberoses, emperor's crowns, hyacinths, tulips, auriculas, fritillaries, and ranunculus. The sweet-smelling auricula was something of a novelty. It is unknown who brought it from Switzerland, its native home; but it was sold largely in Brussels and much improved in color and fragrance in Holland. The amaryllis was another favorite flower of the period; but nothing compared with the tulip in popularity.

The tulip mania began in France in 1635, and soon spread to the Low Countries.

It was only natural that the Dutch colonists should bring to the New World a love for and knowledge of flowers. Seeds and bulbs and scions for grafting came over in many a ship, and soon the gardens of New Amsterdam were bright and fragrant with blossoms. Adrian Van der Donck tells us:

> The flowers in general which the Netherlanders have introduced there are the white and red roses of different kinds, the cornelian roses and stock roses; and those of which there were none before in the country, such as eglantine, several kinds of gillyflowers, jenoffelins, different varieties of fine tulips, crown imperials, white lilies, the lily frutularia, anemones, baredames, violets, mari-

golds, summer sots, etc. The clove tree has also been introduced; and there are various indigenous trees that bear handsome flowers, which are unknown in the Netherlands. We also find there some flowers of native growth, as for instance sun flowers, red and yellow lilies, mountain lilies, morning stars, red, white and yellow maritoffles (a very sweet flower), several species of bell-flowers, etc.; to which I have not given particular attention, but *amateurs* would hold them in high estimation and make them widely known.

The Company had a garden outside, but not far from the Fort, on Broadway, which was cultivated by the Company's negroes for the benefit of the Director and the other servants of the Company. Its situation is explained in Jan Damen's lease (see page 15). From time to time the Bowery, of which this formed a part, was leased to various tenants. Many of the settlers who took up the Company's land used it solely for their own profit and pleasure, notwithstanding reiterated orders to the contrary. An ordinance of 1658 calls attention to this abuse, reciting that

many spacious and large Lots, even in the best and most convenient part of this City, lie and remain without Buildings, and are kept by the owners either for greater profit, or for pleasure, and others are thereby prevented to build for the promotion of population and increase of Trade and consumption, as well as for the embellishment of this city, whereunto many newcomers would be encouraged in case they could procure a Lot at a reasonable price on a suitable location, which neglect, if not contempt, thereof, is owing principally to the fact that no penalty fine or amende is imposed by the forementioned Edicts.

A surveyor was therefore appointed, who found " some hundreds of lots inside the walls of the city vacant and not built on." Lots were therefore ap-

GARDENS, HOUSES, AND STREETS

praised and taxed, the proceeds applied to the fortification of the city and repairs thereof, and

The Director General and Council ordain and command that, from this time forward, no dwelling-houses shall be built near or under the Walls or Gates of this City before or until the Lots herein mentioned are properly built on.

Gardens were so important in New Netherland that they were cultivated not merely by the owners, but sometimes by men whose exclusive occupation was that of gardening. We hear of a gardener as early as 1639, when P. de Truy, P. van der Linde, and Jan Hendricksen declare that Edward Wilson had kicked the wife of Truy's gardener. In 1665 William the Gardener (de Tenier) lived in the Prince Graft.

In Holland the fruit and vegetable sellers displayed their wares in baskets in their shops, and also carried these around from door to door, even on a Sunday. Fruit was also exhibited by the venders in trays or porcelain dishes under the broad verandas of the shops, while on the sidewalk baskets of apples and pears were also temptingly set out. The favorite apples of the day were the red and white " calvillen," the gray and white " renetten," and golden pippins. The best-liked pears were the " little muscat," " poire Madame," the large and small banquets, the robin, russet, rousselettes, beurrés, bergamot, long-green, muscat fleury, ambrette, Saint Germain, Saint Augustin, and Martinsec. Smaller baskets and trays were filled with red, black, and yellow plums; sweet and sour cherries; black and red morellos; green, white, and black berries; raspberries " full of juice and flavour "; medlars, figs, peaches, and apricots. The melon was rare, although Hondius had some in his garden. Still rarer was the pineapple, said to have been first brought from America in 1514, and presented to King Ferdinand, who ate it and considered it the finest fruit on earth.

The attractive specimens of pears, peaches, grapes, melons, plums, nectarines, cherries, strawberries, raspberries, etc., as shown in the pictures by De Heem, Mignon, W. van Aelst, Rachel Ruysch, and other artists of the Seventeenth Century, prove what the Dutch horticulturists were able to produce. Therefore, when the early travelers speak with enthusiasm of the fruits of the New World, we know that they have a high standard for criticism. Van der Donck says:

> The indigenous fruits consist principally of acorns, some of which are very sweet; nuts of different kinds, — chestnuts, beechnuts, mulberries, plums, but not many medlars, wild cherries, black currants, gooseberries, hazel nuts in great quantities, small apples, very large strawberries throughout the country, with many other fruits and roots which the Indians use. There is also plenty of bill-berries or blue-berries, together with ground-nuts and artichokes, which grow under ground. Almost the whole land is full of vines, as well in the wild woods as the mowing lands and flats; but they grow principally near to and upon the banks of the brooks, streams and rivers. . . . The grapes comprise many varieties, some white, some blue, some very fleshy and only fit to make raisins of, others, on the contrary, juicy; some are very large and others small. . . . In regard to other fruits all those which grow in Netherland, also grow very well in New Netherland, without requiring as much care as is necessary there. Garden fruits succeed very well, and are drier, sweeter, and more pleasant than in Netherland; for proof of which we may instance particularly muskmelons, citrons or watermelons, which in New Netherland grow readily in the open fields if the briars and weeds are kept from them.

The garden products in the New Netherlands are very

GARDENS
OF THE VAN CORTLANDT MANOR HOUSE, CROTON-ON-HUDSON

GARDENS, HOUSES, AND STREETS

numerous; some of them have been known to the natives from the earliest times, and others introduced from different parts of the world, but chiefly from the Netherlands. . . . They consist of various kinds of salads, cabbages, parsnips, carrots, beets, endive, succory, finckel, sorrel, dill, spinage, radishes, Spanish radishes, parsley, chevril (or sweet cicely), cresses, onions, leeks, and besides whatever is commonly found in a kitchen garden. The herb garden is also tolerably well supplied with rosemary, lavender, hyssop, thyme, sage, marjoram, balm, holy onions (*ajuin heylig*), wormwood, belury, chives and clary; also pimpernel, dragon's blood, five finger, tarragon (or dragon's wort), etc., together with laurel, artichokes and asparagus, and various other things on which I have bestowed no attention.

The pumpkin grows with little or no cultivation, and is so sweet and dry that it is used, with the addition of vinegar and water, for stewing in the same manner as apples; and notwithstanding that it is here generally despised as a mean and unsubstantial article of food, it is there of so good a quality that our countrymen hold it in high estimation. I have heard it said, too, that when properly prepared as apples are with us, it is not inferior to them, and when baked in ovens it is considered better than apples. The English, who in general think much of what gratifies the palate, use it also in pastry, and understand making a beverage from it.

The natives have another species of this vegetable peculiar to themselves, called by our people *quaasiens*.[1] It is a delightful fruit, as well to the eye on account of its fine variety of colours, as to the mouth for its agreeable taste. The ease with which it is cooked renders it a favourite too with the young women. It is gathered early in summer, and when it is planted in the middle

[1] Roger Williams, founder of the colony of Rhode Island, describes the plant as "*Askutasquash*, their vine apples, which the English from them call squashes; about the bigness of apples, of several colours, a sweet, light, wholesome refreshing." Key into the Languages of the Indians (London, 1643).

of April, the fruit is fit for eating by the first of June. They do not wait for it to ripen before making use of the fruit, but only until it has attained a certain size.

Cucumbers are abundant. Calabashes or gourds also grow there; they are half as long as the pumpkin, but have within very little pulp, and are sought chiefly on account of the shell, which is hard and durable, and is used to hold seeds, spices, etc. It is the common water-pail of the natives, and I have seen one so large that it would contain more than a bushel.[1] Turnips also are as good and firm as any sand-rapes that are raised in the Netherlands. There are likewise peas and various sorts of beans.

The Dutch also had the Indian maize, or corn, and soon learned to appreciate the famous *succotash* made of corn and broad beans.

The Dutch, unaccustomed to the management of vineyards, did not succeed very well with the cultivation of the grape and making of wine. However, they introduced foreign stock and sent to Heidelberg for vine-dressers; and in some instances they were rewarded with success. The Swedes on the South river had succeeded in making several kinds of excellent wine and had white, red and blue grapes.

The citrull or water citron (*citerullen ofte water limoenen*) also grows there, a fruit that we have not in the Netherlands, and is only known from its being occasionally brought from Portugal, except to those who have travelled in warm climates. . . . They grow ordinarily to the size of a man's head. I have seen them as large as the biggest Leyden cabbages, but in general they are somewhat oblong. Within they are white or red; the red have white and the white black seeds. . . . Women and children are very fond of this fruit. It is also quite refreshing from its coolness and is used as a beverage in many

---

[1] A Dutch bushel (*schepel*) is about three pecks.

GARDENS, HOUSES, AND STREETS 35

places. I have heard the English say that they obtain a liquor from it resembling Spanish wine, but not so strong.

Melons, likewise, grow in the New Netherlands very luxuriantly, without requiring the land to be prepared or manured; there is no necessity for lopping the vines, or carefully dressing them under glass as is done in this country; indeed scarcely any attention is paid to them, no more than is bestowed here in the raising of cucumbers. . . . Melons will thrive, too, in newly cleared woodland, when it is freed from weeds; and in this situation the fruit which they call *Spanish pork* grows large and very abundant. I had the curiosity to weigh one of these melons, and found its weight to be seventeen pounds.

The mulberries are better and sweeter than ours, and ripen earlier. Several kinds of plums, wild or small cherries, juniper, small kinds of apples, many hazel-nuts, black currants, gooseberries, blue India figs and strawberries in abundance all over the country, some of which ripen at half May and we have them until July; blueberries, raspberries, black-caps, etc., with artichokes, ground-acorns, ground beans, wild onions and leeks like ours, with several other kinds of roots and fruits known to the Indians, who use the same which are disregarded by the Netherlanders, because they have introduced every kind of garden vegetables which thrive and yield well. The country also produces an abundance of fruits like the Spanish capers, which could be preserved in like manner.

On observing that the climate was suitable to the production of fruit trees, the Dutch imported both seeds and apple and pear trees. The English introduced quinces. Orchard cherries also throve well and produced large fruit.

Spanish cherries, forerunners, morellæs, of every kind we have, as in the Netherlands and the trees bear better because the blossoms are not injured by the frosts. The peaches, which are sought after in the Netherlands, grow wonderfully well here. If a stone is put into the earth, it will spring in the same season, and grow so rapidly as to bear fruit in the fourth year, and the limbs are frequently broken by the weight of the peaches, which usually are very fine. We have also introduced morecotoons (a kind of peach), apricots, several sorts of the best plums, almonds, persimmons, cornelian cherries, figs, several sorts of currants, calissiens and thorn apples; and we do not doubt but that the olive would thrive and be profitable, but we have them not. Although the land is full of many kinds of grapes, we still want settings of the best kinds from Germany, for the purpose of enabling our vine-planters here to select the best kinds and to propagate the same.

Orchards, as we have seen, had become not only numerous but valuable possessions of the Dutch colonists, who cultivated the native and foreign stock. When the Labadist Fathers visited the country in 1679-1680, they were perfectly amazed at the fine specimens of pears, apples, and peaches offered to them, and the abundance. This fruit they describe as "exceedingly fair and good and pleasant to the taste; much better than that in Holland or elsewhere." They saw many gardens on the island of Manhattan and on Long Island so laden with apples, peaches, and other fruit that "one might doubt whether there were more leaves or fruit on them." They confessed they had never seen in Europe, even in the best of seasons, anything to equal it; for though "quantities had fallen off, the trees were still as full as they could bear." Again they were astonished to find peach trees "all laden with fruit to breaking down, and many of them actually broken down"; while hogs and other animals were enjoying their fill. On both sides of the Hudson near Spuyten Duyvel they also found delicious peaches, and in such quanti-

GARDENS, HOUSES, AND STREETS

ties that the road was lined with them, and they were told that the hogs were so satiated with them that they would not eat any more. Here they also found blue grapes "as sweet and good as any in Fatherland." They also remarked a fine orchard belonging to the tavern near the church in the Fort on Manhattan Island. "Among other trees," they say, "we observed a mulberry tree, the leaves of which were as large as a plate. The wife showed us pears larger than the fist, picked from a three years graft, which had borne forty of them."

A typical orchard was that found by Tienhoven, Secretary, who in 1639 "went and behind the house which Anthony Jansen from Salee sold to Barent Dircksen, found 12 apple trees, 40 peach trees and 73 cherry trees, 26 sage plants and 15 vines."

Montanus, 1671, says that some plants imported from Holland thrive better than at home, especially the apple, pear, quince, cherry, plum, currant, apricot, buckthorn, medlar, peach, and onion.

Vines grow wild everywhere and bear in abundance blue and white muscatels and pork-grapes (*spek-druiven*). Some time since, the wine press was successfully introduced. The wine was equal to any Rhenish or French wine. Every vegetable known to the Dutch is cultivated in the gardens. Water melons as savory as they are wholesome, are, when ripe, as large as cabbage. The English extract a liquor from them which would be no wise inferior to Spanish wine did it not turn sour too soon. Gourds when cleaned out serve as water vessels. Tobacco produces leaves five quarters long. Pumpkins grow luxuriant and agreeable. Corn, sowed in hills six feet apart, sprouts up readily and prosperously if properly weeded. Turkish beans, planted beside the corn, wind themselves around the stalk. Grey peas prosper here so well that two crops are gathered in the year from one field. Medicinal plants and indigo grow wild in abundance. The barley can be tied above the head. Furthermore, all sorts of flowers have a pleasant odour and appearance.

The products of orchards and gardens were fully appreciated by others as well as their rightful owners. Robbing orchards was a pleasant, popular, and presumably profitable pursuit, until the authorities stepped in and discouraged the pastime with heavy penalties. We read under date Nov. 25, 1638:

Whereas complaints are made that the gardens of many persons have been robbed and their poultry taken away, if there be any one who can give information of the thieves, he shall be paid 25 guilders as a reward [if an accomplice, pardoned and name concealed].

Again, July 1, 1647:

Everyone is warned against doing any damage to Farms, Orchards and Gardens, either to the fences or fruits. [Penalty, "100 guilders besides an arbitrary correction."]

Four-footed intruders were even more destructive than human marauders, as we gather from the ordinance of 1648 forbidding goats or hogs to be pastured between the fortifications and the Fresh Water.

Mr. Woolley, in his *Two Years Journal in New York* (1678–1680), gives us a description of a bear hunt in an orchard:

I was with others that have had very good diversion and sport with them [Bears] in an orchard of Mr. John Robinson's of New York, where we followed a Bear from

GARDENS, HOUSES, AND STREETS   39

Tree to Tree, upon which he could swarm like a Cat; and when he was got to his resting-place, perch'd upon a high branch, we dispatc'd a youth after him with a Club to an opposite bough, who knocking his Paws he comes grumbling down backwards with a thump upon the ground, so we after him again. His descending backwards is a thing particularly remarkable.

The first care of the West India Company was naturally for the safety of its servants and storehouse, and therefore a fort was built of sufficient size to inclose barracks, a church, a windmill, a may-pole, the Company's buildings, and a gibbet. Into this the settlers could retire in case of Indian attack. Beyond it a small town was laid out, and further protected by a strong palisade with gates that were shut at night.

Michaëlius wrote in 1628:

They fell much wood here to carry to Fatherland, but the vessels are too few to take much of it. They are making a windmill to saw the wood: and we also have a gristmill. They bake brick here, but it is very poor. There is good material for burning lime, namely oyster shells in large quantities. The burning of potash has not succeeded; the master and his labourers are all greatly disappointed. We are busy now in building a fort of good quarry stone, which is to be found not far from here in abundance. May the Lord only build and watch over our walls.

The houses gradually increased and were planted along the lines of the Fort and shores of the river. The river front in these days came up to Pearl Street, and from Whitehall to Broad, the border of the river was called the Strand.

In 1642, two very important buildings were erected, — the city tavern, constructed of stone or brick, two or three stories high, with sloping roof and dormer windows (which at a later date became the Stadt Huys, or City Hall, for both Dutch and English); and the church in the Fort. There was also a road to the Ferry from the Fort, and a line of pickets where Wall Street is now situated. We learn that on March 31, 1644, "a good solid fence was ordered to be erected from the great Bouwery across to the plantation of Emanuel." All persons who wished their cattle pastured in security were called to assist in erecting the fence with proper tools, and those who failed were excluded from the privileges of the inclosed meadow (see page 18).

The forests supplied magnificent timber for building purposes, and so the first houses were usually built of wood with thatched roofs. Some houses, however, were built of brick and stone with tiled roofs, and some wooden houses had brick chimneys. The Company at first supplied the bricks and tiles from Amsterdam, but very soon there were brick kilns on Manhattan Island, at Fort Orange, and in the Dutch settlement on the Delaware. Jan A. de Graaf owned a brick kiln in New Amsterdam in 1658; and ten years later 1250 hard bricks cost twenty-four florins in Fort Orange. Not only brick but stone was used in the construction of the more important edifices. The price of brick and the extent to which it entered into the building of the early houses of New Amsterdam may be gathered from the records. When the West India Company leased the Bouwery at Hoboken to H. C. van Vorst in 1639, 4000 bricks were delivered to him to build the chimney; all other necessaries were at his own expense. On May 29, 1643, Laurens Cornelissen delivered with his house " stone enough to build an oven capable of baking a *schepel* and a half of wheat." On Nov. 2, 1643,

VAN CORTLANDT MANOR HOUSE (1681)
CROTON-ON-HUDSON

GARDENS, HOUSES, AND STREETS

Dirck Cornelissen received a note for twenty-five guilders for building a chimney.

Tienhoven's requisitions to the West India Company in 1650 include "three or four house carpenters who can lay brick"; and in 1659 the "list of materials, particularly required" contained the following items:

12,000 tiles @ 18 g	fl. 216.00
100,000 hard brick @ 4	400.00
20 hogsheads lime @ 3¼	65.00
10 chaldron smith's coals	174.00

The records contain several lawsuits regarding bricks. On May 29, 1657, Peter Bosboom was fined for breach of contract in refusing to manufacture brick for Peter Bent.

In 1642, John and Richard Ogden, of Stamford, contracted to build a stone church in New Amsterdam, seventy-two feet long by fifty-two feet broad, and sixteen feet high above the ground, for 2500 guilders.

La Montagne, in 1661, reports to Stuyvesant that he has bought at Fort Orange 3000 bricks at ten guilders in beaver the thousand and 3000 for twenty-two guilders in wampum.

In 1660, "Cornelis Barensen, baker, requests to be appointed Teller of the Bricks and Tiles coming from Fatherland and other places, as he cannot support his family as measurer of grain and lime and similar things." His petition was granted, and "for fee shall draw four stivers per thousand."

In 1653, a very good brickmaker came out in the *Graft*, with the Directors' recommendation to Stuyvesant "to allot for him so suitable a place as his circumstances and the fitness of it for a brickyard require." In April, 1658, we find an order extending the time for covering W. P. de Groot's house in New Amsterdam with tiles until he received them from Holland or Fort Orange.

Stuyvesant himself, not liking the governor's house in the Fort, built a fine stone house about where State and Whitehall Streets now are. He had a pretty garden here with ornamental shrubs and flowers, had his grounds neatly inclosed by a wall and strengthened by wooden sidings as a protection from the river, and had a private dock for his barge of state. The house received the name *Whitehall*. He also had a country home, the Bouwery.

There is ample evidence that glass was used in the windows of all but the humblest houses. Much of it, but by no means all, was imported from Holland. The pane in general use measured twelve inches high by eight inches wide. The glazier's craft was well worth following, and was not confined to imported labor. In the court records we read, for example, "Oct. 6th, 1648, Cornelis Jansen was indentured to Evert Duyckkink to learn the trade of a glazier."

On Jan. 12, 1654, Hendrick Hendricksen complains that Claes Croon " sometime back took with him six panes of glass out of his house to make them somewhat smaller so as to fit, which up to the present date he has not returned, whereby he suffers great inconvenience at this wintry season." Defendant was ordered to set in the panes within three days, but was contumacious, and the shivering Hendricksen had to go to court again. On March 23, 1655, Mr. Croon was summoned by another customer, Poulus Heymans, for not delivering ten panes of common glass for which he had been paid seventy guldens and was fined twenty-five guldens.

In 1657, the Directors notify Stuyvesant that they

GARDENS, HOUSES, AND STREETS

are sending out a consignment of leaden window frames.

In numerous pictures by the Little Masters we see coats-of-arms in colored glass in the windows of the prosperous class. This taste was undoubtedly indulged also in New Netherland. One of the earliest workers in this art was the above Evert Duyckinck. On Oct. 9, 1656,

Evert Duycking requests by petition to be informed from whom he is to receive payment for the glass which he put in the Church for Schout, Burgomasters and Schepens, demanding 2½ beavers for each. The Court decides that petitioner shall go to each one for whom the glass was for his payment either in trade, or as he can agree for the same.

Evert had two sons, one of whom was the mate of the ship that brought over the Labadist Fathers, and the other, Gerrit, who followed his father's business. When the Fathers visited Esopus, they had the companionship of Gerrit, who was going there with colored glass for the church windows. In 1658,

De Sille and Van der Vin, Churchwardens, report that they have agreed with Claas Marschalk to repair the glass in the church which he undertook for a reasonable price; but he rendered unto them an unreasonable a/c therefor, producing the same, with a request that the magistrates examine the same. Claas Marschalk says he calculated according to the Church work, and has had great trouble to set the lozenges in the arms in their proper places. Burgomasters and Schepens refer the matter in question to Cornelis Steenwyck, old Schepen and now Orphan Master of this City, and to Adolf Pietersen, to take up the a/c, to discuss and decide the same; to reconcile parties if possible; if not, to report their conclusion to the Court.

The following contract to build an inn is descriptive of house-building here in 1655:

We, Carpenters, Jan Cornelisen, Abram Jacobsen and Jan Hendricksen, have contracted to construct a house over the ferry of Egbert Van Borsum, ferry-man, thirty feet long and eighteen inches wide, with an outlet of four feet, to place in it seven girders, with three transome windows and one door in the front, the front to be planed and grooved, and the rear front to have boards overlapped in order to be tight, with door and windows therein; and a floor and garret grooved and planed beneath (on the under side); to saw the roof thereon, and moreover to set a window-frame with a glass light in the front side; to make a chimney mantel and to wainscot the foreroom below, and divide it in the centre across with a door in the partition; to set a window frame with two glass lights therein; further to wainscot the east side the whole length of the house, and in the recess two bedsteads, one in the front room and one in the inside room, with a pantry at the end of the bedstead (*betse*); a winding staircase in the fore-room. Furthermore we, the carpenters are bound to deliver all the square timber — to wit, beams, posts and frame timber, with the pillar for the winding staircase, spars and worm and girders, and foundation timbers required for the work; also the spikes and nails for the interior work; also rails for the wainscot are to be delivered by us.

For which work Egbert van Borsum is to pay five hundred and fifty guilders, one-third in beavers, one-third in good merchantable wampum, one-third in good silver coin, and free passage over the ferry so long as the work continues, and small beer to be drunk during work.

We have subsequently contracted with said Egbert Van Borsum to build a cellar-kitchen under said house, and to furnish the wood for it — to wit, beams and frame timber. There must be made two door frames and two

GARDENS, HOUSES, AND STREETS

circular frames with windows therein, with a stairway to enter it, and to line the stairs in the cellar round about with boards, with a chimney mantel in the kitchen, and to groove and plane the ceiling. Egbert must excavate the cellar at his own expense. The carpenters must furnish the nails. For this work one hundred guilders are promised, together with one whole good otter skin. Moreover, Egbert must deliver all the flat woodwork required for the house — to wit, boards and wainscotting.

A typical dwelling of the middle of the century is also seen in the

Conditions and terms on which Jacob Kip proposes to sell publicly, to the highest bidder his house kitchen hen or hog yard and lot lying in the City of [New] Amsterdam over against the house of Heer Oloff Stevense [Van Cortland], as the same is occupied by him. The house two and thirty feet long and twenty feet broad inclosed with thick planks and a glazed pantile roof, has a garret and floor, cellar walled up three four or five feet with stone, and has a brick chimney in the front room, also a shop, the partition walls of bricks, the inner room built up with brick all around (*rondtom*) bedstead, counting-house and larder therein; besides the aforesaid house, there is a kitchen eight or nine feet wide and seventeen or eighteen feet long, on the side of the house, with a brick chimney, in use by him, together with a hen or hog yard in the rear, and the place paved with bricks and an apple tree therein, also a common gangway on the west side of the house six feet wide and a common well, and what more is thereon and fast in earth and nailed except the andirons (*handizer*) and hearth stone.

In John Josselyn's *Account of Two Voyages to New England*, 1674, we read:

New York is built with Dutch brick *alla-moderna*, the meanest house therein being valued at one hundred pounds; to the landward it is compassed with a wall of good thickness.

The house (facing page 40) which stands on Croton Point, has suffered little change since it was built in 1681. It was originally a block house built by Governor Dongan as a rendezvous for his fishing-parties and conferences with the Indians. It was bought from the Indians by Stephanus van Cortlandt, son of Olaff Stevenson, who came to Manhattan, a soldier from Courland, with Kieft. The estate, which consisted of 85,000 acres, extending into Connecticut, was erected into a manor and lordship in 1697. The walls are of reddish freestone, are three feet thick, and pierced with loopholes, which are seen in the illustration facing page 48.

A famous farm and dwelling was that of Frederick Philipse (or Flypsen, as it was originally written), who, born in Friesland in 1626 and a carpenter by trade, sought fortune and found it in New Amsterdam. In 1662, he married the energetic Margaret Hardenbrook, widow of Peter Rudolphus De Vries, a merchant-trader of New Amsterdam, who left her a large fortune. Margaret Philipse went repeatedly to Holland in her own ships and bought and traded in her own name. Philipse soon became the richest man in New Amsterdam; and soon after Margaret's death remarried, in 1692, another heiress, Catharine van Cortlandt, widow of John Derval, and daughter of Olaff Stevensz van Cortlandt. His house, built in 1682, altered and enlarged by his grandson, is still standing; and is now used as the Town Hall of Yonkers. The original staircase was brought from Holland. The house was surounded by fine trees and gardens in its early days. Philipse also had two hundred and forty square miles,

GARDENS, HOUSES, AND STREETS 47

— Fredericksborough (Sleepy Hollow), where he built, in 1683, Castle Philipse, a stone fortification for protection against the Indians; and in 1699 he and his wife, Catharine van Cortlandt, built the church at Sleepy Hollow. Other houses of the period face page 24.

Stuyvesant appointed surveyors of streets and buildings; and in 1655 Allard Anthony, burgomaster, and Dr. La Montagne, councilor, were a committee to report on the work of the surveyors. A dock was constructed on the East River side, and the streets were regularly laid out and named. New Amsterdam now began to assume the appearance of a town.

At this period was also constructed the Schœyinge, a sort of sea wall, or siding of boards, that reached from the City Hall at Coenties Slip to the Water Gate at Wall Street. The boards were placed in endwise and then elevated. The Schœyinge was begun in 1655, and in the next year, it being determined that the whole Strand should be thus protected, the burgomasters and schepens ordered all dwellers or owners of yards on the East River between the gate and the City Hall to build up and line their property with boards. If they failed, a fine of twenty-five guilders was exacted. On the northern side of Wall Street from the East to the Hudson River a line of defense was erected, called the Palisades.

In 1653, the Committee decided that the Palisades must be twelve feet long, eighteen inches in circumference, sharpened at the upper end, and be set in line. At each rod a post twenty-one inches in circumference was to be set, to which rails, split for the purpose, were to be nailed one foot below the top. The breastwork was to be four feet high, four feet at the bottom, and three feet at the top, covered with sods, with a ditch three feet wide and two feet deep, two feet and a half within the breastwork; the length of the ground to be lined with palisades 180 rods, "the end of the rods being the last of the money." Thomas Baxter undertook to deliver all posts and rails for twenty stivers for each post and rail together.

On Jan. 4, 1655, a petition was presented for enlarging the city gate at the East River so as to permit the passage of a cart and for repairing the road.

We have already seen (page 25) that the average burgher was not careful in keeping the streets clean, nor did he hesitate to cumber the way with building material or any other bulky goods if convenient for his own business. In the inventory of the effects of Cornelis Steenwyck, for example, we notice considerable lumber in the street, consisting of fir planks, iron anchor, boards, Holland pan tiles, etc. In 1656, Stuyvesant made a formal and personal complaint, among other things, of "crowding of the streets with stone and timber, so that no carts or wagons can pass."

The first street, or dirt road, in the city to be paved by the authorities was paid for grudgingly by those even who had petitioned for the improvement. In 1658, Schepen Isaack de Forest appears in court complaining that the "Inhabitants of the Brewer's street (now Stone Street) who imposed on themselves the tax for the benefit of the street in order to its being paved, are unwilling to pay, requesting that the Magistrates be pleased to order payment."

In 1660, when the account for making and sheeting the Heere Graght (the Canal) was rendered in court, it was ordered that each resident or occupant of a lot on both banks should pay "in discharge of said expenses on so much as he possesses, the sum of Forty guilders in Zewant per rod, and the foot in proportion."

WALL OF THE VAN CORTLANDT MANOR HOUSE
SHOWING LOOPHOLES

GARDENS, HOUSES, AND STREETS

There was great trouble in collecting this tax. Nearly all the dwellers along the canal refused to pay, and, when summoned, obstinately said they would neither pay the assessment nor the fine, — they would rather go to prison. The authorities were fain to treat the offenders with considerable leniency. It would seem that the work was not done, after all, for twelve years later (1672) we read:

Whereas his honn^r the Gouvern^r hath severall times Recommended to this Court the Makeing up of ye Mote or Graft of this Citty, the Worshipp^{ll} Court have therefore thought fit and do hereby Strictly Order that ye s^d Mote or graft schall be made up by ye Owners of ye houses or Lotts that do live about uppon ye s^d mote or otherwise by ye tennants of ye houses for ye Owners accounts in manner and forme following, viz.
Imprimus from ye Waterside upwards to the bridge over against ye Stone Street to be Repaired and made and finished in ye same forme and manner as Mr Johannis de Peyster hat already begunn to be made and finished the s^d owners of ye Houses and Lotts or ye Tennants for ye Owners accounts wch in ye space of two months next Ensuing ye date hereof.

A paved street in New Amsterdam was like many a one still to be seen in old towns in Europe, where the gutter is a broad gully in the middle of the street, which must be crossed by stepping-stones when rain turns the thoroughfare into a brawling stream. We may gain a clear idea of a model street of the day (1670) from the "Orders and Instructions for Mr Johannes de Peister, Isaacq Greveraet, Coeuraet ten Eyck and Hendrick Willemsen Backer, Overseers appointed for the Laying out and Paveing of the Streets":

Imprimis: The sd. Overzeers are hereby required to order that the Streetes wch are to be paved be laid out as level and even as possible may be, according to the Convenience of the Streets.

2ndly. That the Passage be Raised about one foot higher then the Middle of the Streete to the end the Water may take its Course from the passages towards the Middle of the Streets aforesaid.

3rdly And in Case the Neighbours are Inclined to wards the paveing of the Whole Streetes, they have liberty soo to doe, provided that all the Neighbours do Jointly agree about the same.

Flimsy construction led to the appointment of firewardens in 1648:

The Honble Director General and Council having seen and observed that some careless people neglect to keep their Chimneys clean by sweeping, and do not pay attention to their fires, whereby recently two Houses were burned and greater damage is to be expected in future from fire, the rather as the houses here in New Amsterdam are for the most part built of Wood and thatched with Reed, besides which the Chimneys of some of the houses are of wood, which also is most dangerous; Therefore the Honble General and Council Ordain, enact and command as they hereby do, that from now henceforward no Chimneys shall be built of wood or [lath and] plaister in any houses between the Fort and the *Fresh Water*, but those already enacted may remain until further order and pleasure of the Firewardens; and in order that the foregoing shall be well observed, to that end are appointed Fire-wardens — from the Honble Council, Commissary Adriaen d' Keyser; from the Commonality, Thomas Hall, Marten Crigier and George Wolsey, with power at their pleasure to see if the Chimneys in all houses situate and standing within this city every where around, between this Fort and the *Fresh Water*, are kept well cleaned by sweeping, and if any one be found negligent he shall, every time the Firewardens aforesaid examine and find the Chimneys foul, pay them forthwith, without any contradiction, a fine of three Guilders for every flue found on examination to be dirty, to be expended for Fire ladders, Hooks and Buckets which shall be procured and provided at the earliest and most convenient opportunity, and if any one's house be burned, or be the cause of fire, either through negligence or by his own fire, he shall forfeit 25 florins to be applied as above.

Jan Vinje complains (Aug. 28, 1656) that "Kint in 't Water's wife goes carelessly night and day with fire through her own and her neighbours lots, whereby they are in great danger of fire; and that he has not repaired his house nor erected chimneys. Kint in 't Water says he brought the plank; the stone and nails he cannot yet obtain; he promises to do all in his power to prevent any disaster." The court ordered him to inclose his house and make chimneys according to the order of the Street Inspectors, allowing him fourteen days' time at the farthest, provided that meanwhile he take good care that no misfortune occurs.

It will be noticed that the dweller in New Amsterdam was not particularly docile under his paternal rule, nor did he take kindly to the various ordinances that interfered with his doing what seemed to him good in his own eyes regarding his own house and grounds. The fact that municipal ordinances on the same subject were repeated with little apparent effect, more in sorrow than in anger sometimes, shows this. It would appear that the officers who were appointed to see that the rules and regulations were observed were not always treated with the respect that was their due. For instance, in 1658 Solomon La Chair was called up for correction. On being visited by the Fire Inspector he had called him a chimney-sweeper, and in his *patois* had exclaimed, "Is it to have a little cock booted and spurred!" Their Worships decided:

As it is not seemly that men should mock and scoff at those persons who are appointed by the Magistracy to any office — yea a necessary office, they therefore condemn Solomon La Chair in a fine of twelve guilders.

No Dutch town, however small, could exist without its *schuttery;* and consequently we find at quite an early period the Burgher Wacht (Citizen's Watch or Guard), consisting of two companies, one of which carried a blue and the other an orange ensign. As they had trouble to get fire-arms, Stuyvesant supplied them from the Company's chest. At a later period the Rattle Watch was instituted, consisting of six men whose duty was to patrol the streets at night, to arrest thieves, to give alarm in case of fire, and all other warnings. They carried a large rattle. In 1658, on going the rounds the watch was required to call out "how late it is at all the corners of the streets from nine o'clock in the evening until the reveillé beat in the morning." Each man received eighteen guilders a month. In January, 1674:

From now henceforward the Burgher Watch of this City shall be set and commence at drumbeat about half an hour before sun down when the train bands of this City then on guard shall parade before the City Hall of this City.

The City gate shall be closed at sun down by the Mayor of this City and his attendant trainbands and in like manner opened at sun rise.

The Burghery and inhabitants of this City and all others of what quality soever they may be, the watch alone excepted, are strictly interdicted and forbid to attempt coming from sunset to sunrise on the bulwarks, bastions or batteries of this City on pain of bodily correction.

It is strictly forbidden and prohibited, that any person, be he who he may, presume to land within this City or quit the same in any other manner, way or means than through the ordinary City gate on pain of DEATH.

In 1697, the streets were first lighted. At every seventh house a pole was projected on which hung a lantern. When there was a "light moon," the candle was not lighted in the lanterns. A night watch of four men with the old rattle patrolled the streets.

In February, 1670, all the city carmen were summoned to court because of a complaint that several of them neglected their duty "in taking good care for the goods which they do cart for the burghers and strangers, as also, that some of them do many times use ill and bad language to the burghers." They were warned to mend their ways on pain of dismissal.

On Dec. 16, 1659, Romein Servein was fined twelve guilders because he "was found one Sunday riding with his cart on the strand; also whilst driving his cart was sitting on his cart." The court also granted the Schout's request "for himself and the Under Schout that they may seize the cart whenever they find any carters sitting riding on their carts along the streets." Thomas Verdon, another delinquent, pleaded "he sat on the cart while riding through the mud, and until he should have time to drive up to the hill." The court fined him six guilders, "because driving on the street he remained seated on the cart."

In 1678, Governor Andros says: "Our principal places of trade are New York and South'ton except Albany for the Indians, our buildings most wood, some lately stone and brick, good country houses and strong of their several kinds." Governor Dongan, nine years later, reports:

The principal towns are New York, Albany and Kingston. All the rest are country villages. The buildings in New York and Albany are generally of brick and stone. In the country the houses are mostly new built, having two or three rooms on a floor. The Dutch are great improvers of land.

In 1685, William Byrd writes:

To Bro. Dan'l per Ruds.

I was a great part of last Summer at N. Yorke, about 100 Leagues to the Northward of this place, and found a very Honorable reception there from the noble Governor (Col Thomas Dongan) and all the Gent. of that place. It is a prety pleasant towne consisting of about 700 Houses, and a very handsome strong forte, wherein is the Governor's House, a great Church, Secretary's office and convenient Lodgings for the officers and Soldiers of the Garrison, with other conveniences. The Inhabitants are about six eighths Dutch, the remainder French and English.

When Madam Knight visited New York in 1707, the city was still characteristically Dutch. She writes:

The Cittie of New York is a pleasant, well compacted place, situated on a commodious River wch is a fine harbour for shipping. The Buildings, Brick generally, very stately and high, though not altogether like ours in Boston. The Bricks in some of the Houses are of divers Coullers and laid in Checkers, being glazed look very agreeable. The inside of them are neat to admiration, the wooden work, for only the walls are plastered and the Sumers[1] and Gist are plained and kept very white scowr'd, as so is all the partitions if made of Bords. The fireplaces have no Jambs (as ours have). But the Backs run flush with the walls, and the Hearth is of Tyles, and is as farr out

---

[1] Sumers is "the central beam supporting the joist," sometimes called the "bearing-beam."

ENTRANCE DOOR OF THE VAN CORTLANDT MANOR HOUSE
CROTON-ON-HUDSON

into the Room at the Ends as before the fire, wch is generally Five foot in the Low'r rooms, and the peice over where the Mantle tree should be is made as ours with Joyners work, and I suppose is fastened to iron rodds inside. The house where the Vendue was had Chimney Corners like ours, and they and the hearths were laid with the finest tile that I ever see and the stair cases laid all with white tile, which is ever clean, and so are the walls of the Kitchen wch had a Brick floor.

Two years later, also, John Lawson says:

The buildings are generally of a smaller sort of Flemish brick, and of the Dutch fashion (excepting some few houses). They are all very firm and good work, and conveniently placed, as is likewise the town, which gives a very pleasing prospect of the neighbouring islands and rivers. A good part of the inhabitants are Dutch.

CHAPTER III
COSTUME

THOUGH the wives of the rich merchants of New Amsterdam did not pay $80 a yard for cloth of gold for a dress, as did some ladies of the period in Holland, there is evidence that they dressed in the rich style of their relatives at home. The Dutch government tried in vain to check what it considered the waste of money in over-dressing, and even prohibited gold and silver fringe. Poets, too, deplored the increasing lavishness in dress, and the splendor was ridiculed on the stage, as it was denounced from the pulpit. Robes of silk, sarcenet, velvet, satin, and serge in all the fashionable hues of the day, — scarlet, purple, amaranth, fire color, rose color, dead leaf color, ash gray, and fawn and mauve, — trimmed with bows and knots of ribbons, braids, gold, silver, or silk fringes, pendants, bugles, and lace; petticoats lined with taffeta and bright with golden flowers embroidered by skillful fingers; black velvet lined with cloth of gold or silver; filmy ruffs and crisp, sheer caps; innumerable chains of gold and strands of pearls; gold bodkins for the hair; scented gloves and high-heeled shoes; muffs, fans, masks, and fine handkerchiefs, and a *châtelaine* upon the various chains of which hung scent-bottles, pomanders, writing-tablets, pencils, seals, charms, and other trinkets — formed a costume that was full of beauty, elegance, and charm.

The rich petticoat and the overdress, the sets of extra

sleeves embellished with lace ruffles, and the flowered calicoes that came from the East, the night-rails, the love hoods, the flowing robes, the fine furs, the laces, and the jewels that we see in the portraits of the day, were sent across the ocean, or made here by native seamstresses and tailors.

Among his shop goods Dr. De Lange had an East India waxed (lacquered) cabinet with brass bands and hinges, worth £4; and within it were the delightful small trinkets that so delight the heart of woman. Gloves, ribbons, laces, fourteen fans, and seven purses were contained in the first partition; laces, buckles, and ribbons in the second; cloth in the third; caps in the fourth; garters, scarfs, bands, fans, and girdles in the fifth; fringe, calico, and silk in the sixth; silk and materials for purses in the seventh; and spectacles, etc., in the eighth. In another small "waxed East India trunk" he kept "hat bands, chains," etc.

Five women's fans are also mentioned in Cornelis Steenwyck's inventory; and three tortoiseshell combs appear in Matthew Taylor's. Mrs. De Lange had a mask, and Mrs. Asser Levy, a muff. The fan was rarely absent from a lady's hand; and from the East the folding fan arrived, with its sweet-scented sandalwood or carved ivory sticks and its beautifully painted gauze or paper mounts. Fans were also made of rounded cardboard upon which feathers of various colors were artistically fastened.

Towards the end of the century the following articles could be purchased in a New Amsterdam shop: five Holland sleeves with lace ruffles; six pairs of sleeves with Holland ruffles; thirteen pairs of sleeves with Holland ruffles; six cravats; twenty-five cravats with neckbands; twenty-seven with neckbands; two white handkerchiefs; two hats with cases; one pair of boots; one cane; two pairs of shoes; one bottle of Hungary water; one pair of red slippers; one girdle, four pairs of woolen mittens; five white woolen nightcaps; one pair of leather stockings; four pairs of silk stockings; one pair of yarn stockings; three pairs of woolen under stockings; two pairs of thread stockings; three pairs of leather gloves; two calico stomachers; twenty-nine shirts; six calico nightcaps; fifteen linen women's petticoats; three pairs of linen petticoats; one blue cloak; one calico waistcoat with white fringe; two white flannel shirts; one white lined ditto with ivory buttons; one silk waistcoat; one cloth waistcoat; two pairs of cloth breeches; two pairs of striped linen breeches; one pair of leather breeches; six pairs of coarse linen ditto; two nightgowns; nine red silk handkerchiefs; sixteen white and twelve blue handkerchiefs; six gray neckcloths with gold; nineteen white neckcloths with gold; fifteen dozen without gold; one piece of white handkerchief; twelve pieces of gray handkerchief, half silk; nineteen ditto, red; three ditto gray, half red silk.

In another shop, in 1692, there are fourteen children's coats, six pairs of boys' woolen stockings, six pairs of men's scarlet worsted stockings, one pair white stockings, nineteen yards black gauze, three pairs of silk stockings, 186½ yards black crape, two dozen ivory combs, four dozen ditto, five dozen ditto, 4000 pins for lace.

One of the chief articles of a lady's dress was the petticoat. This *petit cotte* was originally what is now termed the skirt, over which was worn a silk, velvet, or cloth jacket, often trimmed with fur; or a kind of *polonaise,* the skirt of which was looped up or turned back to show the handsome petticoat.

When Washington Irving accused the Dutchwomen

of New Amsterdam of wearing half a dozen petticoats, he seems to have thought, in the first place, that a petticoat was an undergarment in those days, as it now is; and, in the second place, that a Dutchwoman wore all the petticoats she possessed at the same time.

The petticoat was of silk, satin, velvet, cloth, or linen, and was, moreover, sometimes trimmed around the bottom with gold or silver braid, embroidery, or lace. Wealthy ladies in Holland wore scarlet cloth petticoats, but less rich burghers' wives contented themselves with purple or blue serge, or linen. The fashionable scarlet occurs in many New Amsterdam wardrobes. The "widdow Elizabeth Partridge" in 1669 has six petticoats; a red cloth one is valued at £2 and one of red camlet at £10. She also has a black gros grain petticoat; a "blew silk petticoat," worth £6; and a handsome embroidered white petticoat, worth £2 10s. od. Mrs. Asser Levy, 1682, had six petticoats. One is described as blue, another scarlet, and a third silk, and she "also has one woman's suite with a red petticoat." Mrs. De Lange had a handsome red cloth petticoat with black lace, a black "pottosoo" petticoat with black silk lining, a black pottosoo petticoat with black "taffety" lining, a black silk petticoat with ash gray silk lining, two petticoats with gray lining, two petticoats with white lining, one with printed lace and one without lace, one colored drugget petticoat with a red lining, one striped stuff petticoat, one scarlet petticoat, and one under petticoat with a body red bay.

Fifteen linen women's petticoats are mentioned in John Coesart's inventory. The petticoat was worn over a large circular hoop that rested on the hips, giving "a pleasant round appearance to the figure." A heavy linen underskirt was worn beneath the petticoat. Mrs. Matthew Clarkson had two white petticoats, three black petticoats, and one "curland petticoat with fringe."

The petticoat occasionally figures in court. The following gives a good description of the garment. On Dec. 7, 1647, Lysbet Tyssin sued Goodman Karriman for the purchase of a red petticoat with blue lining and trimmed with cord. The matter was referred to Mr. Ochden and Lieutenant Baxter for arbitration. Again we read: Oct. 19, 1638, Declaration of Cornelis Petersen that Annetje Jans, wife of Rev. Everardus Bogardus, had sold him a hog and purchased in return of him purple cloth sufficient for a petticoat. Oct 13, 1638, Declaration by Jacob van Curler that Rev. Everardus Bogardus's wife had, when passing the blacksmith shop in New Amsterdam, placed her hand on her side and drawn up her petticoat a little, in order not to soil it, as the road was muddy.

Every Dutch lady of the Seventeenth Century owned a "rain dress," to save her skirts from getting wet; and when the streets were dry and the rain had ceased to fall, this was tucked up in a special way to show the costly petticoat underneath. This "rain dress" originated in France, and was worn in all countries by the rich middle classes as well as by the nobility. Instead of this garment another garment was sometimes worn, called a *huik*, which was a long cloak made of serge or cloth, to cover the whole dress, and which was furnished with a hood to protect the head from the rain. In other words, it was a kind of *pelisse*. Mrs. De Lange also owned "a black silk rain cloak," which, of course, is nothing more nor less than the fashionable *huik*.

Of handsome long robes Mrs. De Lange had six, known as *samars:* "one black silk potoso-a-samare, with lace; one black silk crape samare with a tucker;

one black tartanel samare with a tucker; and three flowered calico samare." The night-gown, which was so fashionable at this period, was the name given to an evening dress. "Three calico nightgowns — two flowered and one red" — are evidently made of some Eastern material. We also read of one silk waistcoat, one red calico waistcoat, one bodice, and five pairs of white cotton stockings, besides lace, sleeves, caps, hoods, aprons, and a "black plush mask."

"One embroidered purse with a silver bugle and chain to the girdle, a silver hook and eye," must have been very handsome, because it cost as much as the "black silk crape samare with a tucker" and the "two pair of sleeves with great lace." Little trinkets were probably kept in "five small East India boxes," unless the lady preserved in them the next article on her inventory, "five hair curlings," which were valued at seven shillings!

The apron at this period was not a mere protection for the skirt, but was considered as a decoration. The apron frequently appears in the inventories. Mrs. Partridge has several: a blue linen apron and three woolen aprons are of less value than some others in her wardrobe. Mrs. De Lange has six calico aprons; Mrs. Asser Levy, a black silk apron; and Ann Watkins has four aprons. Lawrence Deldyke had for sale in 1692 six dozen silk aprons with gold, four dozen black aprons with silver, and six dozen blue aprons with gold.

Mrs. Partridge had a black silk gown worth £5; a black cloth waistcoat, a handsome lace handkerchief, and a red coat and a loose gown. Among other items four silver clasps, a gold ring, and a silver button are mentioned. Mrs. Clarkson owned one stuff gown lined, one pair of "stayes," one calico gown, "one silk waistcoat for a woman," one " pair of gloves and topknotts," and one black crape gown.

Among Asser Levy's belongings we find " sixteen women's smocks, one bodice, one colored cassock, one velvet cassock, one hood, one muff, one black silk apron, three pair red women's stockings, two pair silk stockings, six white aprons, and twelve women's caps with lace."

The sleeve was of great importance, and was made separate from the bodice. The great slashed and puffed sleeve was worn over a lace or fine cambric or silk undersleeve, clasped here and there with gold or silver ornaments or jewels, and embellished with a lace or cambric cuff or ruffle at the wrist. Ann Watkins had, for example, in 1688, " thirty-seven pair of old false sleeves "; Mrs. Clarkson owned three pairs of sleeves and one pair of ruffles; Mrs. Partridge, 1669, a parcel of lace and laced bands, and Mrs. De Lange had " two pairs of sleeves with great lace "(£1 3s. 6d.), two pairs of woman's sleeves without lace, five pairs with inner lace, thirteen women's sleeves with lace, and " twenty-five small and great cushion sleeves." She also possessed a tucker and a black silk scarf with lace.

The ruffs, or collars, were of equal importance, having reached such tremendous proportions that they extended far over the shoulders and stood up above the back of the head. In order to keep them in shape after they were starched and ironed, they were fastened on gold or silver wires. The material was the finest cambric edged with lace or *point de Venise* or *point d'Alençon*. When all the plaits of these were smoothed out, they sometimes measured sixty yards! These ruffs were extremely expensive (some of them cost as much as $4000), and were worn only by the rich; but the burghers' wives followed the styles as well as they

HALL AND STAIRWAY
VAN CORTLANDT MANOR HOUSE

could, as the portraits of the period show. The laid or turned down or flat collar was also worn; and also the crossed pleated and rounded pleated, ribbed collars. The making, undoing, washing, starching, and ironing, and remaking was no common work; and many Dutch ladies attended to the making and the doing up of their ruffs themselves.

One of the most costly articles of a lady's toilette was the stomacher, or "breast-piece," which was made of silk, satin, or velvet, and ornamented with pearls and jewels. Some of them were valued at £10,000, being beautifully embroidered or sprinkled with gems or garnished with lace. W. D. Hooft gives a bride four, — of velvet, satin, figured silk, and "lord's serge."

Headdresses were of various kinds. Caps of lace made into various shapes and styles, such as the commode, in which a series of ruffles shaped something like battlements stood erect and high above the forehead, pinners or lappets, "head cloths" wrapped around the head like hoods, "cornet caps," "drawing-caps," and hoods of silk appear in many inventories. Mrs. De Lange, for example, has sixteen cornet caps with lace, thirty-nine drawing caps with lace, eleven headbands with lace, and eleven headbands without lace. She also has twelve white hoods of love, another white love hood, three black love hoods, one yellow love hood, and five of dowlas (coarse linen).

Ann Watkins, 1688, had "twelve capps for a woman," three "calico heads," two pinners, or lappets, for headdress, and ten headcloths. She also had an "alamode hood," which was, of course, silk. She also owned a silk lute-string scarf measuring two yards and a half. The "Widdow Elizabeth Partridge" in 1669 had a parcel of head cloths worth £2, and a "taffety hood." Mrs. Matthew Clarkson had seven plain headdresses, three laced headdresses, four "pinners," and three scarves, one of which was of velvet and lined.

The Dutch ladies were fond of perfumes; highly scented powder and the essence known as Hungary water were to be found on the dressing-table, where the various cosmetics, pins, hairpins, etc., were conveniently at hand in dainty boxes of porcelain, silver, or tortoiseshell. "A small box with some paint," found in the inventory of Mrs. Elizabeth Graveraet, widow of Dr. Samuel Drisius, looks suspiciously like a cosmetic.

Gloves were of leather, silk, cotton (calico), and white openwork thread. A lady always had a good number of "shoe-work." Her out-of-door shoes were of brown or black Spanish leather, with high red heels, called by Huygens "shell-heels." Indoors she wore red slippers, or shoes of gold or silver, leather, satin, or silk, and yellow, green, blue, scarlet, or white stockings with "clocks" at the side.

The jewels of the day were hair ornaments, earrings, brooches, pins, bracelets, chains, miniatures set with gems or pearls, clasps for the sleeves, finger-rings, necklaces, and, last but not least, the *châtelaine* of gold or silver, from which on its several chains and hooks hung the various trinkets, sewing and toilet articles, — little round mirrors, scent-boxes or pomanders containing sweet powder or paste, a patch-box containing the black court-plaster cut in various shapes, all ready to replace a fallen beauty spot, bodkins, an *étui* case, tiny silver-bound pincushion, thimble, scissors, etc. The *châtelaine* was often given as a wedding-present by the father-in-law.

In some inventories we find the characteristic head ornaments that the Dutch and particularly Frisian women have worn from time immemorial, and of which Madam Knight speaks in 1707. These gold or silver head-wearings, ear-wearings, earrings, ear-wyers, as they appear variously, were often studded with jewels, and, if not, were adorned with pendants of delicate filigree work. These peculiar decorations are familiar to all travelers in Holland, and were far from uncommon in the New World. Let us take a few examples: Mrs. Van Varick left to her daughter Cornelia " two gold pieces to wear above their ears." Cristina Cappoens had " a gold ear pendant with ye ear jewels," the weight of which was two ounces and the value £10. This was also described as " one great ear spangle with ear jewels." Among Peter Jacob Marius's belongings we find " one gold earwyer," and " two pair gold pendants." Mrs. Jacob De Lange had a pair of gold *stricks*, or pendants, in each ten diamonds, worth £25; a pair of black pendants with gold hooks, and two small white pendants. Mrs. Elizabeth Graveraet, the widow of Dr. Samuel Drisius, had " one silver head-wearing, or ear-iron," which, with a pint cup, a pint tumbler, and four spoons was valued at £5. Isaac Van Vlecq, 1688, left to his daughters two pairs of gold pendants with crystals, a gold chain, "five double," a gold bodkin, and other jewelry; and Mary Jansen, 1679, left to her daughter Elsie Leisler " a golden ear-ring."

A very handsome headdress forms a bone of contention in court in 1665. The story is as follows: Pieterje Jans said she sold to Hendrickje Duyckingh's daughter, in presence of her husband, an ornamented headdress for fifty-five guilders in seawant, and that the defendant sent it back. She demanded that the bargain should stand good. Hendrickje said her daughter had no authority to buy such without the knowledge of her parents, as she is still under them. Hendrickje's husband, Evert Duyckingh, appeared and " would have nothing to do with it." He said "it is now no time to buy head dresses; also, that it is not worth so much." Parties on both sides being heard, Burgomasters and Schepens decided that the sale of the headdress should stand good, and consequently ordered defendant to pay the sum of fifty-five guilders promised therefor, to receive the headdress and keep it.

Gold ornaments are very numerous, though not always described in detail. John Spratt, 1697, had gold ornaments weighing 2¾ ounces, which were appraised at £13 15s. od.

A curious case came up in court on Dec. 7, 1669, when Jan Hendricx van Gunst said that Jannetie Jacobs had a pair of gold ornaments which were heretofore stolen from him, and demanded restitution. She claimed she bought them from a Frenchwoman, whose name she did not know, and paid forty-eight florins seawant for them. Thereupon the court ordered her to prove from whom she had bought them. On Jan. 11, 1670, Jan Hendricx van Gunst and Jannetie Jacobs again appeared in court, when one Elsie Barentsen declared that the ornaments in question formerly belonged to Aeltie Marishalls, from whom the plaintiff bought them. Barentie Moulenaers declared on oath that she heard the plaintiff say that he had not lost the ornaments, but believed he let them fall, and that his sister found them and had seemingly sold them. Sara Peters declared she heard the plaintiff say he believed the ornaments in question were not stolen, but fallen, and were found by his sister and sold by her. On February 8, Jannetie Jacobs produced the following declarations. Harmen Hendricx van Weyen testified and declared "to have seen one fytie Dirx residing at Breukelen on Long Island wear the ornaments in question now about a year ago." Anna Dirx, wife of

Dirck Claessen Pottebacker, declared the same in writing. On March 1, 1670, the "Court found that the ornaments in question are not stolen by the defendant. However, since she cannot sufficiently prove that she bought them, but only that they were seen on Fytie Dircx, from whom defendant in the first instance declared she bought them, therefore the W: Court decide and order that the ornaments in question shall be delivered to the plaintiff and retained by him, on condition of paying to defendant twenty guilders zewant and the costs incurred herein."

Diamonds seem to have been the favorite jewels of the Dutch; they sparkle in rings, lockets, earrings, chains, and pendants of various descriptions. The wife of Dr. De Lange had a jewel box described as a "silver thread wrought small box, wherein: a gold boat wherein thirteen diamonds to one white coral chain (worth £16); two red stones; two diamond rings (worth £24); a gold ring with a clapbeck, and a gold ring or hoop bound with diamonds (worth £2 10s. 0d.)." Peter Jacob Marius, 1702, has two gold diamond rings and six other rings; Dr. De Lange had two very valuable diamond rings and a handsome gold ring, or hoop, bound round with diamonds; Mrs. Van Varick had no less than seven diamond rings; John Coesart, "a gold diamond ring and a gold hoop." Mary Jansen in 1679 left to her son Jacob a diamond rose ring; Anne Richbell, "Gentlewoman, of Mamaroneck," to her daughter, Elizabeth, in 1700, "my gold ring with an emerald stone in it"; and Cristina Cappoens has one gold rose diamond ring, worth £5. Matthew Taylor in 1687 has an enameled stone ring.

Among many instances of those whose jewel boxes were by no means empty Mrs. Margareta Van Varick is conspicuous. She has a pearl necklace, a gold chain with a locket with seven diamonds, a gold ring with seven diamonds, a gold ring with a table diamond, a gold ring with three small diamonds, two gold rings each with a diamond, two small gold rings with diamonds, three more gold rings, one pair diamond pendants, two gold drops for the ear, two gold chains, two gold buttons, one comb tipped with gold, one pair crystal pendants edged with gold, two gold pins headed with pearls, one gold bodkin, one chain with gold bell, another gold bell and chain. Cristina Cappoens, 1693, owns a gold rose diamond ring worth £5 and a large hoop ring, a " chain of great beads," and " gold hooks and eyes for a night rail." Anna Vandewater, 1684, left her daughter her gold " Stricke, or pendant."

Asser Levy in 1682 had " fourteen gold rings, one gold bodkin, two silver bodkins, two pairs gold pendants, one silver watch, one silver hatband, two pair of silver buckles, one silver earring, one pair silver buttons, one ducatoon with a ring, one silver knife, and silver to a belt for a sword." Peter Jacob Marius had in 1702 two diamond rings, one amber necklace, four pair gold buttons, three gold chains, one bodkin, and three buckles.

Cornelis Steenwyck owned a great deal of valuable jewelry, including several gold chains. Jacob De Lange kept much of his valuable jewelry in a very costly " silver thread wrought small trunk," and, moreover, owned a watch of great value, " a testament with gilt hooks and gold hangers and a gold chain." Lawrence Deldyke owned silver shoe buckles and silver shirt buckles and a silver seal in 1692, and in 1700 John Coesart had a silver snuff-box, a silver powder-box, a silver watch, and twenty-three ounces of amber beads. Among her treasures Mrs. Van Varick owned "one small gold box as big as a pea," one gold medal, one small mother of pearl box, and four small boxes with beads and shells, one gold Arabian ducat, and one gold piece the shape of a diamond.

Some pearl pins figure in a lawsuit in 1656 between two women who are evidently relatives, Helletie Jansen, plaintiff, *versus* Pietertie Jansen, defendant. The latter requested, " as defendant has bought from Indians here within this City some goods belonging to her and her sister, that she be condemned to return the same to her on receiving what she has given therefor; being one small box with divers linens, as a pair of linen sheets, two shirts, some frills, coifs, children's caps, pocket handkerchiefs, three pearl pins and other things, that she does not know precisely." Specimens of watches from the Rijks Museum face page 70.

Children were dressed like miniature grown people. The little daughters of the wealthy wore long dresses, ruffs, lace cuffs, caps, and often a good deal of jewelry. Boys were dressed in the style of their fathers, even to the large felt hat with plumes. It is not often that children's clothes are specially listed in the New Amsterdam inventories; but occasionally we find such an item as " two children's stript caps," as in that of Mrs. Elizabeth Graveraet, and in the inventories of shop goods. Cornelis Steenwyck's is rather unusual in this respect, for we find " one red silk fringe belt and one children's ditto; two children's waistcoats, one coate and one pair breeches for children, one dozen children's caps, a parcel of linen for children, four dozen children linen caps, one dozen children's shirts, four children best linen shirts, three laced cuffs for children, two boyes' bonnets, three whisks for children, two pair children's sleeves of silk, six children tufted holland waistcoats, old, one dozen small linen children's hoods, one dozen children linen cuffes and one gold child's whistle." "One silk child's cloak and five child's aprons" appear in Matthew Clarkson's inventory.

The peasant-women, or farming-class, were more varied in costume than the wealthy burghers' wives and daughters who followed the fashions of Paris and Amsterdam. Generally speaking, the dress consisted of a woolen skirt, a jacket reaching nearly to the knees, with puffed sleeves, a standing collar, and a large woolen cloak. There were slight variations according to the country from which the women came. The Purmer women wore a tight-fitting jacket with narrow sleeves fastened around the wrists with silver buttons, a "breast cover," or stomacher, trimmed with small rosettes or bows, a standing collar, a short skirt, and a silver *châtelaine* with keys, a purse, knives, knitting-needle holders, and other trinkets. The Edam women might be distinguished by their flat linen collars turned back over their jackets. The wives of the South Holland farmers wore a laced jacket, with a flowered or velvet "breast cloth" pinned over it, which sometimes was adorned with a collar and fastened in front with buttons or loops. The North Holland women wore a white starched bonnet, with a high bodice laced up to the chin; while the very large and gaudy colored neckerchief was not worn round the neck but pinned on the bodice. Their skirts were longer than those of the South Holland women, which were so short that the poets poked fun at them. These last did not wear collars, but velvet neckerchiefs, or neckpieces, with thick golden clasps. The aprons were of blue linen with green binding; the skirts generally of brown material or black linen.

Stockings were red, blue, yellow, brown, and other

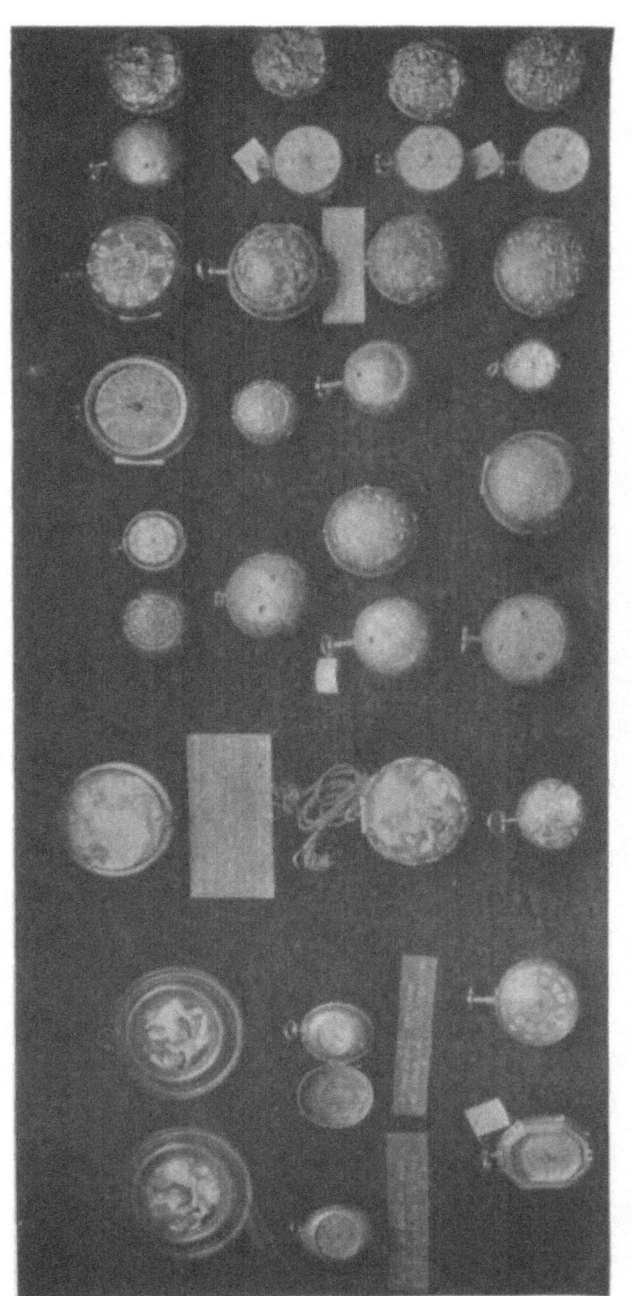

OLD DUTCH WATCHES
RIJKS MUSEUM, AMSTERDAM

colors, and slippers were generally worn as well as the wooden shoes.

The hair was combed back smoothly over and braided at the back of the head, after which this braid was twisted around the head. Over this was sometimes worn a velvet hat, not unlike a man's hat, with a rim, straight in front and turned upwards in the back. These hats were generally worn to market, but the richer women often wore "embroidered bonnets" and "cornet-caps," of which Mrs. De Lange had several (see page 63). The Alkmaar girls went bareheaded, but they had a knack of braiding their golden hair in a captivating way.

The suit of clothes for men consisted then, as now, of breeches, coat, and waistcoat. Baggy breeches were characteristic of the Dutchmen. They were usually of the same color as the waistcoat, and were extremely wide and reached to the knee. These were made in a great variety of shapes and colors, except in the case of the city magistrates, who rarely wore anything but black. There was no article of clothing on which more work and care were bestowed and which was made in so many different styles and called by so many different names, most of which were foreign. "Do you wish your breeches in the French or the German style? a flesh-colored pair woven in the German style, or one of the French fashion?" the tailor would ask. The breeches were elaborately trimmed with buttons. Cloth buttons were sometimes used; but if the gentleman could afford it the decorative buttons were of silver. Wrought silver buttons were often given as christening presents for future use. Innumerable buttons of silver, metal, thread, silk, and other materials are found in the shops of New Amsterdam. Mrs. Van Varick had seventeen dozen colored buttons, twelve dozen black, ten gross white, twelve and a half light thread, twenty-six dozen silk breast buttons, one gross silver breast buttons, seventeen dozen gimp coat buttons, eight dozen thread coat buttons, four dozen and ten pewter, twenty-two dozen hollow buttons, five pairs shirt buttons, four gross bell metal buttons, and four gross bell metal hollow buttons.

Coats were of bright colors and often lined with silk. Tail coats came into vogue towards the last of the century and were made of fancy materials. The coats were also ornamented profusely with buttons. The waistcoat was bright and gay. Young noblemen, who set the fashion, selected very costly materials, such as gold and silver cloth, silver damask, white satin with golden stripes and embroidered with flowers, and fastened with three or four rows of handsome buttons.

The burgomaster usually wore a simple black cloth suit on week days; on Sundays and on holidays, a velvet one. In summer he wore a black satin waistcoat, which fitted tight around the chest and waist and was fastened in front with small golden buttons. This black costume was frequently worn at christenings and other ceremonial occasions. One or more black suits of velvet, satin, or broadcloth are conspicuous in the inventories of the prosperous citizens of New Amsterdam.

Cornelis Steenwyck has a long list of rich and expensive clothes. He is beautifully dressed in his portrait (see Frontispiece) painted by Jan Van Goosen about 1667, and now owned by the New York Historical Society. For instance, one cloth coat with silver plate buttons is worth £4 15s. 0d.; another "stuff coat with silver plate buttons" is appraised at £4, and a black cloth coat and breeches at £2. Then he has a pair of cloth breeches, a cloth coat with gimp buttons (£2 10s. 0d.), a black cloth coat (£2 10s. 0d.), a black velvet coat, old (£3), "a coloured stuff coat," a silk coat, and one pair of silk breeches, black, and one old silk doublet (£1 5s. od.), a silver cloth doublet, an old velvet waistcoat with silver lace, a pair of "stockins" and linen breeches, a buff coat and silk sleeves (£1 10s. od.), a yellow scarf silk with silver fringes (£1 5s. od.), two cloth coats and breeches, a pair of breeches, and four fustian waistcoats.

Dr. Jacob De Lange could make a fine appearance. He had a black broadcloth suit (£1 5s. od.), a "cull'd serge, ye new suit with silver buttons" (£5), "a cullered cloth west coat with silver buttons" (£1 4s. od.), one "Japons coat lining with red say" (£1 15s. od.), two old "coates" (£1 10s. od.), and one black gros grain suit (£1 17s. od.). Asser Levy, 1682, had a black velvet jacket, a pair of black gros grain breeches and coat, one gray ditto, one dark broadcloth suit and coat, breeches; two linen breeches. Francoys Rombouts, 1691, owned two black coats, one colored coat, one waistcoat with silver buttons, three fustian waistcoats, and one pair of plush breeches and a linen coat. Lawrence Deldyke, 1692, had six coats, five waistcoats, two pairs of breeches, two pairs of plush breeches, and one morning gown. In his inventory we also find one pair of drawers. Francoys Rombouts had ten pairs of drawers and also a pair of crape drawers; Asser Levy had six linen drawers; Dr. De Lange has three silk drawers, two calico "mixt checkard" ditto, and three white calico drawers.

Mr. Joseph Farral, 1702, was also elegant in matters of dress. His wardrobe included one light colored cloth suit (£3 10s. od.), one pair plush breeches with cloth buttons, one pair woolen and three pairs striped linen breeches, one "French druged coat" and red striped waistcoat (£4 9s. 10d.), one "Capitation coat," one silk "wasecoat," one fustian "wasecoat," and six pair Holland breeches. Tymen Vanborsen, 1703, owned two coats and a pair of "britches" and another pair with silver buttons valued at £8. Thomas Davids, 1688, had three waistcoats and seventy-six silver buttons worth £48. Colonel William Smith, of St. George's Manor, Long Island, had in 1704 one hundred and four silver buttons worth £5 10s. 0d.; and a silver watch and silver buttons, £10.

Sleeves were often separate from the coat and were very handsome. Cornelis Steenwyck has three pairs of sleeves; Dr. De Lange's inventory mentions "nine and a half pair men's sleeves"; Francoys Rombouts, 1691, had six, and Lawrence Deldyke, 1692, three pairs of sleeves.

Turning now to shirts, we find Captain Cæsar Carter with seven plain shirts (£4 18s. 0d.), three new laced shirts (£4 10s. 0d.), and three laced shirts worn (£4 10s. 0d.); Dr. De Lange, thirteen linen men's shirts worth £2 15s. 0d. and three worth £1; Tymen Vanborsen, 1703, with twelve men's shirts (£4 10s. 0d.); Matthew Clarkson, 1702, with no less than twenty-five; Asser Levy, "twelve new shirts and twelve worn shirts"; Francoys Rombouts, fourteen shirts; Lawrence Deldyke, "eight white and blue shirts"; and Joseph Farral, a "callico" shirt and three Holland shirts, worth £13, and five coarse linen and one flannel shirt (£1 10s. 0d.).

The men of the period, as we know from the many portraits showing ruffs, collars, and cuffs of various styles and beautiful materials, were particularly elegant in the matter of neckwear. Whether of Brussels or cambric, lace or needlework, embroidered or plain, they were very costly. One of the oldest styles was the simple rimmed collar with either large or small plaits. Then there was a collar shaped like a horseshoe, flat in front and round at the back; also a stiff standing upright collar. About 1638 the Spanish collars were displaced by the not less costly French ones. These reached with long embroidered points down the back, and were fastened in front with cords, terminating with small acorn-shaped balls. They were first worn by Prince Frederick Henry and his Court and later by all the patrician families. Later, when the long wigs, which hung over shoulders and back, became fashionable, these collars went out of fashion, and the band took their place, which also was finely embroidered and likewise fastened with a cord with acorn-shaped balls.

A beautiful set of collar and cuffs was one of the presents a bride gave to her husband on the wedding-day, preferably made by her own hands.

The New Amsterdam inventories contain many examples of neckcloths and cravats. Dr. De Lange was very elegant in this accessory of dress. He had two neckcloths with great lace, two pairs of gorgets with lace, six long neckcloths with lace, six short neckcloths with lace, two long neckcloths without lace, eight striped neckcloths, twenty-nine pairs of gorgets, and seventeen bands. Cornelis Steenwyck had " six men's linen neckcloths (12 shillings), twenty bands (£1), seven neckcloths (12 shillings), and three laced cuffs for men (3 shillings). Asser Levy's wardrobe included twenty neckcloths with lace and without, three hals (neck) cloths, eight ditto, and eight ditto of another sort. Captain Cæsar Carter had two laced neckcloths (£2 4s. 0d.), one laced neckcloth, worn (£0 7s. 6d.), and six neckcloths (18 shillings). Lawrence Deldyke, twelve muslin cravats and two lace cravats; and F. Rombouts, twelve neckcloths.

In the old inventories the word "handkerchief" sometimes is used for the neckcloth; but in some of the New Amsterdam inventories the two articles are distinct. Captain Carter, for example, had five plain handkerchiefs and three laced handkerchiefs; Mr. Joseph Farrel, three handkerchiefs and three neckcloths; Matthew Clarkson, ten handkerchiefs; Francoys Rombouts, twelve handkerchiefs; Lawrence Deldyke, four handkerchiefs; and Steenwyck has only one.

Stockings were of great importance, and were generally of the same material as the trousers. Sometimes they were elaborately embroidered or trimmed. We read of silk, cotton, woolen, satin, flannel, and roll stockings; stockings with clocks and ribbed stockings; stockings of white, black, blue, and, above all, scarlet. The stockings were held in place by garters, and garters contrasted with or matched the stockings. There were garters of satin, silk, or cloth. A pair of ribbon garters occurs in Steenwyck's inventory, and are worth eight shillings. Steenwyck had three pairs of stockings, two pairs of thread and one of woolen stockings (8 shillings); Dr. De Lange had "five pairs white calico stockings, one pair of black, and one of gray worsted stockings"; F. Rombouts, six pairs of stockings; and Lawrence Deldyke, five pairs of stockings. Captain Carter had a large assortment: "two pair thread stockings (6 shillings), one pair scarlet stockings (18 shillings), one pair blue worsted stockings (10 shillings), one pair white worsted and one pair coarse blue stockings (8 shillings), one pair old black silk (3 shillings), and one pair white cotton stockings (5 shillings)."

Stockings were sufficiently valued to be often bequeathed to friends and relatives. For example, in the will of Thomas Exton, gentleman, 1668, we read:

COSTUME

I give unto Captain Sylvester Salisbury a new pair of silk stockings and a new pair of gloves that lye in the till of my black trunk. I give unto Mrs. Abigail Nicholls, my silver boat, a silver meat fork and a silver spoon.

In 1689, Lawrence Deldyke, the London merchant, writing his will on board the *Beaver*, leaves a pair of scarlet stockings to Lieutenant Matthew Shanks (a very appropriate name for such a bequest!), and another pair to Lancaster Symes.

Shoes were of brown or black Spanish leather. Some were cut open at the top and adorned with rosettes, or a bow of ribbon on the toe, and, as a rule, the heels were high. Indoors, slippers ("quiet walkers") were worn and also sandals.

There were many shoemakers in New Amsterdam, and for expensive boots and shoes the leather was often imported. On Sept. 27, 1656, we read:

On the complaint of the Fiscal, William Brouwer, shoemaker, was ordered to pay duty on Russia leather, etc. imported by him and to make a pair of shoes for the Fiscal.

Among the shoes and slippers we may note that Asser Levy, 1682, had two pairs of shoes and one pair of "pantoffles"; Captain Carter, two pairs of shoes and one pair of slippers; F. Rombouts, two pairs of shoes; Lawrence Deldyke, two pairs of shoes, one pair of boots, and one pair of shoe buckles; and Joseph Farrel, one pair of new shoes and one pair a little worn.

Gloves also occur frequently. Cornelis Steenwyck had two pairs of gloves; Dr. De Lange, a pair of "yellow tand gloves with black silk fringe," worth fourteen shillings; Francoys Rombouts, three pairs of gloves; Lawrence Deldyke, one pair of gloves; and "one pair white leather men's gloves" are found in Mrs. Elizabeth Graveraet's inventory.

The hat was of fine felt, round, low of crown and wide of rim, but not as low and flat as those of the Quakers; and very often it was trimmed with one large feather or several plumes, or it was ornamented with a chain of gold or row of pearls.

The tall hats (called sugar-loaves) were worn by the staid burghers, and the hats trimmed with laces, pearls and diamonds, feathers and plumes, were worn by the fashionables. In the inventory of a rich merchant of Develshem appear some "armosyn-colored, silver gray, and Sabin hats, hats with feathers and birds natural and imitations, allonges, cavalieres, carrees; wigs à la Mousquetaire, wigs of goat, buck's and camel hair, etc." Towards the end of the century the long wigs became fashionable, the curls of which sometimes reached down to the waist, while the "toupet" or "coif" often rose a foot above the forehead. It was blond, weighed sometimes more than five pounds, and frequently cost from two to three thousand guilders.

Hats and wigs occur in the wardrobes of the burghers of New Amsterdam. A few examples will give an idea of the headgear worn here: Captain Cæsar Carter had one campaign wig (£1 5s. 0d.), one short bob wig (£1 5s. 0d.), and one old bob wig (10 shillings). He also had one lacker hat (£1), and one old hat (10 shillings), and one fur cap. Mr. Joseph Farral, 1702, had "three bob wiggs" (9 shillings); Matthew Clarkson, 1703, had a "hat with a mourning hat band"; Cornelis Steenwyck had four old hatts (12 shillings); Dr Jacob De Lange, one black fine hat, one old gray hat, one black ditto, all worth £1 1s. 0d. Francoys Rombouts, 1691, had two hats and two periwigs; Lawrence Deldyke, 1692, two hats and one cap. Asser Levy, 1682, one hat, four coarse hats, two "capps," three man's "capps" with lace, a belt and a hat, and a gray and black hat. Two pearl cords mentioned in the inventory may have been trimming for one of these hats.

To wear a cloak with elegance was the mark of a gentleman; and it was not an easy thing to throw it over the shoulders in the proper folds and to keep its graceful lines. The burgomaster wore it to church and to the meetings of the Council and kept it on with his hat when paying a call. On arriving home it was removed with the shoes, for which slippers were substituted. Some of the cloaks of the day were richly trimmed with gold or silver lace, or embroidered, but, as a rule, they were handsome cloth lined with silk, and sometimes ornamented with buttons.

A number of cloaks appear in the New Amsterdam inventories, some of which are rich and costly. For instance, Dr. De Lange had a handsome heavy silk gros grain cloak lined with silk; Cornelis Steenwyck, a " light coloured gros grain cloak," a dark cloak with lining, a cloth cloak with lining of bay and wrought silver buttons; Francoys Rombouts had a " new black cloak " in 1691; and Lawrence Deldyke left a camlet cloak to Major Richard Ingoldsby.

Swords and belts and walking-sticks and canes occur among the possessions of the wealthy citizens. Dr. De Lange had a sword with a silver handle and one with an iron handle, and two canes, one with a " silver knot or head " and one with an ivory head. Colonel William Smith, of St. George's Manor, Long Island, had a silver-headed cane, three handsome swords, and eleven embroidered belts worth the extraordinary sum of £110. Asser Levy, 1682, a silver-hilted sword, one sword with a belt. Captain Cæsar Carter, 1692, an old embroidered belt with silver buckles (£1 10s. 0d.), a white silk waist belt (8 shillings), a pair of pistols

(£4), and a silver-hilted sword (£3 12s. 0d.); Matthew Clarkson, 1703, two walking-canes, two silver-handled swords, and a mourning-sword.

A melancholy wardrobe now confronts us. This belongs to Jaques Cosseau, once a prosperous merchant of New Amsterdam, but reduced to sad days at his death in 1682. Everything is "old" but one item, — "a *new* pair of stockings." The inventory reads: "one old serge coat, one old kersey coat, one old pair kersey breeches, one old black hat, one pair old black breeches, one pair old red breeches, and three old shirts." One red waistcoat without that opprobrious adjective was perhaps more presentable than the other articles. He also owned one neckcloth and "thirteen skeins of silk." Perhaps the latter were used for darning!

The dress of the farmers consisted of a waistcoat with sleeves, or a shirt-coat and an over-frock of black linen called "paltrok." The "hemd-rok" was cut short or long, and was made of serge, wool, cloth, or other materials. In some cases it was cut so low that it hung in lapels over the hips. The breeches were wide and short; but sometimes they were long and hung down to the shoes. Some people wore fringes at the bottom of the short breeches, with large silver buttons, shields, or silver ducats as clasps. The collars were low and flat. The hats had a flat crown, rather high, with a short fringed rim in the shape of a sugar-loaf, such as the Quakers wore. Some people wore what is called a "skipper's cap," and others wore hats with wide rims. Some were made of flowered velvet, with a bow at the side or ornamented with a peacock's feather. The hair was cut very short. Leather shoes were worn only on Sundays, and wooden shoes on week days.

CHAPTER IV

ROOMS AND FURNITURE

NOTHING was too good for the prosperous New Netherlander. He emulated to the best of his ability his brothers, the merchant princes of the Spice Islands, whose luxury aroused the apprehension of the home authorities and induced sumptuary laws. In furniture and upholstery he demanded the latest fashion. The looms of the East supplied him with silken fabrics for his hangings and fine raiment, and painted calico and other fine cotton goods for the comfort and elegance of his apartments. Venice and Bohemia provided him with exquisite glass; and China, Japan, and Delft with ceramics that to-day would be priceless. With lacquer (or varnish) ware he was quite familiar, and his wrought silver was rich and plentiful. Most of his fine furniture was imported, but there were many able turners, joiners, and cabinet-makers here who were capable of making artistic use of the exotic woods and ivory brought into this port from the East and West Indies, from the Gold Coast and Madagascar. From the middle of the century, when the chairs, tables, cabinet-stands, and other articles of furniture became light and graceful with side posts, rails, and supports made of turned work, beaded or spiral, we find many evidences of the new style in the inventories. Ebony was used here, as in Holland, for the expensive furniture, and ivory for inlaying. As early as 1644 we find brought into the port of New

Amsterdam a prize laden with sugar, tobacco, and ebony. In 1663, the *Gideon* was chartered for a voyage from Holland to Africa to procure slaves, copper, and elephants' teeth for New Netherland.

In the Albany County Records for 1654 we read:

Jan Gouw and Harmen Janse wish to sell a certain casket inlaid with ebony and other woods, on the following conditions, to wit: That the payment shall be made in good whole beavers; which payment shall be made within twenty four hours, without one hour longer delay.

Jacob Janse Flodder remained the buyer for thirty beavers and nineteen guilders.

As a beaver skin was worth eight to ten guilders in 1654 ($3.50 to $4), this was a rather good sum, $120; and the casket must have been a very handsome article to command such a price.

In 1681, the Royal African Company of England complained of Robert Allison for infringement of their charter by importing negroes, elephants' teeth, etc., into New York from Africa. Again, in 1702, Henry Jourdaine, mariner, owned sixty-one elephants' teeth marked "H. J."

Mahogany was undoubtedly known and used here as a cabinet wood towards the end of the century. A handsome table of this wood was brought from Holland in 1668 by Olaf Stevenson Van Cortlandt (see facing this page). The great *kasten* were usually made of oak, "French nutwood," or other kinds of walnut. In 1687, Mary Mathews has "one great walnut cupboard."

The native walnut was greatly praised by all early writers, as we have seen, but it was probably not so good for cabinet purposes as the Dutch. Be that as it may, we find that in 1658 a duty was imposed on walnut imported from Holland.

MAHOGANY TABLE BROUGHT FROM HOLLAND IN 1668
BY OLAF STEVENSON VAN CORTLANDT

The presence of Oriental goods is very noticeable in the houses of New Amsterdam: ebony chairs and mirror frames, picture frames, chests and boxes, East India cabinets, caskets and boxes, waxed and lacquered trunks, beautiful articles of silver work, fine porcelains, carved ivory, and many exotic articles occur.

A great many of these doubtless were obtained from the Madagascar pirates. Governor Fletcher himself did not disdain to accept presents from the daring sea-rovers. The pirate, Giles Shelly, had, naturally enough, a fine collection of Eastern treasures; and we may particularly note Dr. De Lange and Mrs. Van Varick. The latter's house was full of such things. She had thirteen ebony chairs, one East India cabinet with ebony feet, two East India cabinets with brass handles, one small black cabinet with silver hinges, ten India looking-glasses, two East India cane baskets with covers, one fine East India dressing-basket, one East India square gilt basket, one round East India dressing-basket, two wooden East India trays lacquered, one "round thing" lacquered, one small black cabinet with silver hinges, one "carved wooden thing," one East India wrought box, three silver wrought East India "cupps," one silver wrought East India dish, one small ebony trunk with silver handles, one East India wrought trunk, one East India wrought box, and "eleven Indian babyes."

The most striking objects in the Dutch room are the chimney-piece, the bed, and the *kast*. If the bed was a separate piece of furniture, it was domed or tent-shaped or box-shaped, and tastefully draped or inclosed with curtains of simple or rich materials. Sometimes, however, the bed formed part of the woodwork of the room and was closed in with folding doors or sliding panels (see page 44). The movable bed often had its feet and posts artistically carved or turned. Many of these were imported, but some were made here. Thus, in 1656, Jan Picolet sued Jan Schagger for payment for a field-bed. Schagger admitted having ordered it, but said that Picolet made it larger than desired, and consequently demanded more money. The court ordered that if they could not come to an agreement it should be valued.

In the wills we constantly find beds being bequeathed to relatives and friends. Thomas Halsey, of Southampton, 1677, leaves among other things to his son Thomas "the bedsted and curtains in the porch chamber." Eliza Burroughs, of Newtown, Long Island, gives to her son, John, " one feather bed which I now ly on, with all the furniture thereto belonging."

Beds of the latest style were often imported. We learn, in 1653, that Lucas Elderson sues for "forty florins for bedsteads received by Captain G. Tysen." Very handsome beds were owned by Colonel Lewis Morris in 1691. One in the "Great Room" was valued at £25, one in the "Dining-Room" at £18, one in the "Lodging-Room" at £15, four others at £36, and five "without furniture," £20.

Typical beds of the period are seen in Jan Steen's *Parrot Cage* and *St. Nicholas Eve* (see facing pages 202 and 300), and a cradle faces page 254.

The most elaborate piece of furniture in the Dutch house was the great cupboard, or *kas*, or *kast*. It was a feature of the "show" room and a necessity in the living-rooms. Wealthy persons had a number of cupboards; and it is hard to draw a distinction in the inventories between the innumerable cubberts, cupboards, clothes-presses, etc. The Dutch word *kast* (cupboard or cabinet) included a number of pieces of furniture; for the word *kasten makker* means cabinetmaker or joiner. *Kast,* of course, is the old word for case, box.

In the great *kasten* the most valuable silver was kept, — the spoons, forks, platters, dishes, mugs, beakers, silver-mounted horns, bridal and christening gifts, and handsome pieces of glass. On the broad flat top were displayed the choice porcelains or the products of the Delft factories.

The great cupboard was made in a variety of styles: it was heavy, massive, and four-square, and equipped with drawers and doors, and sometimes shelves. It was carved, inlaid with mother-of-pearl, ivory, or porcelain; ornamented with pearwood stained to represent ebony or innumerable knobs and spindles of ivory. It was made of oak, plum, cherry, or nutwood, and stood on great round balls for feet. These were sometimes called "knots," and were often repeated on the four corners of the top. Van Nespen termed them "guardians of the porcelain ornaments which decorated the top."

The *kast* was always a prized heirloom; and we often find it left to a favorite child or grandchild. In 1678, Judith Stuyvesant, widow of the Director-General, left to her son, Nicholas William Stuyvesant, "my great and best casse or cobbert empty, exclusive of what might be found therein." He also received all his mother's china except "the three great potts." Mrs. Stuyvesant left to her cousin Nicholas Bayard "my black cabbinett of ebben wood with ye foot or frame belonging to it, together with the three greate China pots before reserved." Mrs. Van Varick's "great Dutch *kas*" was so large that it could not be removed from Flatbush and was sold for £25. The name was well known in England. Many an inventory of the Seventeenth Century lists a *kos*. It lasted all through the Queen Anne period. In 1714, Jan Hendrickse Prevoost left to his daughter, Janettie, wife of Thomas Sickelsen of the outward of New York, "my new cupboard commonly called a kass."

We find the great cupboard in evidence in many homes in New Amsterdam. Andries Bresteed as late as 1723 had six large presses or cupboards of the familiar type with the great round ball feet: an oaken chest without a lock; an oaken chest with two balls under without a lock; a chest of cedar with two balls and brass handles; a chest-of-drawers; one Dutch press; and a small painted cupboard. Humphry Hall had "a chest-of-drawers with balls at the feet" in 1696, valued at £1 16s. 0d.; and another that had lost one of these feet, worth £1 10s. 0d.

In Holland, during the Seventeenth Century, the cupboard made of "nutwood" was particularly cherished. When a certain pastor was asked what he would take for his translation of Cicero's *Epistolæ ad familiares,* he replied: "Sir, not being in a position to charge anything for my labour, I will listen to the advice of the wife that the Lord has given me for a helpmate. She wishes to possess a nutwood cabinet with a set of porcelain to go with it, and ornaments for the top, if the consistory will grant."

We find the "nutwood" cupboard or cabinet highly appreciated in New Amsterdam. Cornelis Steenwyck had "a nutwood cupboard" that was valued at £20. "Nutwood" was usually hickory, which was so valued by the first colonists, and exported to Holland; but sometimes it was walnut.

The cabinet, as a rule, was intended for the exhibition and guardianship of treasured articles. Provided with a glass door, the collection of porcelains, ivories, curios, and silver toys could be seen to great advantage. Sometimes it was of the plainest and cheapest wood painted green, red, or yellow, and sometimes handsomely inlaid or carved. Examples of Dutch cupboards and cabinets face pages 90 and 98.

Next in value was the small casket or coffer, — the tiny trunk, made of ebony, ivory, " silver wrought," sandalwood, painted, gilded, " waxed," or lacquered, and mounted with beautifully chiselled brass, silver, or gold locks, handles, and feet.

The plain chest, or coffer, was made of lignumvitæ, *sacredaan* (Java mahogany), cherry, plum, oak, walnut, or pine. It was also covered with leather, in which case it was really nothing more nor less than a trunk. It was frequently lined with linen or cloth, and sometimes was furnished with handsome metal mounts and stood on ball or square feet. Chests and trunks occur, naturally enough, in the old inventories; and many of these were undoubtedly sea-chests.

The long oak " drawing-table " was a species of extension table, the leaves of which fell in the center when the two ends were pulled apart. This had heavy black bulbs, or massive and heavily carved acorn-shaped ornaments on the legs. The form popularly known to-day as " the thousand-legged " with its twisted legs connected by twisted stretchers and drop leaves, was also coming into favor, and was made of the Java mahogany, walnut, oak, and pine painted to suit the owner's taste (see facing page 82). It may be noted that the drop-leaf, or " hang ear," table became common about the middle of the Seventeenth Century.

Tables were oval, round, and square, and were covered, as a rule, with a Turkey rug, known as the " table carpet." These rich and handsome rugs are frequently represented as table coverings in the pictures of the Little Masters. The chairs of the period were the high and low leather, the first with high backs and the second with low square backs.

The legs of the chairs were connected by stretchers and the seats were rounded or square. The X-shaped chair was also in use during this period. In old inventories we read of Russia leather and Prussia leather chairs, table chairs, ebony carved chairs, chairs of *sacredaan*, and chairs covered with Turkey-work red or green cloth. There were also the simple three, and four, and five-backed chairs with rush, or mat seats. These were painted in any color that the owner wished. A loose feather or down-filled pillow or cushion was always placed on the seat; so high was it, in fact, that a child standing on tiptoe could not see over it. A type of chair that was coming into fashion is seen in the hall of the Van Cortlandt house, facing page 62; and ordinary low-backed chairs and a form appear in the old print facing page 120.

The great number of window-curtains, valances, and cushions of bright colors and rich materials must have given an air of warmth and luxury to the homes. Dr. De Lange's hangings and cushions are noticeable; and still more so are Mrs. Van Varick's. She has six satin cushions with gold flowers (£4 10s. 0d.), one suit serge curtains and valance with silk fringe (£6), six scarlet serge ditto (£4 10s. 0d.), two chimney cloths of flowered crimson gauze and six window curtains of the same (£6 10s. 0d.), one green serge chimney cloth with fringe (£2 14s. 0d.), one painted chimney-cloth, one calico carpet, one chintz carpet (fine), one calico curtain.

Mirrors were framed with crystal borders beautifully cut or inlaid with variously colored glass. Lustres for candles not unfrequently branched from either side of the frame. Occasionally, too, the mirror was placed in the large space over the chimney-piece. The looking-glass was universal in New Amsterdam; and, as a rule, several were found in the house, with "black lists" or "gilded lists." Abraham De Lanoy must have had a very handsome one, for in 1702 his "great-looking-glass" is worth £5.

The ordinary Dutch house in New Amsterdam contained a Cellar and sometimes a Cellar Kitchen. The ground floor consisted of a Shop, a "Fore Room" (*Voorhuis*), a Back Room, a Kitchen, and sometimes an Office. Sometimes also there was an extra Kitchen, and other offices in the yard as well. The floor above was occupied by chambers, a combination of sitting-rooms and bedrooms. The larger houses also had cock lofts and garrets above these in which various stores were kept.

The *Voorhuis* in New Amsterdam corresponded with the hall in New England and the Southern States. Till comparatively late in the Seventeenth Century, the hall of even the wealthy settlers contained a bed as well as dining-room and sitting-room furniture, and in the Dutch house this general sitting-room also contained a bed, as is to be seen in the innumerable pictures of that day. In the houses of the richer merchants there were more than one sitting-room or parlor, in which case the bed naturally was banished from the apartment in which visitors were received.

The rooms on the ground floor of a prosperous merchant of New Amsterdam consisted of a *Voorhuis*, a Shop, or a Counting-House (*Comptoir*), sometimes both, a small Back Room behind the *Voorhuis*, a big Kitchen behind the Shop, and a smaller Kitchen adjoining in the yard.

The Fore Room was always comfortably and frequently sumptuously furnished. Let us take a few examples. The inventory of Dr. Jacob De Lange, 1685, shows that the doctor's Fore Room was quite an elaborate apartment. Here we find two of those great wardrobes known variously as the press, the *kas*, the *armoire*, and the cupboard. One is a hat-press, and the other a clothes-press. There is also a large black walnut chest that stands on large black balls. A large looking-glass with black frame hangs on the wall, with nine pictures, and the family coat-of-arms all in black frames. A square table, a round table, a small table, and an oak " drawing table " — the first form of the extension table — and a small square cabinet, twelve chairs with seats of red plush and six with seats of green plush, and a cupboard with a glass, make a dignified and comfortable room. An additional touch of luxury is contributed by a " waxed " (lacquered) East India small trunk, a " silver thread wrought small trunk," and an " ivory small trunk tipped with silver," which are, of course, small coffers for the preservation of jewels and other small articles of value. Red striped silk curtains and green striped silk curtains drape the windows and match the seats of the chairs.

Cornelis Steenwyck's *Voorhuis*, or Fore Room, was furnished with seven Russia leather chairs and one mat chair, a marble table in a wooden frame, a wooden table with " carpet," or cloth, a " foot banke," eleven pictures, a clock, and a " children's ship." The latter in all probability hung from the beams.

It will be noticed that neither Dr. De Lange nor Mr. Steenwyck had a bed in the Fore Room; but Mr. Cornelis Van Dyck, of Albany, 1676, had in his Fore Room a painted chest of drawers (worth 26 beavers),

DUTCH CHINA CABINET WITH PORCELAIN
OWNED BY MR. FRANS MIDDELKOOP, NEW YORK

a bed and suit of green say hangings (72 beavers), a looking-glass (8 beavers), an oak bedstead, a wooden table, a desk, a "painted eight-cornered table," two chests and a "blue cotton chest," ten matted chairs, "four racks that the pewter stands on and earthenware," an "old Spanish leather stool," and much pewter, silver, and earthenware.

Another room is even more characteristically Dutch. It contained a bedstead of "south walnut, with a dark say hangings and silk fringe" (42 beavers), "a feather bed with a checkered-work covering about it, and a dark rug and white blanket" (69 beavers), a "painted chest-of-drawers" (48 beavers), a "chest-of-drawers of southwalnut with a press for napkins atop of it" (22 beavers), an oak chest-of-drawers (12 beavers), an "oak table with a carpet" (6 beavers), a capstock of South walnut" (to hang clothes upon) and "eight Spanish stools" (26 beavers), an old case without bottles, a "red table that folds up" (9 beavers), a "southwalnut chest" (18 beavers), "a serge suit bed hangings" (16 beavers), "a flannel sheet, a small bed and a hanging about a chimney" (16 beavers), tablecloths, napkins, etc. (16 beavers), and brass, pewter, earthenware, and glass (32 beavers). Mr. Van Dyke's possessions were valued at 1428 beavers. The last item reads: "Before the door a wooden slee."

Dr. De Lange's house shows that a man of wealth was able to indulge his tastes not only for fine furniture, but for silver, pictures, porcelain, etc. Besides the Fore Room, his principal apartments were a Side Chamber, Shop, Chamber, Kitchen, and Cellar. The Shop was stocked with a varied assortment of porcelain and East India goods.

The Side Chamber was almost a picture and porcelain gallery. Eleven paintings of great value hung on the walls, and a handsome "East India Cupboard" was filled with fine porcelain and earthenware. On the chimney-piece covered with a blue valance stood a number of basins, flagons, pots, bowls, a small china dog, a duck, two swans and six white figures of men. The windows were hung with blue curtains, and a handsome looking-glass in a gold frame also brightened the room with its reflections. In this room Dr. De Lange kept his library of ninety books and from the presence of his "chest with medicines," a "chest containing dry herbs and salves," sundry instruments and a white alabaster mortar, we may assume this was the barber-surgeon's office.

Dr. De Lange's Chamber was evidently a very large room and very luxuriously furnished. "Sixteen curtains of linen before the glass windows" show that there were eight windows. The Chamber, therefore, in all probability occupied the greater part of the second floor. It would also seem, from the enumeration of the other curtains, that the outer curtains were in pairs and made of different materials, for we read of two striped calico curtains, "two small calico valions before the glass windows," two calico curtains with silk fringe, and two green silk curtains; and there was a ninth of calico with red lining and woolen fringe. The room also contained a very handsome bedstead with white calico hangings and a number of pillows and cushions, etc., and several spreads and counterpanes; for example, one calico spread laid with calico, one calico spread laid with red crape, one ditto without lining, one flowered calico upper spread laid with red calico, one spread with white and calico squares and eight East India filled spreads. There were no less than fourteen cushions in the Chamber, three gray striped chair cushions, two great blue striped and three "for the loynes," etc. Four pieces of tapestry for chests show that the chests were draped attractively. A flowered tablecloth covers the table.

The number of valances and chimney-cloths would indicate that the room was draped differently on occasions. There is " one white valion before a chimney, one redd chimney-cloth, two ozenbrig chimney valance, one blue calico mixed checkard valance, one redd ditto, one ditto white with red pointed lace, one ditto red flowered calico valance, one ditto flowered with red lining one blue say fringed valance and two valance carpet work."

The most important article of furniture in this room was a large wardrobe or *kast*, described in the inventory as " one great cloth case covered with French nut wood and two black knots under it " (£13). This was probably of French walnut, carved in the Renaissance style, and as there were " six cloths to put upon the boards in the case," we may conclude that there were six shelves within the case; a seventh " cloth with lace " would seem to indicate that a cover ornamented the top. This fine *kast* was used as the receptacle for caps, aprons, handkerchiefs, and neckcloths.

Cornelis Steenwyck's house consisted of a Fore Room, Withdrawing Room, Great Chamber, Kitchen Chamber, Chamber above the Kitchen, After Loft, Cellar Kitchen, Garret, and Cellar.

As the Fore Room has already been described, we will pass to the Withdrawing Room. This contained a cabinet worth £4, a chest, a trunk, a close stool, two chairs, a "capstick," a cushion, a shop ladder, eight pictures, "five earthen china dishes," and drygoods.

The Great Chamber contained an enormous case, or cupboard (*Kasten*) of French nutwood, valued at £20;

twelve Russia leather chairs and "two velvet chairs with fine silver lace"; a cabinet worth £6; a "great looking-glass," £6; a very handsome square table, since it was worth £10; a round table (£2); a bedstead and furniture (£25); a dressing-box; a carpet (£2); a flowered tabby chimney cloth; a pair of flowered tabby curtains for the glass windows; five alabaster images; fourteen pictures; a "harthe iron with brass handles"; two earthen flowered pots; a "piece of tapestry to make twelve cushions"; sixty-four yards of "striped linen to cover the beds"; "nineteen china, or porcelain, dishes"; seven hundred and twenty-three ounces of silver plate (£216 18s. 0d.) and seven ditto (£2 2s. 0d.); and much jewelry, money, and household linen.

In the Kitchen Chamber he had a case for clothes, a lantern with glass, a looking-glass, five Russia leather chairs, "four old stripe chairs," three "old matt-chairs," three "wooden racks for dishes," one "cann-board with hooks of brass," two small children's trunks, a bed, bedstead, and furniture (worth £25), iron rod and two curtains, a pair of andirons and hearth iron, an oval table, two linen cloths, two woolen cloths, a chimney cloth, two "cussions," a tobacco pot, and much valuable earthenware.

In the Chamber above the Kitchen we find a cupboard, or case-of-drawers (£9); one small children's case; a bed, bedstead, bolster, six blankets, and a silk quilt (£12 10s. 0d.); ten "chyers" (£2 5s. 0d.); six "chyer" cushions (£1 10s. 0d.); a carpet, green flowered (£1 5s. 0d.); a small piece of tapestry; a chimney-cloth; a wooden table; six pictures; three fine wicker baskets; seven earthen dishes, and a great deal of household linen.

In the After Loft were kept glasses, earthenware, and pewter; a piece of "carpett or tapyt, old," which must have been good, for the value (£1 5s. 0d.) is extraordinary for a banished article; twenty-four pounds of Spanish soap, and forty-six scrubbing and rubbing brushes. Here were also two tin water-spouts and " an old basket with tin ware to bake sugar cakes."

The Cellar Kitchen contained a great deal of pewter, brass, iron, and tin ware; a mustard querne, a paper-mill, wooden utensils, a wooden press, a table, ten chairs, and two cushions. In the Garret, brass, iron, powder, locks, leather, paint and such articles, and fourteen French nutboards, valued at £3 3s. 0d., were stored. The Cellar was well stocked with wines and liquors.

There was also an upper chamber for merchandise, where were dry-goods, pewter, iron, etc., guns, saddles, and books, a tick-tack board, two tables, two benches, and two painted screens (the latter worth £3).

Mr. Peter Jacobs Marius, who died in 1702, was very wealthy. His house consisted of a Shop and Fore-room; a " Writing Closet," or office; a " Lower Back Room," a " Great Kitchen," an Upper Chamber above the Great Kitchen, a " Little Chamber on ye left," a Loft and " Cock Loft." There was also a " Kitchen in the Yard," a small Store House in the Yard, a Great Store House, and a Cellar.

In the Lower Back Room there were " Three blew curtains for the windows " which tell us that there were three windows; " one screen covered with ozenbrigg," two feather beds, one bolster, six pillows, two blankets, two "blew curtains and valance," one white, one "blew," and " four speckled valance for the chimney," " two pare of Rollows," six glass bottles, " one large Dutch Bible tipt with brass," one " small Dutch Byble tipt with silver and a chain," five earthen cups on the cupboard, one black framed looking-glass, sixteen small pictures, one black walnut table and carpet, six Turkey leather chairs, one "blew" elbow chair, one matted ditto, thirteen old matted chairs, one red cedar chest, one old-fashioned clock, one dressing-basket, one brass warming-pan, eight "stoole" cushions, old and new, nineteen earthen dishes great and small "on ye mantle tree," two earthen painted bottles, one small hair trunk, four cases with square bottles, and a money scale and weight. In this room the household linen was kept, also the silver.

"In the Upper Chamber above the Great Kitchen" we find eight black walnut chairs covered with blue, a black walnut table and carpet, a large cedar chest, a red cedar cupboard, an old-fashioned linen press, a bedstead with iron rods, six blue curtains, valances, tester, and head cloth, feather bed, bolster, and pillow, "a callico valance for the chimney, a blew chest cloth, a green and flowered table cloth," two green curtains, two ditto valances, a "white calico hammake"; eight pictures, two blew curtains, two ditto valances.

In the "Little Chamber on ye Left" are one small bedstead with iron rod and two blue curtains and valance, one green rug, one white blanket, one white and two calico curtains for the windows.

In the Loft are stored a small oak cupboard and calico cloth, a small red cedar chest, without hinge and lock, a Dutch hamper, a bedstead with sacking-bottom, two large and two small pillows, a blanket, two rugs, and a woolen cover for a rug, a close stool and basin. In the Cock Loft are an iron fender and five iron curtain rods.

The Kitchen contains a goodly number of fine utensils, among which we may note five brass kettles (44¾ pounds), three copper kettles (31½ pounds), three brass new pans and covers (31 pounds), two tart pans, two brass scales, one small metal pot and cover, five iron pots with covers (54 pounds), two iron chains, two spits, a brass mortar and pestle, a rolling-pin, two ladles, a kneading-trough, a tin apple roaster, a tin grater, twenty-four pewter dishes, two porringers, two chafing-dishes, a copper pail, a skillet, a saucepan, two brass skimmers, three brass frying-pans, two "old tin pye pans," a cullender, an iron dripping-pan, a flesh fork and ladle, and "one gridding iron," a brass bowl and ladle, and 1521¼ pounds of pewter.

In going over the inventories of the citizens of New Amsterdam of the Seventeenth Century, the student would not need to look at the heading to determine which was English and which Dutch. The early Jacobean and even Elizabethan flavor persists in the furnishings of the Englishman's chief living-room, whether the appraiser calls it "Fore Room," *Voorhuis*, or "Hall." Just as the bed was a familiar object in the living-room of the Dutch well-to-do classes all through the century, so was it also in that of the English merchant. Thus, in 1692, we find a bed in the hall of Thomas Crundall, a rich merchant, whose hall must have been a large one to have accommodated a large "cupboard," a large oval table, a small square table, a black walnut chest-of-drawers, a black walnut glass case, a bed with all appurtenances, a chamber screen, a small black walnut box, seven leather chairs, six Turkey work chairs, two calico window curtains, a fringed calico chimney cloth, two large landscapes, three small landscapes, two andirons, two earthen bowls, two earthen dishes, a large silver tankard, a silver cup, two large spoons, a small spoon, four glasses, and a great deal of household linen.

Another rich Englishman, John Winder, who died

twenty years before Mr. Crundall, had, on the other hand, no bed in his hall, which contained four Spanish tables, twelve Turkey chairs, a leather chair, one King's arms, two Turkey-work carpets, two brass screens, two leather Bristol carpets, two looking-glasses, a screen, two stands, a pair of andirons with brass heads, a pair of bellows, a framed table, two trunks, and two earthen pots.

Mr. William Cox owned about £2000 in 1689. His house was completely furnished. He had two bedsteads, twenty-four Russia leather chairs, a black walnut chest, a desk and box, three looking-glasses (one large), three cedar tables (two with a "carpet"), a "dansick table," another table and carpet, a Turkey carpet, a "pendula clock," an "old screene," a chest-of-drawers and frame, a side-table and drawer, a silver frame looking-glass, a glass case, rugs, etc., six rocking-chairs, a chimney clock, a fine hammock, a great copper (65 pounds). Tall clocks as well as chimney and wall clocks were also used. One brought from Holland in the Seventeenth Century by the Van Cortlandts appears in this book.

In the Widow Cox's Chamber were stored one hundred and fourteen ounces of silver plate, including a silver tankard, cup, plate, sugar box, and spoon, salt-cellar, two porringers, tumbler, and twelve spoons. This room was luxuriously furnished, for it contained a bed with bedding and appurtenances, serge curtains and valance with silk fringe, a chest-of-drawers and frame, side table and drawers, a large looking-glass, a silver looking-glass, a dressing-box, a glass case, and twelve Turkey-work chairs.

Some of these articles doubtless appeared again in the inventory of Mr. Cox's widow Sarah, who married John Ort, and took for her third husband Captain Kidd,

DUTCH CHINA CABINET AND PORCELAIN
OWNED BY MR. FRANS MIDDELKOOP, NEW YORK

the noted pirate. In 1692 her plate and furniture were valued at £255 14s. 0d. Her possessions consisted of furniture, linen, pewter, glass, and earthenware. She had no less than fifty-four chairs, eighteen of which were " Turkey-work," and owned a Turkey-work carpet, four looking-glasses, four bedsteads, four tables, four other carpets, dressing-boxes, screens, stands, desks, linen, a coat-of-arms, three chafing-dishes, pewter, tin, four handsome brass candlesticks, hearth-furniture, rugs, and a fine clock. She also had five leather fire buckets.

In Nathaniel Tompson Barrow's Best Chamber, 1688, he had a bedstead with " sacking bottom," bolster, feather bed, pillows, blankets, and curtains and valance (£10). A round table, a chest-of-drawers, a close table, a small dressing-glass, and six chairs come to £2 13s. 0d. In the " Next Chamber " we find a bedstead, two feather beds, bolsters, pillows, rugs, quilts, etc., a small chest-of-drawers, two trunks, a looking-glass, and four chairs (£7 15s. 0d.), household linen (£13 8s. 6d.), and a suit of white curtains.

Nathaniel Sylvester, 1680, worth £322 16s. 0d., is another good type. He has a " Turkey-wrought couch " and twelve chairs, six green chairs, ten leather chairs, a " Turkey-work carpet," a clock, four tables, two great chests, two great trunks, two cupboards with drawers, a clock, ten feather beds and furniture, and four handsome looking-glasses, besides beds, table-linen, etc.

The handsomest piece of furniture Mr. Francoys Rombouts owned was a " Holland Cubbert furnished with earthenware and porcelain " (£15). He also had a " cubbert and earthenware pots and cups," two other " cubberts," and a kitchen " cubbert." The beds in his house were: one bedstead and furniture (£12); another bedstead (£10), which was draped with white curtain and valance; another (£7), hung with blue curtains; and a little bedstead, a pair of curtains for a close bedstead, a rug and blanket (£3). Of looking-glasses he owned four; of tables he had five, including a little table and cloth, and one oval; and he also possessed a press, a dressing-basket, a desk, a cradle, a chest-of-drawers, a wooden press, several trunks and chests, a house screen, a fire screen, a hat-press, two clocks, one a "chimney clock," clothes in a linen case and an old chest and trunk (£16 16s. od.); two chimney cloths with fringe and lace; seven white calico curtains and two mats; one large chair (£6 2s. od.), seven matted chairs, fourteen chairs, and eight cushions (£5 10s. od.), four chairs and cushions, four leather chairs (£1 5s. od.), two chairs and cushions, eight other chairs, four chair cushions, fifteen pictures, a "perriwig-head," a "hat pin," "earthen jugs and hanging-board" (£2), a lantern, and two leather pails, iron backs for the hearths, five baskets, three hampers, one "capstick," one Dutch Bible, one psalm book, one "history book," and a "parcel of books." He owned silver plate worth £20 17s. od., and a great deal of pewter, brass, iron, hearth-furniture, cutlery, and earthenware; innumerable brushes, and much fine household linen.

Some of his cooking and cleaning utensils were expensive; for instance, a wooden dish, a brush, a still and churn, are valued at £5 10s. od. Among the kitchen articles we find two gridirons, one dripping-pan, one candle-box, "two whetting boards for knives," three brooms, one brush, four tubs, one butter firkin, two rolling boards for linen, one glass spout, thirteen "wooden Pools for lining [linen] and one board." He also had two nets and about one hundred old bags and odd things. Mr. Rombouts's two dwellings were appraised at £600.

Anthony De Milt, who died in 1693, worth £176 7s. 10½d., and who was *Schout* in 1672, had, at the time of his death, two great chairs, fourteen chairs, ten pictures (£2 10s. 0d.), one looking-glass, silver plate, linen, earthenware, one desk, two tables, one oak case, six stoves, one trunk, two chests, two bankes (benches), a wooden box, two pails, two great wooden boxes, one small ditto, one spit-box (worth 3 pence), and three Bermuda baskets.

CHAPTER V

PICTURES, SILVER, CHINA, GLASS, AND CURIOS

ANY one who studies the Little Masters cannot fail to be impressed with the great number of paintings of interiors of the ordinary homes of the period; and many works of Jan Steen, Gerard Dou, Teniers, Pieter de Hooch, Van Mieris, Metsu, Ter Borch, S. van Hoogstraaten, and others give us an exact impression of the rooms and houses of the Seventeenth Century. From Hoogstraaten and Pieter de Hooch particularly we learn the interior construction, — how the stairs led to the floors above; how the rooms led from one to another; how the beds were built in the panels and wainscoting; how the windows and doors opened upon courtyards, streets, and back gardens; how the halls were arranged, and how the chimney-pieces were built; — while other masters show us how the furniture was disposed, and how rich were the carvings and the porcelains, and how thick and brightly hued the "table carpets" and hangings. Innumerable would be the hints given to us by De Heem, Van Huysam, Mignon, Van Aelst, Rachel Ruysch, Snyders, and others of the rich vases of china and glass owned by the Dutch of three centuries past, even if the museums and private collections were not full of splendid examples of the potter's and glass-maker's arts. Priceless silver beakers, loving-cups, and great tankards, too, appear in many convivial scenes and reunions of gay arquebusiers, and show us what the silversmith could do. The Dutch painters, as every one knows, excelled in representing all the familiar objects of daily life; but they painted such things not merely for their own pleasure, — there was a great demand for exact representation of persons amid familiar scenes. The Guilds of Surgeons and members of Saint Andrew's, Saint George's, and other shooting-societies liked to be represented at their banquets, glasses in hand, attacking game pasties, munching pork chops, and toasting each other in slim-necked beakers half full of liquid amber or topaz wine, while jokes and laughter went the rounds. Celebrated and mediocre masters and brilliant painters, who had at that time little reputation, were called upon — in a day when photography was unknown — to paint the homes of the well-to-do, in exactly the same spirit that the latter had dolls' houses made in miniature.

The stranger who visited the Dutch cities was perfectly amazed at the "many interiors and landscapes which were exhibited in the booths at the fairs and under the verandahs in front of the houses of the painters, and often bought them for a small sum to sell them in his own country at a considerable price."

Many of the Dutch artists so highly esteemed to-day were, when living, unappreciated and poor. The great Ruisdael died in an almshouse; his pupil, the now famous Hobbema, discouraged, ceased to work, and was buried at the expense of the parish. Aert van der Neer, painter of landscapes by moonlight and winter scenes of charm, died in a garret; the wife of Adriaen van de Velde had to carry on a hosier's business in order to support him and her family; and Jan Steen probably made more money out of his tavern than he did from his painting.

It would, then, not be extraordinary if many pictures of a high order of merit were brought across the Atlantic by the Dutch sea-captains and if New Amsterdam were quite in touch with the art productions of the day. When we critically examine Dr. De Lange's, Mrs. Van Varick's, and Mrs. Cappoens's collections with their *Evenings, Countreys, Zea, Banquet, Bunch of Grapes with a Pomegranate, Break of Day, Apricots, Winter, Flower Pot, Country People Frolic* (Kermess), *Plucked Cock Torn, Abraham and Hagar, Picture of Roots, Fruit, Burd Cage and Purse*, a *Rummer, Shippes, Landskip ye City of Amsterdam, and Rosen*, it is certainly not fanciful to attribute them to the now famous landscape, genre, and still-life masters of the day. If so many pictures passed from Holland to England, why should not a certain number cross from the parent Amsterdam to the child New Amsterdam? Some were purchased and some were sent as presents; but, undoubtedly, many came. Not only pictures but tapestries, coats-of-arms, and maps adorned the homes of this city. Many of the merchants and officials of New Amsterdam crossed the water more than once, and while in their old home had their pictures painted by artists of the day. Fortunately, one of the most important portraits of a civic notability is still in existence (see Frontispiece). The tremendous supply kept down the prices, and it is no wonder that the strangers were astonished at the pictures that they saw with other ornaments in the homes of the Netherlands. Brickman says:

Their interior decorations are far more costly than our own (English) not only in hangings and ornaments, but in pictures which are found even in the poorer houses. No farmer or even common laborer is found, that has not some kind of interior ornaments of all kinds, so that if all were put together it often would fill a booth at the fair.

De Parival remarked:

The furniture of the principal burghers, besides the gold and silver ware, are tapestries, costly paintings of the best and most celebrated masters of the country, for which no money is saved, but rather eked out in economizing in living, beautifully carved woodwork, such as tables, treasure-chests, pewter, brass and earthenware, porcelains, etc.

The finest collection in New Amsterdam appears to have been that of Dr. De Lange. He had no less than sixty-one pictures, many of which are described as "large." The inventory distinctly mentions the rooms in which they were hung. Entering the Side Chamber, we find one picture, an *Evening;* a small *Zea;* four pictures, *Countries;* and five East India pictures with red lists (frames). We may note that a large looking-glass with gold frame also took up some of the wall space. In the Fore Room he had "A great Picture, being a *Banquet* with a black list; one ditto, something smaller; one *Bunch of Grapes with a Pomegranate;* one *Picture with Apricokes;* one *Picture, a small Countrey;* one *Break of Day;* one small *Picture, Winter;* one small Picture, *a Cobler;* one *Portraturing of my Lord Speelman;* and one board with a black list wherein the coat-of-arms of Mr. De Lange." This was appraised at nearly twice the value of a great *Banquet*. The Great Chamber contained one great picture, *Banquetts;* one ditto; one small ditto; one Picture *Abraham and Hagar;* four small *Countreys;* two small *Countreys;* one *Flower Pot;* one smaller ditto; one *Country People Frolic;* one *Sea-Strand;* one *Portraiture;* one *Plucked Cock Torn;* two small *Countreys;* one *Flower Pot*, small, without a list; one "small print broken," and "thirteen East India prints past upon paper." In the Cellar were a portrait of Mr. De Lange, portraits of two men, and four *Countreys* without lists, unframed.

Mrs. Margarita Van Varick had one large picture of *Images, Sheep and Shippes;* one *Picture of the Apostle;* one *Picture of Fruit;* one *Picture of Battell;* one *Picture of Landskip;* one *Picture of large Flowr Pot;* one *Picture with a Rummer;* one *Burd Cage and Purse,* etc.; one large *Horse Battell;* one *Picture of Roots.* She also had two *Pictures of Shippes* in black ebony frames, and two similar ones in black frames also, two small painted pictures in black frames, and two maps in black frames. Moreover, there were eight prints in black frames and four in "guilded frames"; and no less than fourteen "East India Pictures," large and small, framed, some of which were framed in black and some in gilt frames.

Cornelis Steenwyck had fourteen in the Great Chamber, six in the Chamber above the Kitchen, eleven in the Fore Room, and eight in the Withdrawing Room.

Cristina Cappoens, 1687, also had two small pictures, one great one with "a broken list," four small pictures, two small pictures, three small gilded pictures, and four that are described sufficiently to suggest perhaps a De Heem or Rachel Ruysch, a Van de Velde, and a Berck-Heyde or a Bakhuysen. These are "two Rosen pictures," one "a ship," and one "of ye city of Amsterdam."

Two years later, in 1689, John Van Zee had four pictures: one was *Scipio Africanus,* and another *Julius Cæsar.* These were probably a pair painted by the same artist. The names of the other two are not mentioned. Dirck Benson had "four pictures of four quarters of the World."

Other instances are: Dominie Nicholas Van Rensselaer, of Albany, had thirteen pictures — The King's Arms, five small printed pictures, and an "almanach" worth eighty beavers; Cornelis Jacobson had one picture in 1680; Cornelis Dericksen, seven pictures (£2) in 1681; Asser Levy had nine pictures in 1682; Cornelis Van Dyck, three pictures in his Fore Room in 1686; and Jacob Abraham Sanford, four pictures in 1688, and Thomas Davids, ten. The widow of Nicholas Burdene had two pictures in 1690; Philip Smith, a chart and a picture in 1692, in which year Francoys Rombouts had fifteen pictures. Anthony de Milt had ten in 1693; and Annitie Van Bommel, two in 1694.

One constantly comes across the mention of maps, prints, and almanacs, which probably hung upon the walls also; and "thirty pictures of King William and Mary," in Lawrence Deldyke's shop in 1692, show that the Dutch rulers of England were popular in New Amsterdam. Dr. De Lange's East India prints pasted on paper were undoubtedly valuable Eastern pictures. A flower-piece of the period, by Jan van Huysum, such as was owned by the rich New Amsterdam collectors, faces page 196. The tulip is noticeably important.

The silver of the period was massive and heavy. Great tankards and beakers with lids, such as face page 272, great porringers, caudle-cups, bowls, dram-cups, tumblers, and cups were marked with the family coat-of-arms, or the name, initials, or monogram of the owner, and bequeathed from generation to generation. Apostle-spoons, too, were much in favor and highly valued, and special spoons for the sugar-box, pap-bowl, mustard-pot, etc., were also known (see facing page 262). Forks were gradually coming into general use, and so were the pepper-box, saltcellars, spice-boxes, and other delicate articles for table use. Special presents were given to brides, and the christening gifts were also numerous, including spoons, bowls, cups, and rattles with silver bells. Spoons were sometimes presented for souvenirs at funerals. Silver toys of all kinds were also highly valued, and at this period the silversmith was able to reproduce in miniature every known article, from a coach and six horses to a chair of the period (see opposite). The cabinets of the rich were filled with these little articles. Mrs. Van Varick, who had a great many of these beautiful and costly miniature toys (see page 119), owned a very remarkable collection of silver. Much of it was evidently of beautiful workmanship and from the East. Her treasures included one silver spice-box, one silver egg-dish, one small silver knife and fork, one silver knife, three silver wrought East India boxes, one silver tumbler, one silver knife, "one silver fork, studded handle," one silver wrought East India trunk, one silver saltcellar, one silver wrought East India box, two silver-headed canes, one china cup bound with silver, two scissors tipped with silver, one hundred and eighty-five ounces silver (£69 7s. 6d.). She also had three silver wrought East India "cupps," one silver wrought East India dish, one small ebony trunk with silver handles, a silver thimble, silver medals, and a great variety of current coins of foreign mintage and Oriental curios.

Asser Levy also had an unusual collection of silver in 1682. Among his fine articles we may note twenty-two silver spoons, one silver fork, three silver goblets, one silver tankard, one silver mustard-pot, one silver cup with two ears, four small silver cups, one small silver goblet, two silver saltcellars, two silver cups, two silver saucers, one silver spice-box, one silver tumbler, one silver bell, and "one Cornelia tree cup

MINIATURE SILVER ARTICLES AND SILVER TOYS
RIJKS MUSEUM, AMSTERDAM

and two dishes with silver." William Pleay had, in 1690, a silver "jocolato pot."

Another fine collection was that of Peter Jacob Marius, who died in 1702. Among other things he had one silver tankard, two large and one small silver saltcellar, one large and one small silver beaker, two large and one small mustard "pott" and spoons, twenty-five large and two small sweetmeat spoons, four silver tumblers, seven large and small cups with two ears, one silver old-fashioned server, one silver mug and cover, one "babyes silver chaffendish" and cradle, one silver fork and cup, with a parcel of buttons and other broken silver (218 ounces). He also owned two silver-handled knives and a pair of silver-handled "sizers."

Charles Morgan, of Gravesend, Long Island, had one "sylver dram cup" in 1668; and in the same year Thomas Exton left to Mrs. Abigail Nicholls "my silver boat and a silver meat fork and a silver spoon." John Winder owned four hundred and forty-seven ounces of plate in 1675 (£111 15s. od.); George Cooke had £40 of silver plate, including an inkhorn and fork; in 1680 Cornelis Jacobson had "a silver cup and two hooks for a cloth"; and in 1681 Cornelis Derickson, fourteen spoons, the handle of a spoon, the handle of a fork, two little spoons, a dram cup and a "currell" (26 ounces), all amounting to £7 16s. od. The same year, Cornelis Steenwyck had seven hundred and twenty-three ounces of silver plate worth £216 18s. od. and seven ounces worth £2 2s. od. In 1689 William Cox had one hundred and fourteen ounces of silver plate and a "case of silver hafted knives"; John Van Zee possessed plate valued at £9 11s. od.; Anthony de Milt also possessed a little silver. Madame Blanche Sauzeau, widow of Jaques Dubois, had six silver spoons, six forks, and six small spoons in 1690; and two years later Philip Smith had one hundred and fourteen ounces of silver plate, worth £12 2s. 3d. Francoys Rombouts had £20 17s. 0d.; and Sarah Ort, soon to be Mrs. Kidd, one hundred and four ounces of silver, worth £101 9s. 0d., including a tankard, cup, plate, sugar-box and spoon, saltcellar, two porringers, a tumbler, and twelve spoons. Margaret Duncan, 1702, owned £98 worth of silver, including a porringer worth £10 19s. 9d. and six silver spoons; Francis Hulin in the same year had a dozen silver spoons and a dozen silver forks, valued at £14 8s. 0d.; Abraham Delanoy, 1702, nine silver spoons, worth £5 6s. 0d. John Haines, 1689, had sixteen silver spoons worth £9 12s. 0d. Colonel William Smith, of the manor of St. George, Suffolk County, 1704, owned silver plate to the value of £150; and Cristina Cappoens, 1693, had three silver beakers, two silver cups, one having a silver cover, a silver pepper-box, a silver mustard-pot, a silver saltcellar, and nine silver spoons. In 1700, Cornelis Van Dyck had four silver "tummelers."

Tankards and beakers were highly valued and frequently bequeathed to the eldest or favorite son and grandson. Thus we find Philip Udall, of Flushing, in 1711 bequeathing a silver "Beeker," about a pound weight, to his son, Joseph, " for the use of my grandson Philip Udall, after the death of my son, Joseph." Derick Clausen, 1686, had a silver beaker (worth £3) and a silver cup (18 shillings). Margaret Duncan, 1702, owned a tankard; Cristina Cappoens, 1693, owned two old family beakers: one, weighing twelve ounces, was worth £4 4s. 0d., and the other, weighing sixteen ounces and marked with the name Christina Rasselaers, was valued at £5 12s. 0d. John Haines, merchant, 1689, had a silver tankard worth £10.

SILVER

Four handsome pieces that belonged to Olaf Stevenson Van Cortlandt face page 112; a silver tankard that belonged to Sara de Rapelje, the first child born of Dutch parents in the colony, faces page 116, on which is also a curious drinking-cup known as the "clover-leaf."

Silver frequently excited the cupidity of servant, guest, and relative, if we may judge from the many thefts that occur in the court records. A very peculiar case appears in 1656, when the Honorable N. de Sille appears with a charge against two ladies of position, — Neeltie van Couwenhoven and her sister Mrs. Nicholaes Boot. "For that N. Boot's wife cunningly took, with the said Neeltie, a silver goblet from their father's house and refuse to restore it; whereupon they being complained of, plaintiff caused the goblet to be brought and laid before the Court, maintaining that it is a species of theft or violence." The court ordered that the goblet be delivered to Couwenhoven, which was done in court.

Silver was always a great temptation to the thief. Many instances came into the court, among which was the case of Marten Van Weert, who was a notorious thief who had visited the homes of some of the most important burghers of New Amsterdam. In some way he made off with half a dozen spoons at a wedding at the house of Cristina Cappoens. Marten van Weert was accused by the officer Pieter Tonneman " for his grave and shameful act of theft committed at various times and divers places according to his own voluntary confession and acknowledgment without torture or force; first having stolen seven or eight years ago a quantity of zeewan from the house of Pieter Kock dec'd; having stolen from Cornelis Steenwyck's house at divers times a quantity of otters and beavers together with some pieces of manufactured or Haarlem stuffs and a piece of fine napped cloth, also a piece of fine linen; having lately stolen from Cristyntje Cappoens's house at the feast or celebration of the marriage of Lauwerens Van der Spygel and Sara Webbers, to which wedding he was invited, half a dozen silver spoons." It was considered important to make him an example to others; and Marten van Waart was condemned to be "severely scourged with rods in a closed chamber, banished ten years out of this jurisdiction and further in the costs and *mises* of justice." Owing to his youth, the first punishment was later remitted.

In rich houses in Holland pewter was generally used in the place of silver tableware. The silver, when families were so fortunate as to own it, was kept for ornament and for occasions of ceremony. The pewter, of good design and often engraved with the family coat-of-arms, shone as brightly as the silver itself, and was kept in a special pewter cupboard (or *tinkasten*) in the dresser, or in rows in the wooden racks on the wall.

Pewter was universally possessed in the New Netherlands. Annitie van Bommel, 1694, had a great amount, including sixteen pewter platters, seven plates, sixteen porringers, ten pewter spoons; Cristina Cappoens, 1687, four pewter dishes, eight pewter plates, six pewter cans, and seven funnels, ten pewter dishes, two small pewter dishes, one pewter beaker, three pewter cans, and one "pewter cop"; Cornelis Jacobson, 1680, eight pewter dishes (35 pounds), twenty-four pewter trenchers, two small dishes, a pepper-box, and many other dishes and spoons; George Masters, 1686, a pewter tankard and five old porringers, eleven pewter plates, three small and three larger deep pewter dishes,

DUTCH SILVER FROM THE VAN CORTLANDT MANOR HOUSE

three large pewter platters, a small " pye plate," and a pint pot. Dominie Nicholas Van Rensselaer, of Albany, had seventeen small and great pewter platters, two dozen plates, a saltcellar, a mustard-pot, two pewter candlesticks, four dozen cans or tankards, and four dozen small cups. John Haines, who had £26 of silver, also had " 77 lbs. pewter 10^d lb." (£3 4s. 2d.), four porringers, and two dozen pewter plates. He owned, moreover, seventy-seven pounds of brass. George Underhill, 1691, possessed twenty pounds of pewter and eight porringers. Charles Morgan, of Gravesend, Long Island, 1668, was particularly well stocked. We read of three pewter platters, two basons, four plates, one pewter flagon, one pewter bottle, three beakers, four small pewter dishes, a mug, and two porringers. He also had three brass candlesticks, two lamps, two brass kettles, and " a great copper kettle," which he valued very highly, because it was the subject of special bequest. In his will of 1668 he says: " I do give and bequeath one great copper kettle for and to the use of all my children during the tyme that they or the greatest part of them shall reside or live together and upon the said land aforementioned in this town." The " great brass kettle " and " the great copper kettle " appear in many an inventory, and they are always appraised at high figures. Judging from the prevalence and the amount of pewter, brass, and copper listed in the old documents, the homes of the Dutch residents must have been filled with brightly shining metal articles for domestic use.

During this century the Delft potteries reached the height of their activities and imitated with the greatest skill the blue and white, the black, the red and variegated porcelains and earthenware that the ships brought almost daily from the East. The collecting of porcelain became a craze with the Dutch burgher at home and abroad.

The inventories of New Amsterdam prove that the colonists shared this luxurious taste. Dr. Jacob De Lange had articles both for use and ornament. In his Side Chamber the "Purcelaine in the chamber before the Chimney" consisted of seven half basons, two belly flagons, three white men, one sugar-pot, three small pots, six small "porrengers," and one small goblet, one great goblet, two great basons, two pots, two flasks, four drinking-glasses, five dishes, six double butter-dishes, thirty-three butter-dishes, seven red small teapots, two white teapots, one hundred and twenty-seven teapots, three small men, one can with a silver joint, one can with a joint, two flaskets, one barber's bason, five small basons, sixty-seven saucers, four saltcellars, three small mustard-pots, five oil-pots, one small pot, two tobacco boxes, one small spoon, four small cans, six small flasks, two small oilcans, one small chalice, two fruit-dishes, one earthenware bason, two small cups, one small oilcan, one small spice-pot, five saucers, four small men, one small dog, two small swans, one small duck, and two small men. One small East India rush case contained nineteen wine and beer glasses. This china-ware was probably arranged upon innumerable wall-brackets in the Marot style.

In the Shop we find the following earthenware: ten white dishes, seven white and blue dishes, two flat white basons, one white cup, one saltcellar, one mustard-pot, twenty-one trenchers of red earthenware, five small saucepans, three stewpans, four pots, one strainer, two small dishes, and two jars.

Cristina Cappoens owned a good deal of porcelain in 1687. She had eleven "great cheenie dishes," worth £1 15s. 0d., "four cheenie cups," two marble images, seven painted dishes, one small can and two cups, five white plates and two cups, two bottles and glass, two painted cups and five earthen white and painted cups.

Another fine collection was that of Françoys Rombouts, who had a " Holland cubbert furnished with earthenware and porcelain " (worth £15), eighteen pieces of earthenware and porcelain, one case of bottles, twenty-six earthenware dishes and other earthenware, a " cubbert " with earthen and porcelain pots and cups, six porcelain cups, seven earthen dishes, six earthen jugs, and a hanging-board, eight earthen dishes, fourteen porcelain cups, four earthen jugs, and two great glass bottles.

Mrs. Van Varick had " ten china dishes; three large china dishes, crackt and broke; four china dishes, crackt; six bassons (three crackt) ; two fine cups, one fine jug, four saucers, six smaller tea-saucers, six painted tea-dishes, four tea-dishes, eight teacups, four teacups painted brown, six ditto smaller, three teacups painted red and blue; eight East India flower-pots, white (one crackt) ; one china ink-box and two sand-boxes; eight white earthen plates; a tea-dish and two cups; one china image and one lyon; three teapots; one cistern and bason, and three china basons."

In 1668, Charles Morgan, of Gravesend, Long Island, owned three earthen dishes, two saltcellars, and one glass bottle; in 1674, Arent Everts had eight earthen platters; in 1675, John Winder, six earthen platters; in 1679, Nicholas Van Rensselaer, " five chany " plates, six cups, nineteen fine earthen platters, twelve butter-dishes, two earthen saltcellars, eight fine little earthen dishes, two ditto flower-pots, one ditto can and one ditto mustard-pot, — all together worth eighteen beavers.

In 1680, Nathaniel Sylvester had a case with bottles; and in the same year Cornelis Jacobson owned an earthen pot, one case of bottles, forty earthen dishes, thirteen earthen pots, five earthen dishes, one stewpan, and seventeen pots. Cornelis Derickson had four earthen cups and seven cans in 1681. Dr. De Lange had two fruit-dishes, fifty-three glass bottles, and two glass bottles tipped with silver. John Budd had earthenware, four glass bottles, and a case with bottles in 1684; Derick Clausen, a white pot with cover and five blue dishes in 1686; Cornelis Steenwyck had, in the same year, five earthen china dishes, five alabaster images, seven earthen dishes, two cases with bottles, and nineteen china or porcelain dishes worth £4, besides some earthenware worth £3 7s. 0d. In 1687, Glaunde Germonpré van Gitts had three white earthenware cans and five gray ones; in 1688 Thomas Phillips had glass and earthenware worth £6 5s. 0d.; and Frances Richardson, earthenware and a glass case and glasses. In 1689 William Cox had a dozen "pharnish plates," worth £1 4s. 0d., six new saucers and six old saucers. Simeon Cooper had two cases with bottles in 1691, and in the same year Dirck Theunissen possessed seven earthen dishes and basons, six earthen platters, one "boter dish," two earthen cans, seven earthen pots, and two glass bottles. Sarah Ort, the wife of Captain Kidd, had in 1692 twelve drinking-glasses. In 1694, Annitie van Bommel had four earthen pots, five dishes, and one great earthen jug. In 1700, John Coesart had for sale in his shop "20 red figured pots, 135 red mugs, one case with wine glasses, two earthen water pots, one earthen pot and one spitting-pot."

Examples from the Rijks Museum face pages 178 and 232, and a group in which appears one of the

SILVER TANKARD
OWNED BY SARA DE RAPELJE

grotesque ornaments brought from China and called by the French collectors *magots* faces page 190. Other fine specimens are contained in the cabinets facing pages 90 and 98.

Any one who visits the Rijks Museum in Amsterdam will see a wonderful collection of glass of this period, — of all shapes and sizes, white, green, ruby, amber, and opalescent tints, — loving-cups, tumblers, wineglasses, chalices, beakers, cordial glasses, jelly and syllabub glasses, beautifully cut in innumerable facets, or engraved with a delicacy that rivals the touch of the frost fairies on the wintry panes; hunting-scenes, biblical scenes, mythological scenes, landscapes, proverbs, coats-of-arms, and mottoes are etched upon them with marvelous skill. Here we see the shapes and forms that so often appear in the pictures of Metsu, Van Mieris, Ostade, Jan Steen, Van der Helst, and others. What pleasure the Dutch artists took in painting the Bohemian glass and the transparent wine or beer that fills them! Particularly with Metsu do we meet with tall oblong glasses of elegant form in which the wine sparkles or the beer froths, — glasses cut and shaped in twenty different ways — octagon glasses each facet of which ends with a curve and which cut the light with their sharp edges, or glasses the calyx of which forms a reversed cone on a heron's claw, or elongates into a swan's neck, and finishes like a trumpet; lastly glasses, sometimes of an imperishable thickness and solidity, sometimes as delicate, light, and thin as an onion skin. Specimens of glass of the period face pages 184 and 216.

The old Dutch were great stay-at-homes, and although economical with regard to the expenditure of money on travel or pleasures, considerable sums were spent on beautifying and decorating the home. Godewyck said, somewhat gloomily, that "the home is like a grave wherein we always dwell." A great part of the Dutchman's pleasure in life lay in the acquisition and care of choice possessions. When his home was furnished to his taste, he liked to have it perpetuated on canvas, and he even had it reproduced in miniature with all its furniture and belongings in tiny articles of gold or silver.

Realism was carried to such a pitch that the doll's house had its kitchen, lying-in room, and gloomily draped death-chamber with the tiny coffin containing its wax corpse. The little garden of "coral work" with its hedges, trees, flowerbeds, shell walks, paths, and statuettes was added.

One of the most attractive houses of this character is in the Antiquarian Museum in Utrecht. It consists of several rooms, furnished in the period of 1680, and contains real paintings in miniature by Moucheron. First comes the *Voorhuis*, or Vestibule; then a *Gang*, or passage-way with staircase leading to the next floor; third, the Little Back Room; fourth, an Office, *Comptoir;* fifth, the *Saletkamer*, or Drawing-room; and, sixth, the Art Gallery. The other rooms are the Bedroom or Chamber; the Lying-in Room, the Nursery, the Kitchen, the Cellar, the Scullery, the Storeroom, the Maidservant's Room, the Garret, the Laundry in the Garret.

A doll's house, also of the Seventeenth Century, said to have been made for Peter the Great, is preserved in the Rijks Museum. It is encased in tortoiseshell. The general view is shown in the illustration facing page 172, and other rooms appear facing pages 144, 150, 156, and 162.

Hundreds of miniature trinkets are to be seen in the Rijks Museum in silver and gold filigree work, ivory, ebony, brass, porcelain, earthenware, and Delft; for to the doll everything was given that human beings need for use or pleasure. The illustration facing page 108 will suffice to give an idea of the variety of these silver toys. These charming curios were known in New Amsterdam. Mrs. Margarita Van Varick left eighteen pieces of silver children's toys to Johanna; twenty to Marinus; seventeen to Rudolphus; "twenty eight silver playthings, or toys, to Cornelia"; and besides there was a chest full of "childrens babyes playthings and toys" to be divided equally among them; and also for Johanna and Cornelia there were "two glaasen cases with thirty-nine pieces of small chinaware and eleven Indian babyes"; also "six small and six larger china dishes." Some of these may have been playthings; but they were evidently much prized treasures.

CHAPTER VI

NEW AMSTERDAM HOUSEKEEPING

ALL through the night the watch had been crying the hours and describing the condition of the weather. Soon after daybreak the family arose, sometimes even before the bell of the city rang, for early rising was the custom. The first to get up, as a rule, was the head of the house, who would go downstairs in his dressing-gown and slippers, with nightcap on, open the door and the shutters, look at the weather, bid his neighbor good morning, and call the servant. While she lit the fire and got things ready for breakfast, the rest of the family would get up. The maid set the table, shook up the pillows in the chairs, heated the foot-warmer for the mistress, and placed the Bible before the master's chair. The family now came downstairs, — parents, children large and small, — washed, combed, and dressed, and took their places at the table. The servant also took hers at the end of the board. Then the father stood up, uncovered his head, and all followed his example and with folded hands joined in the prayer which he led. All repeated the "Amen," covered their heads, and sat down to breakfast, during which the father at the table, or one of the sons at the reading-desk, read a chapter from the Scripture. After the meal and at the end of the reading all stood up, sang the hymn, and the father said grace.

Bread, butter, and cheese always appeared upon the

From an old print

A FAMILY MEAL
SEVENTEENTH CENTURY

NEW AMSTERDAM HOUSEKEEPING

table, but breakfast did not consist of these staples alone, by any means. In many families there were pasties of venison and meat. Fried fish was a favorite dish at breakfast, and smelts were called the "breakfast fish" by preference. The bread was different in size, quality, and shape from that of the present day. Rye, wheat, or white bread was used, and also bread made of oats, barley, and beans. Fancy bread was baked on festive occasions. At Christmas, presents were given of Christmas "Wights," in the shape of a child in swaddling-clothes; and at Easter, round Easter "Egg" loaves. At Twelfth Night a cake was given called *duive-kater*, derived from the French *deux fois quatre*, consisting of two four-cornered currant-loaves, baked together; and on Saint Nicholas Eve, the "St. Nicolaas brood."

Burghers seldom ate two relishes at once. Butter and cheese on a "piece" of bread was considered a wicked extravagance. With the bread milk was drunk, and sometimes small beer. It was not until the end of the Seventeenth Century that the coffee-pot made its appearance on the table. Many people used to make a milk-sop with white bread soaked in milk. The farmer himself was satisfied with buttermilk, while his wife was clever in adulterating the milk. Beer was the most general beverage. The common people drank *schenkel* (pouring), "sharp," or sharp beer (*scharre-bier*), leakings, and "thin beer." The citizens had stoops, of four or eight quarts, and pewter cups on the table; the richer class used silver and English pewter and poured the beer out of jugs with covers.

After breakfast everybody went her or his way,—the husband to his office or his business, the boys to their offices, shops, or schools; but the girls usually helped their mother and the servant in the housework. The husband and wife attended to their special duties and hardly met, except at meals and at night. Before going to market the mistress saw that the kitchen was put in order. This was first thoroughly cleaned and all the cooking utensils scoured. The mistress would help the servant, working as hard as she did, and talking to her on equal terms, just as the husband was on a familiar footing with his clerks. The hearth also required great attention to keep it and its utensils bright and free of dust and ashes. Andirons or firedogs were of brass and copper, as were also the tongs and shovel. Steenwyck had a " hearth iron with brass handles " which may have been a species of grate or perhaps a fender. Mrs. Van Varick had two hearth hair brushes with wooden handles, one with a brass handle, and a chamber hair brush. The brass and copper chandeliers also required constant polishing. The rooms in well-to-do homes were lighted from chandeliers that hung from the centre of the room, sconce arms that were placed on either side of the mantelpiece, and standing candlesticks. Mrs. Van Varick had five brass hanging and handle candlesticks worth eighteen shillings, a double brass ditto, which with snuffers and extinguisher was worth £1 4s. 0d.; a pair of brass standing candlesticks, worth sixteen shillings, and a standing candlestick with two brass candlesticks to it, worth twelve shillings.

Another pleasurable duty was the care and arrangement of the flowers. Potted plants stood on windowsills and tables, and there were handsome vases and jars in which to place cut flowers. Cornelis Steenwyck had two earthen flowerpots, and Mrs. Van Varick six East India flowerpots, white, three large and three small and two round ones.

After having put the house in order, the mistress, in a simple dress and with a headcloth folded over her head, would go to market, accompanied by the servant with the basket. In the middle of the century the market day was Saturday, and the commodities were offered for sale in the Strand, which, as we have seen, extended along the river shore from the Battery to the Ferry on the east side of the island. On Sept. 12, 1656, the following was issued:

"Whereas now and again divers wares such as meat, pork, butter, cheese, turnips, carrots and cabbage and other country produce, are brought to this City for sale by the outside people; with which being come to the Strand here, they are obliged frequently to remain a long time with their wares to their great damage, because the Commonalty, or at least the greater part thereof, who reside at a distance from the waterside, do not know, that such articles are brought for sale, which tends not only to the inconvenience of the Burgher — but to the serious damage of the industrious countryman, who frequently loses more than he has expended on his wares; Therefore being desirous to remedy this evil, the Director-General and Council hereby ordain that from now henceforward the Saturdays shall be Market days here within this City on the beach, near or in the neighbourhood of Master Hans Kierstede's house,[1] whereby every one who has anything to sell or to buy shall regulate himself.

The importance of the servant as a marketer is shown in the following lawsuit in 1654, when Marretie Trompetters (the Bugler's), plaintiff, *versus* Maria de Truwe, defendant, demands payment of 3.11 florins for fish sold to defendant. Maria insisted that she sent the money by the servant, and that it fell into the ditch. She had no more at present, but promised payment at

[1] South side of Pearl Street.

the earliest opportunity, wherewith, the plaintiff being satisfied, they were reconciled.

In meats and vegetables, fruits, poultry, and dairy products New Amsterdam compared very favorably with the Old Country with regard to supplies for the table. Game was far more abundant, however, and the delicacies of the sea were within reach of all. Early travelers spoke of the waters here as being "very fish rich." They greatly prized the salmon and the striped bass, which were found in large quantities. Having found shad, which in Dutch is called *Elf*, they next discovered the "streaked bass" which they called *Twaalf* (twelfth), and when they found the drum next they called it the *Dertien* (thirteenth). Wissenaer, 1625, wrote:

Very large oysters, sea-fish and river fish are in such great abundance there that they cannot be sold; and in rivers so deep as to be navigated upwards with large ships.

The sheepshead also attracted great wonder and praise. Van der Donck wrote:

The kinds of fish which they principally take at this time are shad, but smaller than those in this country ordinarily are, and are quite as fat and very bony; the largest fish is a sort of white salmon, which is of very good flavour, and quite as large; it has white scales; the heads are so full of fat that in some there are two or three spoonsful, so that there is good eating for one who is fond of picking heads.

It was strictly forbidden to sell fish on Sunday during church hours. In 1660, the following case came up in court:

Schout Pieter Tonneman, plaintiff, demanded from Wessel Everzen, defendant, the fine for having sold fish on last Sunday forenoon. Defendant's wife appearing said, that it happened before the ringing of the bell. The Court dismissed the Officer's suit.

Again:

Schout Pieter Tonneman, plaintiff versus Albert Trompetter, defendant. Plaintiff says that defendant sold fish on Sunday morning and that Resolveert Waldron has subjected him to the fine. Resolveert appearing in Court declares he fined him because he sold fish on Sunday morning. Defendant's wife appears in Court, says it occurred before the ringing of the bell. The Court dismiss the Officer's suit, as the occurrence took place before the preaching.

The cheeses were known by the names of the towns where they were made and were in demand in nearly every country in Europe. The farmers of New Amsterdam made their cheeses according to methods of their own provinces. Occasionally, too, cheeses were imported.

Regarding prices, it is interesting to learn that in 1692 James Latey's Turkey hen was worth one shilling; twenty common hens, ten shillings; and fourteen geese and ganders, fourteen shillings.

Although the Dutch housewife was a very clever cook and superintendent of the kitchen, for great occasions she called in the help of the baker, who was also a confectioner. For every festival or ceremonial occasion there was a special cake. The Saint Nicholas, the Twelfth Night, the gilt New Year's, the wedding and the christening cake were made according to special recipes and beautifully decorated. The Dutch bakers were also expert in the making of pancakes, waffles, oil-cakes, wafers, biscuits of various kinds, *marsepein*, and many kinds of sweets. The cakes and pasties were as different in shape as in composition. They were filled with fish, meat, cheese, ram's kidneys, and even cocks' combs. One of the favorite pasties was thus prepared: a piece of pork the size of a loaf of bread was chopped fine and stewed until done. Then a piece of salted fat pork the size of an egg, and butter the size of an egg, and four salted apples, and four raw eggs and ginger and a little mace and saffron, and with that some powdered sugar, were added.

There were also tarts of apples flavored with wine and spices and tarts of *marsepein*. The pastry-cooks also prepared the jellies. There was a green jelly made out of milk, parsley, eggs, sugar, and cinnamon-powder; apple-jelly; and orange jelly, or marmalade. Spice and sugar were bought at the apothecary's, who sometimes mixed flour in his sugar, as the baker would put bean meal in his flour. On well-provided tables were also found macaroons and "oblies" (wafers) made of thin egg pancakes rolled and hardened in the oven. White-bread sop, waffle cakes, salted almonds, egg-cheese, almond bread, clotted cream, chestnuts, roasted, served with butter, sugar, and cinnamon, after which came blanc-mange, apples, pears, cheese, and aniseed sugar comfits, with which the meal ended.

Innumerable are the pictures of kitchens by the Dutch painters of the period. A very interesting one by Jan Steen faces this page, where the cook is spitting a bird while laughing with the errand boy who brings to her an unplucked bird and a basket of eggs.

All cake-bakers had a sign with the picture of Saint Nicholas, a bishop, Saint Obertus, an oven with the inscription "Delicious and sweet," some biscuits, cakes, and pastry for sale, or various emblems of the trade. Here and there one would find a molasses barrel or

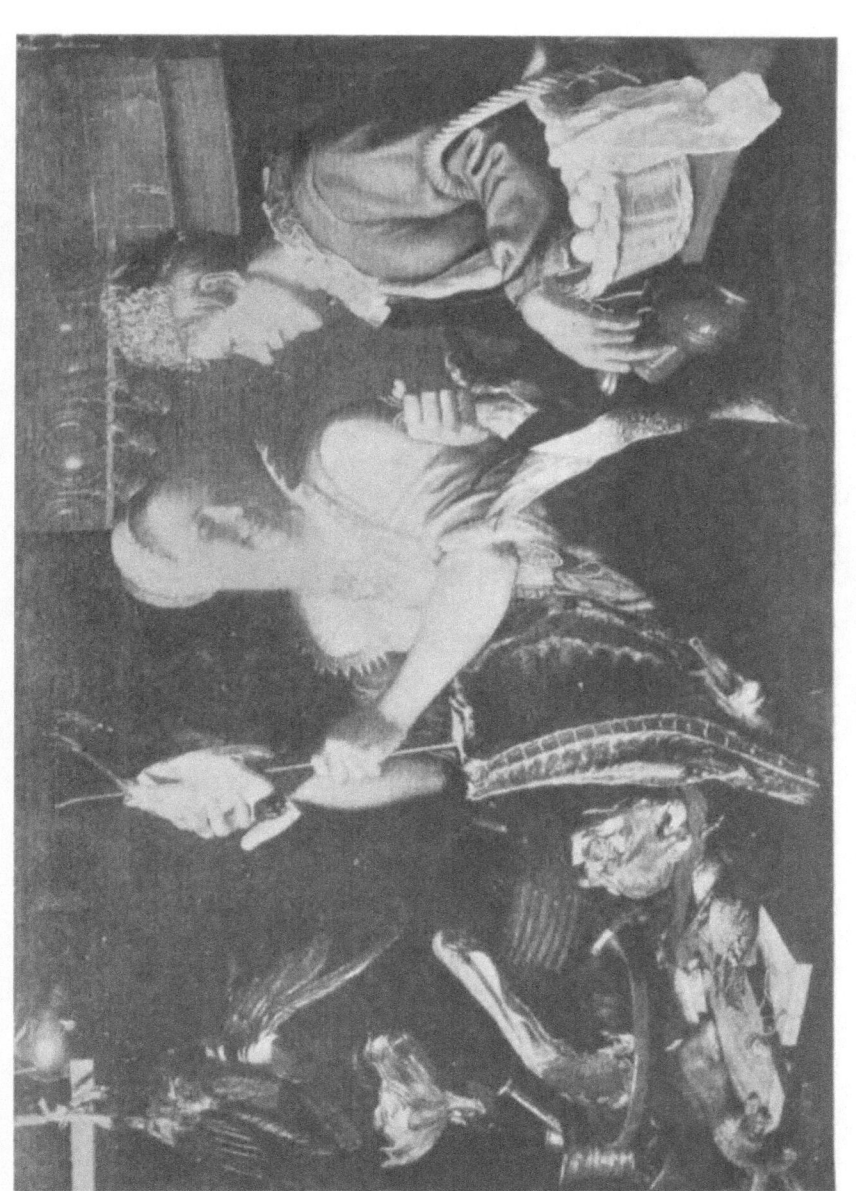

DUTCH KITCHEN
JAN STEEN

a beehive with inscriptions underneath, "what is sweeter than honey," and "Here we sell honey by the jug, while the Holy Land was overflowing with it," and various others. Under the veranda all kinds and sizes of cakes were exhibited, while the shop was filled with boxes of various kinds. In an old print we see the baker descending the staircase, sleeves tucked up, with a skull cap on, while a boy stands on the stoop with an ox's horn and the inscription "Nice and warm." The wife is superintending things, and threatens the cat with uplifted finger because she is licking the honey barrel. On the boxes we read "pasteys, letters, roundels, sugar's, marmelades, spice-cake, *marsepan*, pea-sweets, edge-cake," etc. Among the delicacies we find quartered tarts, tarts with cream and eggs, gin, chevreuil, quinces, pears, jelly tarts, and various others.

The New Amsterdam bakers were subject to the strictest rules and regulations. Their wares were regularly inspected, and baking-hours were strictly enforced. Bakers were not allowed to peddle their bread and cakes in the street, nor to sell to the Indians. They also had to take certain precautions against fire. It was sometimes difficult to become a baker, especially for Jews; for we read in the court records in April, 1657, that "Jacob Cohin Hendricus, a Jew, appeared and requested permission to bake and sell bread within this City as other bakers, but with closed doors." After much deliberation the request was refused.

Let us return, however, to the daily routine. Towards noon the tablecloth was spread on the table, and the *dwaelen* (finger-wipers) put on the plates. The cloth and napkins were woven out of one piece. In rich families a bowl of water and a napkin were first handed to each guest. In the first half of the

Seventeenth Century we find table-sets of flowered damask; damask table-linen, with flowers, borders, scenes, fables, verses, proverbs, portraits, and arms woven in them. The Brussels and Courtray damasks were famous. A set was generally one tablecloth to one hundred and twenty-four serviettes; some had as many as twenty-four such sets in the " linen-kast," which rarely came out of it except to be sent to be washed. During the greater part of the century the wealthiest people still eat with their fingers and helped themselves with the knife.

When setting the table, the servant placed salt, pepper, and sometimes dried ginger on the board, and a knife, spoon, and bread at each plate. The slice of bread was the original trencher, on which the diner cut his meat; but during the Seventeenth Century the trencher was a wooden platter, which is still used in many parts of Holland and Germany. In accordance with the wealth of the householder the plates were now of wood, pewter, earthenware, porcelain, or silver. These are all to be found in New Netherland inventories. The table-ware was decorated variously with scenes from Scripture or history, the parable of the Prodigal Son, the Ten Commandments, the articles of the Creed, the battles of Admiral Tromp, rhymes, dates, and coats-of-arms.

As late as 1680 William Sharpe had seventy-two wooden trenchers and six pewter plates; Madame Sauzeau in 1690 has twenty-four pewter plates; and Elizabeth Partridge, 1669, six pewter platters. Cornelis Steenwyck had forty-three earthenware dishes, great and small, worth £2 3s. 0d.; other earthenware worth £3 7s. 0d.; glasses, earthenware, and porcelain, £16 0s. 0d.; seven earthen dishes, nineteen china dishes, two cases of knives, fifty-eight napkins, and eleven tablecloths. Madame Sauzeau had in 1690 fifty pounds of pewter in dishes; William Sharpe in 1680, four pewter saucers; Elizabeth Partridge, 1669, a saltcellar, five pewter dishes, three pewter dishes, a bason, a pewter plate, a saucer, and two fruiterers; Mrs. Van Varick had three large china dishes, ten china dishes, four china dishes, three large and three small china basons, six wooden tumblers, a silver spice-box, a silver egg-dish, a silver knife, and a silver salt-cellar. Fine silver was also owned by Cristina Cappoens and Peter Marius.

Silver drinking-cups of all kinds were found in all homes of wealth, and silver bowls, jugs, and spoons were also comparatively common. Mrs. Van Varick, who had a large amount of silver, also had " a thing to put spoons in," and Glaunde Germonpré van Gitts, 1687, had " a spoon rack."

Forks were rarities, even in wealthy houses abroad. They are mentioned towards the end of the Seventeenth Century. They were brought from Venice, and used for the first time at the Court of Queen Elizabeth. Though Asser Levy had twenty-two silver spoons in 1682, he had but one silver fork; Madame Blanche Sauzeau had in 1690 six silver spoons, three small spoons, and six forks worth £10. George Cooke had a silver fork as early as 1679. The mention of hand bells in the inventories shows that these articles were used to call servants. In cases where the servant took her meals with the family, the bell, of course, was unnecessary.

When not in use, the porcelain, earthenware, and china were displayed on the tops of the *kasten*, in the glass cases and cabinets, on the mantel shelves, on the tops of doors, brackets, cornices and racks, and hung from hooks on boards. For instance, Cornelis Steenwyck had in his kitchen a "can board with brass hooks," and three "wooden racks for dishes"; and Mrs. Van Varick had a "painted wooden rack to set china on."

After bringing the large pewter dish with boiled food, the servant took her place at the foot of the table, as she did at breakfast. All stood up and uncovered their heads while the father said grace. Everybody repeated "Amen," and the company said to one another, "God bless you," or *"Bon proufaes,"* after which the heads were again covered. The father now served bread, meat, and the boiled dish. As nothing was spoken by the children and very little by the grown people, the noonday meal was soon finished. A typical family gathering at the table faces page 120. Seldom were more than two or three dishes served at the noonday meal. The first cooked dish was generally "potage," made of brown and green peas, mashed, with butter, ginger, and celery; or white beans with prunes and syrup; green or shelled Turkish or broad beans; lentels with meat gravy or butter, vinegar, and parsley. Wheat bread-sop stewed in milk, mutton broth, stewed sweet turnips with fish, medlars with butter, "double bake" or stewed barley, and cold stewed mixed vegetables were the usual dishes. There was also a *hutsepot* (mixed pot) of finely chopped or cut mutton, beef, or veal, boiled in summer with greens and onions, in winter with beans and carrots. Cauliflower and Savoy cabbage were less general and were only found on the table of the rich. Both were first cleaned and then boiled, and afterwards stewed with mutton broth, hot pepper, and nutmeg, sometimes with fine Dutch butter. Sometimes a hard-boiled egg, rubbed to powder, was mixed or spread over it. Artichokes were stewed in vinegar and clear water, butter,

NEW AMSTERDAM HOUSEKEEPING

and ground pepper, butter and salt. The peas were never eaten green or young. The second course was fish; if no fresh fish was to be had, dried codfish, ling, or pickled herring was served. According to reports fried sturgeon was also used, and fried perch, and the pike was roasted at the spit. The carp was stuffed, or prepared in the French way; that is, it was put, after having been washed in water and vinegar, in a thick sauce of butter, Rhine wine, vinegar, mace, pepper, and ginger. With fish turnips were eaten as a vegetable, sometimes carrots, and milk or water was drunk. In case the second course was fish, the third consisted of banquets (pasties) of mussels, oysters, lobsters, crabs, generally eaten with sweet sauces. Oysters and mussels were also stewed or fried in the pan; lobsters and crabs were stewed with parsley, pepper, walnuts, mace, butter, and lemon juice. If no fish was to be had, meat was eaten, fresh in summer but salted in winter, — the pork with greens, sometimes with prunes and currants; the beef, veal, and mutton, with prunes, caraway seed, and mint. Chopped beef was eaten with prunes, currants, and syrup. On *fête* days a beef-stew was made with "olipodrigo" (a mixture of various vegetables). The capon was also one of the choicest dishes. Eggs plainly cooked were used in large quantities, as well as in the cakes that were named after them. "An egg was an evening meal," and very cheap. The egg was the daily food of the poor, who liked it best when well fried in oil; it was seldom fried in butter. But the poor man could not always feed so generously. Sometimes he had to be satisfied with some fried turnips or onions, a dry crust of sometimes mouldy bread, or a bowl of boiled whole barley, with a drink of water or "*scharre-bier*," a thin kind of beer. No wonder he became as lean as Saint Jeronime! Generally, however, the rich ate as simply as the poor.

After the meal the heads were uncovered, the father said grace after meat, and all returned to their work. In many families a chapter from the Holy Scriptures was read after the noonday meal, and a psalm sung. A couple of hours after the noonday meal, the family gathered again to eat the " piece of bread " (*stuk*), cut by the father of the house, with either cold or warm beer or water. Sometimes friends were invited to share this informal meal of cold meat, fried fish, and some sweetmeats. Rich burghers often went into the summer-house in the garden to take the afternoon " piece " of bread, and ate fruit with it, and, after the importation of tea, the family would gather there at a little later hour.

The use of tea was well established in Holland by the middle of the century, and the custom of afternoon tea-drinking crossed the Atlantic. There were many varieties of tea in use, and the hostess as a rule made several kinds in different teapots to please the taste of her guests. Saffron was made, and always in a red pot, to serve with the tea. In the summer peach leaves were sometimes substituted for a flavor. Neither cream nor milk was ever used until the end of the century, and this was a French innovation. The tea-board, tea-table, teapot, sugar-bowl, and silver spoons and strainer were the pride of the Dutch housewife. From the inventories it is evident that tea was in vogue in New Amsterdam. Dr. De Lange had a number of tea-cups and no less than one hundred and thirty-six teapots; Lawrence Deldyke had a tea-board among his articles, and Mrs. Van Varick, a small oval table painted, a wooden tray with feet, a sugar-pot, three fine china teacups, one jug, four saucers, six smaller tea-saucers,

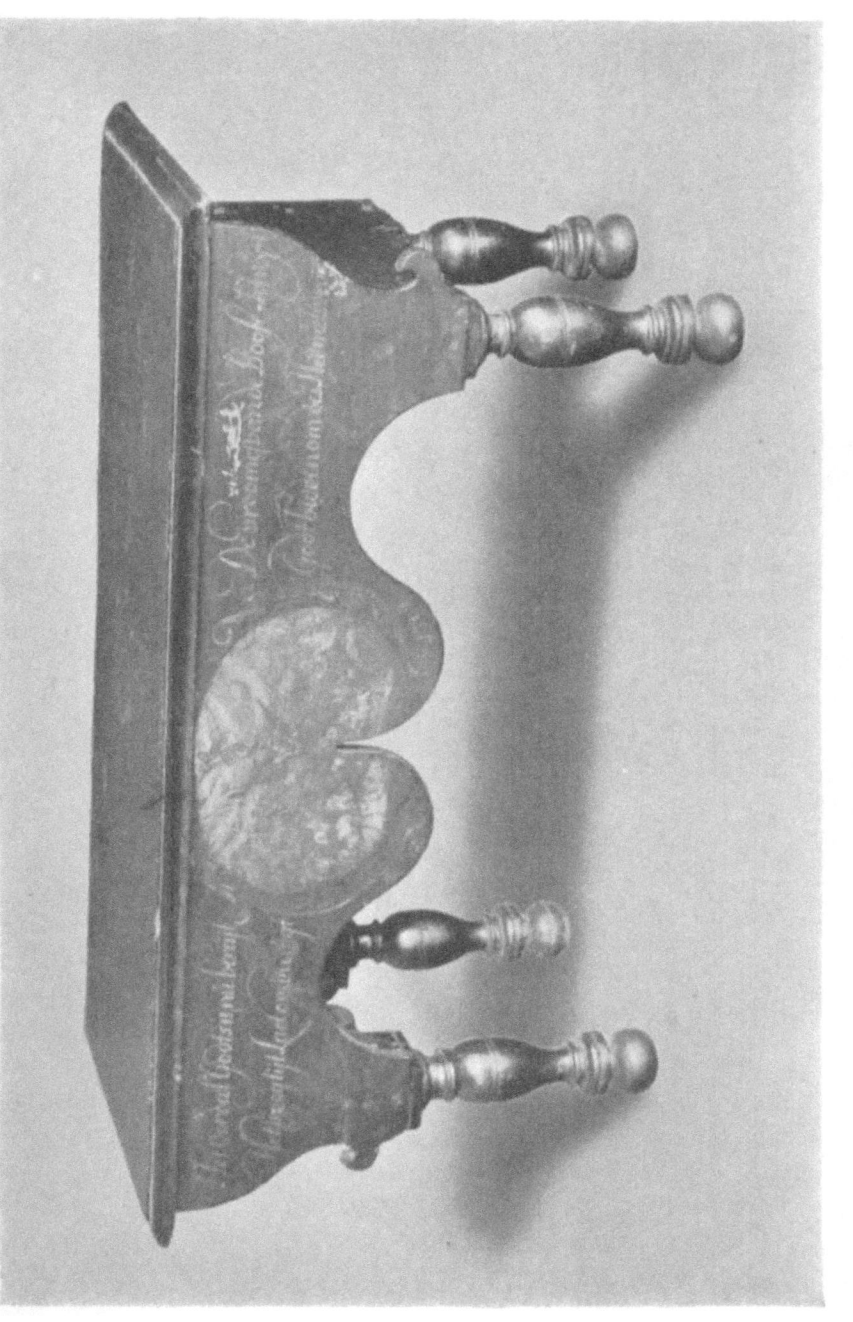

OLD CHURCH BENCH OR STOOL
ALBANY INSTITUTE AND HISTORICAL AND ART SOCIETY

six painted tea-dishes, four tea-dishes, five teacups, three other teacups, four teacups painted brown, six smaller ditto, three teacups painted red and blue, one tea-dish, and two cups finest porcelain.

Tea was known and liked long before coffee, the use of which did not become general until about 1668, when it was drunk with sugar and cinnamon. Coffee was boiled in a copper pot lined with tin, and drunk as hot as possible with sugar or honey. Sometimes a pint of fresh milk was brought to the boiling-point, and then as much " drawn tincture " of coffee was added, or the coffee was put in cold water with the milk, and both were boiled together and drunk. Rich people mixed cloves, cinnamon, or sugar with ambergris in the coffee. At first many conservative families could not accustom themselves to the growing habit of replacing the "must" or beer at breakfast with coffee; but by the end of the Seventeenth Century coffee had taken its place at the breakfast-table once for all. Many families also served coffee regularly at eleven o'clock in the morning. Some doctors considered it a cure for many diseases. Dr. Blankaerd preferred it to wine, drank twelve cups a day, and prescribed it for his patients.

Chocolate was more of a luxury than tea or coffee. It was used at Court towards the end of the Seventeenth Century, but was very expensive and was seldom found on the ordinary table. Chocolate-pots very rarely appear in European inventories in the Seventeenth Century, and therefore the item of " one jocolato pot " in William Pleay's inventory shows that chocolate was known in New Amsterdam as early as it was in Europe.

The winter evenings were passed sociably at the hearth. All sat around the table, — the housewife, daughters, and servant busy spinning, sewing, or knitting, and the boys carving in wood or knitting fishing-nets; while the father read aloud from the Scriptures, Flavius, Josephus, Beverwyck, Cats, the voyages of Schouten, or some other instructive work. Sometimes a scriptural verse would be sung, or some music played. Sometimes a friend, accompanied by his servant carrying a lantern, would make a call. If it was not a clergyman's house and people were not very strict, they would play lansquenet, or the owl or goose board would be brought forward, or lotto or lottery played. At the stroke of nine the maid came to spread the table. The supper was very simple, and consisted in most houses of bread, butter, and cheese; but some people had a *gekookte pot* (a cooked meal), consisting of three courses. The first course was barley with prunes and cinnamon, white-bread sop, rice boiled in milk, or sometimes a salad of different greens and beet roots. The second course was the fish or meat, left over from dinner, fried up or heated anew; and some light dishes, apple-sauce, raisins, and almonds for the third. As at breakfast and dinner, grace was said before and after. At ten o'clock the night bell rang, the "clearing clock"; taverns and gates were closed, and the ordinary burgher would extinguish the fires and lights and retire. Before going to bed, the children received their father's and mother's blessings and a hearty kiss; brothers and sisters also kissed each other good night, and retired after saying prayers at their bedside.

The New Amsterdam home was not devoid of pets. The dog was a favorite member of the household, and, as we have seen, not infrequently appeared in court. In Mrs. Van Varick's inventory there is mention of a "collar for a dog." Steenwyck had a parrot stick, and in 1658 Vice-Director Beck brought to Director Stuyvesant a beautiful parrot from the Spanish Main for Mrs. Stuyvesant. In the same year there is the following memoranda of sundries sent from Curaçao to New Netherland, namely, "salt, preserved lemons, paroquets and parrots, some of which were for Johannis van Brugh, recently married to Miss Rodenborgh."

In all the pictures of Dutch interiors the well-dressed ladies, whether playing musical instruments, making lace on cushions, sewing, or merely engaged in conversation, have one or both feet resting upon the "foot-warmer," or "foot-rest." This little square box covered with perforated sheets of copper or brass, was filled with hot coals, and was no doubt very much needed in the cold houses of the period. It was used so generally that Roemer Visscher, a writer of the period, calls it the "darling of the ladies." "A stove with fire in it," he writes, "is the beloved jewel of our Dutch wives, especially when the snow falls and the hail clatters."

Sometimes the cat is dozing comfortably upon the foot-warmer in the pictures of the Little Masters. In the nursery things were conveniently kept warm upon it, and it was used in the *kermis* booth and tents on the ice to keep the cakes and drinks warm. The foot-warmer was also carried to church by the servant, who also took along the church seat. Mrs. Van Varick had a church chair and cushion; Cornelis Dericksen also had a "church seat." This may have been similar to the one shown facing page 132, now in the Albany Institute and Historical and Art Society. It is painted black with a picture of the Last Judgment in colors, where the angel is separating the sheep from the goats. It is dated 1702, and the inscription reads:

Het oordeel Gotsir nu bereijt
Het is nogtijt Laet onsincingt
De vroome van de Boose Scheyt
Godt beddenom des Heemals ovengt.

(God's judgment is now ready
There is still time to leave folly
The Good Sheep will be separated from the Bad Goats,
God's wisdom encircles the universe.)

The Dutch *vrouw* spent the greater part of her life in keeping clean the house that had been so beautifully furnished and ornamented. Many of the rooms she preferred to scrub and brush and dust and scour with her own hands, for she would not trust her treasures to the clumsy touch of a servant. Some people were so careful of their " show rooms " that they only exhibited them on occasions, and they were only opened every few days, or once a week for the purposes of cleaning. This passion for cleaning was universal; it extended to high circles. In one of his plays Godewyck makes the daughter of an alderman say:

My brush is my sword, my besom is my weapon.
I know no rest; I never go to sleep.
I think of my drawing-room; I never think of my throat.
No labour is too heavy; no trouble too great
To make everything spotless and bright.
I do not want the maid to touch my pretty things
I myself rub and polish; I scrub and splash;
I hunt the speck of dust; I do not fear the pail
Like the showlady.

Many travelers of the Seventeenth Century have noted this national trait. We will see how the French De Parival and the English Brickman were both impressed; the first says:

The wives and daughters scour and rub benches, chests, cupboards, dressers, tables, plate racks, even the stairs until they shine like mirrors. Some are so clean that they would not enter any of the rooms without taking off their shoes, and putting on their slippers. The women put all their energy and pleasure in keeping the house and the furniture clean. The floors are washed nearly every day and scoured with sand, and are so neat that a stranger is afraid to expectorate on them. If the city woman keep their houses clean, the farmer's wives do this no less. The cleanliness is even carried out, into the stables. They scour everything, even the iron chains and mounts until they shine like silver.

Brickman writes:

Now, if you have entered into their houses, the first that will strike your eyes is a large mirror, the other the pewter and brasswork, standing on a ledge along the walls like soldiers in their files — and everything is so neat and snug and clean, that it appears unto you like a golden and silver mountain, for nothing of all Gods good things looses anything of its original beauty. The rooms in their houses are various: some only a few steps, others cornered rooms, others like a ladie's powder box, in which you are afraid to breathe. You have also to remove your shoes or you are not allowed to enter the ladies salon, or best decorated room, but it will be opened and you will be allowed to look in from the threshold. However limited their means, the linen must be fine and clean. Therefore the smith's workshops have been banished from Amsterdam, so that the smoke and soot should not begrime their fine roofs and gables. For some of these are excellent, and show the art and subtleness of the architects. They keep their houses cleaner than their bodies, and their bodies cleaner than their souls. In the one house you will see the fire irons standing in the corner of the chimney, covered with fine netting in another house, the warming pans covered with Italian open work designs and the handles carved, in the third the brass strainer, wrapped in cambric.

This excessive neatness was also found in New Amsterdam, not only among the wealthy, but among the poorer classes, and great numbers of brushes, brooms, and pails are noticeable in the inventories of various grades of households in New Amsterdam. Mevrouw De Lange evidently "hunted the speck of dust"; for in her house we find "one rake brush, one hearth broom, one cloth brush, two Bermudian brooms with sticks, one hay broom without a stick," and in the shop three whiting brushes, a "brush to clean ye floor," three rubbers, two small painted brushes, two hair brushes, two dust brushes, a chamber broom, and a hearth broom. Nor was this all; for in the kitchen were "two dust brushes called hoggs," two whiting brushes, two rubbers, and some other brushes. Cornelis Steenwyck had four brooms and nine brushes in his house, thirteen scrubbing and thirty-one rubbing brushes, and no less than twenty-four pounds of Spanish soap in his garret.

Another passion of the Dutch housewife was for fine household linen, and her great cupboards and chests were not only full of sheets, pillowbeers, towels, tablecloths, and napkins, but of great stores of uncut material to be made into such articles. This taste was shared alike by high and low; every Dutchwoman had the ambition to own a vast amount of such treasure, "saved from grandmother's time with economy," or "inherited from great aunt and kept as precious goods," to be again bestowed as a wedding-gift to some member of the family, or bequeathed to the children of the household. A rich store was greatly prized, therefore, and every penny saved from the household expenses, received as a present, or won at play was

NAPKIN PRESS, SEVENTEENTH CENTURY
OWNED BY MR. FRANS MIDDELKOOP, NEW YORK

used by the housewife to increase that treasure. It was, moreover, her custom to sit every afternoon with her daughters and maids in the kitchen before the spinning-wheel, sewing-cushion, or work-table, or to stand before the ironing-board smoothing and gophering the shirts, neckerchiefs, caps, and ruffs. She was proud to have a rich linen cupboard filled with " mountains of her own make and foreign produced stuff." One rich lady who dwelt in Dordrecht had no less than twenty-four dozen sheets in her cupboard and forty dozen tablecloths, as well as coffers full of uncut linen, while her wearing apparel filled many other receptacles. The rich Mrs. Margarita Van Varick left to her sister, Engeltie, " a spinning-wheel," her clothes, and " a piece of linen, which is at Lucas Renhoven's to make," evidently spun in her own house. Peter Stuyvesant's widow made a special bequest of her linen, dividing it equally between her son, his daughter, Judith, and her eldest son's two children.

The washing of the household linen was also an undertaking. Great hampers and wicker baskets full of articles to be washed were carried away at stated intervals, washed in the canals and rivers, dried on the pasture-land, or special places known as " bleaching-grounds." These existed early in the annals of New Amsterdam, for the first schoolmaster added to his meagre income by keeping a bleaching-ground. It seems that such places afforded a good opportunity for those whose envy was excited by choice damask from Holland. Among the cases of 1653 the following ladies' battle is waged:

Annetie, wife of Age Bruynsen, plaintiff, versus Mrs. Abraham Genes, defendant, complains that on Tuesday last, when four napkins, bought by her of her master Croon from Holland were lying out to bleach, defendant picked them up and carried them away. Defendant says, she has been robbed and plaintiff demands proof that they had been stolen from defendant, or else return of the napkins and suitable satisfaction. Defendant admits having taken up and away from the bleaching-ground 4 napkins in the presence of Martin Loockermans and Engeltie Maus, because they belonged to her, and she says, that she misses other napkins and linen, which she has not yet seen or found; also that neighbours have compared the said napkins with others daily used by her and have found them to be of the same pattern and linen, while upon one of them there is the same mark as shown by affidavit; she has left it with Anneke Loockermans and Tryntie Kips for safekeeping. The latter called into Court with it, state, that it is the same napkin, as left at their house, but is not like the one shown by plaintiff. Having been examined by plaintiff she says that two of the napkins taken by defendant are changed and that the one with the mark may have been mixed with hers by Engeltie Maus at her wedding. The Court examines and compares the four napkins with those of defendant and finds them to be alike.

A few days later:

Madame Genes being summoned into Court by the Schout (concerning the 4 napkins in dispute between her and Annetie, the wife of Hage Bruynsen), is asked (since Madame Genes intends to remove to Fatherland, and Annetie aforesaid intends to go to Fort Orange), whether she can produce any further proof. She gives for answer: No other proof than before; that they are found in all respects like her napkins, and she is willing, if she can retain her napkins and will remain unmolested on that account, to forgive the said Annetie her fault, and never to trouble her on that account.

On being brought home, the various articles of clothing and household linen were passed through the mangle; then, neatly folded, they were put away in the great cupboards and chests. Sometimes they were placed in the napkin-press, a fine example of which faces page 138, which stands on a frame with four bulbous legs. The greater number of New Amsterdam inventories mention linen to the amount of a fairly large, if not a great, sum. A large proportion of one's wealth was sometimes spent in this article; for example, in 1688 Nathaniel Pompson Barrow owned household linen worth £13 18s. 6d., when his whole estate amounted to only £84 10s. 0d. In the same year Mathew Taylor had one hundred and twenty-six napkins and towels (£4 14s. 3d.), seventeen sheets (£8), eleven tablecloths (£4 7s. 0d.), twelve pillowcases, and a cupboard cloth. The linen in Cornelis Steenwyck's kitchen amounted to more than £5 4s. 0d. In the chamber above the kitchen were twenty-eight sheets, fifty-eight napkins, nine tablecloths, twelve towels, and thirty-two pillowbeers. Peter Marius, 1702, owned twenty-three linen sheets, eight calico sheets, thirty-two great and small pillowbeers, two linen tablecloths, seven diaper ditto, sixty-one diaper napkins, three ozenbriggs ditto, and sixteen small linen cupboard cloths. Matthew Clarkson, 1703, had eight fringed napkins. Mrs. Elizabeth Partridge in 1669 owned one dozen diaper napkins, £3 5s. 0d.; one dozen and a half blue strak'd, £3 0s. 0d.; one dozen plain napkins, £2 0s. 0d.; one diaper tablecloth, £2 0s. 0d.; two pair of sheets, £5 10s. 0d.; one round diaper tablecloth, £1; one pair Holland pillowbeers, £0 16s. 0d.; one pair diaper pillowbeers, £0 8s. 0d.; and a parcel of old linen, £0 5s. 0d. This linen must have been very fine, as it was worth altogether £18 14s. 0d., while her house and land was valued at only £45.

Turning now to a weaver named Glaunde Germonpré van Gitts, 1687, we find that the weaver's loom is worth £2 10s. 0d.; and in the modest house there are nine linen sheets (£1 7s. 0d.) and five pillowbeers (£0 3s. 6d.). Six napkins, eight sheets, and fifteen pillowbeers were owned by Derick Clausen in 1686; Dirck Theunissen had nine sheets, nine pillowbeers, and eight napkins in 1691; and twelve tablecloths (£3 15s. 0d.) and nine dozen napkins (£5 8s. 0d.) were owned by Nathaniel Sylvester in 1680. In 1679 Dominie Nicholas Van Rensselaer, of Albany, owned twelve pair of sheets, sixteen pillowbeers, and four large ones, and a cloth to hang before a chimney, all worth together twelve beavers.

CHAPTER VII

SERVANTS AND SLAVES

SERVITUDE in New Netherland was not regarded as demeaning. The mistress and servant were really on a social equality, since the servant was very frequently the daughter of somebody whose station in the community was equal to that of the mistress. In a new country every extra pair of hands was valuable, and when a householder had more children than were required to do the work afforded by his own occupation and his home, he hired them out to others. When the indentures were signed, the chief parental rights passed to the employer. Sometimes the son or daughter took service for a short time only, but more often for a term of years. If the children were not properly treated, the parents or guardians would apply to the court, which seems to have been quick to remedy any real case of abuse, neglect, or cruelty. If the child absented himself or herself from the master, even if only to visit parents, without permission from the master, it constituted a breach of the engagement. Thus, in 1638, when Jan Damen sued Lenaert Arentsen for breach of his son's indentures, Arentsen was ordered to send his son back whenever he ran away. Again, in 1660, Hendrickje Swartwout sued Pieternelle La Montagne for seven months' wages for her daughter, hired by defendant at fifty florins the year. The court decided that the girl should recover only a quarter's wages, because she was at home two days with her parents without the knowledge of her master or mistress.

That a master could not discharge a servant without good and sufficient cause was shown in a case in which the ill-fated Jacob Leisler was defendant; Agnytie Hendricks sued him for a year's wages, amounting to one hundred guilders in seawant and four beavers, because he had discharged her. Mr. Leisler pleaded that inasmuch as Agnytie had consumed almost a whole bottle of preserved strawberries, also biscuit of his; moreover, as it came to his ears that she had two fellows climb over the wall to her whilst he was at church with his wife, and received no good service from her, he would have nothing to do with her. Agnytie denied having Sunday visitors over the garden wall, and declared that the children had eaten the preserves. She was consoled for the loss of her place by a quarter's wages, according to agreement. Having blamed the children for the disappearance of the preserves, it is a wonder that Agnytie did not lay the loss of the biscuit at the door of the cat. She was not as fertile in excuse as a contemporary of the male sex named Elias Jansen, who, when discharged by Jan de Witt, miller, sued his employer for breach of contract. The miller declared Elias had stolen a pound of candles, whereupon " he gave him for answer that it was not true, and that perhaps a dog had been in the mill and eaten them."

Teunis Cray's wife, 1662, sues Jan Jacobzen for a balance of wages for her son, forty-five guilders in corn and four guilders in seawant; also by balance, one breeches and two pair of stockings sold to him for twenty-four guilders. Defendant has nothing against it but deduction of wages for three weeks when the

VOORHUIS IN THE DOLL'S HOUSE
RIJKS MUSEUM, AMSTERDAM

plaintiff's son left before the expiration of his time. It was proved, however, that he had discharged the boy, and so judgment was given against him.

Masters were responsible for the good behavior of their servants; employer's liability was fully recognized by the court. On Nov. 12, 1643, Teunis Nysson sued Peter Colet for injury done to a young animal by Colet's boy; and the master was fined fifteen guilders, payable when the lad should have served him two months. If the boy should die before that time, damages were to be proportionable.

The servants here were undoubtedly subject to rough treatment on the part of their employers; and it does not appear that an occasional beating was regarded by the court as a valid excuse for breaking the contract. In 1657, when Jochem Wesselsen, a baker, was sued by Jan van Hoesum because the baker's wife, Gertrude Jeronimus, had violently kicked Miss van Hoesum, Wesselsen pleaded that his wife had a perfect right to chastise any girl who was in his service. The court, however, agreed with the father, and fined the irritable Gertrude thirty guilders and costs.

In 1659, "Andries Clazen says that Jan Everzen Bout cut two holes with the tongs in his little daughter's head, in service with him about three weeks ago. Jan answers that it is a stiffnecked thing and will not listen to what is said to her, and through hastiness he flung the tongs after her, but not with a view to injure her, — it occurred unintentionally. Clazen says his daughter lay abed some days." Finally Jan had to pay the surgeon's bill, twenty florins damages and ten florins fine.

Caspar Stynmets, 1657, said that his wife's brother served Jan Hendrick nine months, and as the boy was treated harshly and dismissed, he requested that defendant be condemned to fit the boy out decently in clothes as he received him, so that he might engage with other persons; demanding a coat, breeches, two shirts, one pair of stockings, and one pair of shoes, and reparation for having treated the boy so harshly. Hendrick said that the boy earned only whippings, but denied having abused him, treating him only as his own child. He also said that he offered the boy a shirt and leather breeches, and could not give him any more. The defendant was condemned to pay thirty-six florins instead of the clothes demanded. The boy was, further, released from service.

Teunis Tomassen sued Barent Gerrisen for 28.15 fl., according to verbal agreement, because his son had worked with defendant. Being sick himself, his wife pressed the case. Gerrisen admitted having taken the boy at eleven florins per month, and pocket money every week, but said the boy was still bound to him for another half year; also he had not done what he was bound to do, for which he was to receive spending money; therefore no spending money was due. " Plaintiff replies and says that her husband will have the money for the boy every week, and that he the defendant said he will not see the boy at the table. Defendant rejoins and says, that he stated if the plaintiff will have his money every week for the boy, he does not require the boy. Requests that the boy serve out his time, promising to pay him. The Court order the plaintiff to let her boy serve out his time according to agreement, on condition that he be paid according to agreement."

Wolfert Webber, 1657, said he hired his son to Claes Pietersen Kos to dwell with and serve him here in this city; "and whereas the defendant employs his son, not here but mostly over at Pavonia and in journeying to and from that place, where much danger is to be expected both by water as from Indians, etc., of which he has had a sample," demanded that his son should either be employed in the city or sent home; and in case he refuse he declares before God and the "Judge that he, in the capacity of a father, protests that if any misfortune happen his son, either in passing over, or from the Indians or otherwise, he has done his duty and shall avenge himself on him." In reply, Kos said he hired the boy to reside with and serve him "unconditionally as to his going over, or remaining."

In 1662, the Directors write to Stuyvesant about a child being retained in New Netherland by a creditor as security for a debt due by the mother. They order it to be released and sent to Holland.

In the wills we frequently find fathers disposing of the future of their children till they come of age. Thus, in 1680, Cornelis van Bursum leaves "the proper portion of a child to my daughter, Anna; and my wife Sarah is to maintain my daughter Anna decently and cause her being taught reading and writing and a trade by which she may live." Balthazar de Hart, 1672, bequeaths "unto his natural son Matthias 2000 guilders . . . and he is to have maintenance with reasonable vittles and clothes, and likewise to be teached to read and write and in a trade also that thereby he may help himself." John Leggatt, 1679, desires his son to be bred up to the sea for his livelihood. Daniel Pearsall, 1702, devises "concerning my three little daughters, my wife disposed of two of them to their two sisters before she died, and the third, Margery, I do likewise dispose of to my two eldest daughters, desiring that as soon as it is convenient, she may learn the trade of a tailor."

In at least one case we find that a parent would

rather entrust his children to the tender mercies of total strangers than of his own or his wife's relatives. For example, Francis Yates, 1682, wills "to Mr Wm. Richardson my five children, Mary, John, Dinah, Jonathan, and Dorothy, for him to keep so many of them as he sees fit. The rest to be put out to whom he thinks fit, but not to any of my own kindred, or kindred of my wife."

From two or three of the wills both in New Amsterdam and Fort Orange we gather that parents were prejudiced against the officially appointed Orphan Masters. For example, Stoeffel Abeel and his wife Heeltie in their joint will, 1678, exclude the Lords Orphan Masters from all management and do not desire them to meddle with the government of the children.

Judging from some of the wills, fathers were not always entirely satisfied that their widows would treat the children with the kindness naturally to be expected from a parent, or, on the other hand, that sons would be invariably dutiful and affectionate to their mothers. In some cases, at least, the father provided special inducements for mother and children to dwell together in unity. For example, Nathaniel Sylvester, 1698, desires his wife to take care of the children, and they are to be dutiful to her. Richard Terry, 1696, leaves all his children at his wife's command to be educated and brought up "both for the good of their souls and bodies 'till of age." Abraham Jossling, 1669, desires his son Henry to be kind to his brothers, and take one of them to himself to learn his trade, as he had promised. "And Good Wife I would not have you remain where you are with any of my children, but my desire is that my children may be put out to trades where they are."

Captain Sylvester Salisbury, 1679, leaves all to his

wife "with this proviso and restriction, viz. to bring up the children in good education and learning, and further to do what is fitting for good and religious parents to do for their children." Cornelis Van Hoorn's children, 1692, are to be instructed in an art or trade by which they may live. Henry Crevenraedt, 1699, hopes that his wife "will be kind to the children and not rong them, but doe by them as she will answer to God Almighty." On the other hand, Jasper Smith, 1695, wills that "my son John be careful and diligent to seeke to please his mother and goe forth in her business and not grieve her." In that case he is to have £10 more than the others; but if "he bee careless and disobedient" he is to have £10 less.

As the passenger lists of the ships show, many of the settlers brought servants with them who were under contract to work for their masters for a certain number of years for stated wages, and until they had earned their passage money. When their time was up, the Company would allot them a city lot for building a house, and land for farming, on various terms, as we have already seen.

It was a serious offense to lure a servant away from his master; but so many servants did break their agreements and seek other service that stringent legislation was required. The Company promised not to take from the service of the Patroons any man or woman, son or daughter, manservant or maidservant, and though they desired the same they would not be received, much less allowed to leave their Patroons and go into the service of another.

In 1640, it was declared that so many servants daily ran away that the corn and tobacco were rotting in the fields, and the harvest was at a standstill. Both farm and house servants therefore were ordered faithfully to serve out their time on pain of making good all losses sustained by their masters, and serving double the time they might lose. The penalty for harboring runaways was fifty guilders, to be equally divided between the Fiscal, the New Church, and the Informer. In 1658, also, it was ordered not to debauch or incite any person's servants, or to harbor them, or fugitives, or strangers, longer than twenty-four hours.

In 1648, the authorities having daily observed that some of the inhabitants harbor in their homes and dwellings the Company's servants and other domestics, when they run away from their lords and masters, also of those who come hither from abroad, whereby many servants when they are dissatisfied with their employment are afforded a means and opportunity to run away, therefore anybody who lodges or boards such runaways for more than twenty-four hours at the most is to be fined one hundred and fifty florins, to be paid to whomsoever will make the complaint. In 1662, a runaway servant, "a Turk," was hanged and afterwards beheaded, and his head was set on a stake at New Amstel, for resisting arrest.

In 1654, the West India Company considerately thought of a scheme for "taking a burden from the Almshouse of this city and helping to increase the population of New Netherland." They therefore wrote to Stuyvesant: "We recommend you most seriously to take good care of the boys and girls sent from the Orphan Asylum and place them with good masters."

On examining the ages of the children who arrived in 1655 we must confess that the Amsterdam Almshouse of the day could not be accused of turning the inmates out into the world before they were of an age to shift for themselves, the girls especially.

BEDROOM, DOLL'S HOUSE
RIJKS MUSEUM, AMSTERDAM

SERVANTS AND SLAVES

Girls	Age	Boys	Age
Tryntje Peters	23	Guillaume Roelant	17
Tryntje Jans	22	Francis Leigh	17
Jannitje Dircx	19	Mathys Coenratsen	16
Lysbet Jans	18	Hendrik Thomasen	14
Dieuwer Volcherts	16	Peter Stoffelsen	13
Annitje Pieters	17	Otto Jansen	13
Lysbet Gerrits	16	Jan Hendricksen	12
Debora Jans	15		
Marritje Hendrik	16		
Catalyntje Jans	13		

If we follow the career of these waifs who were sent away to relieve the congestion of home charity, we shall find that a fair proportion of them followed the example of the early pastors and schoolmasters in developing into undesirable citizens. The first to be presented at court was Trintje Pieters, the eldest of all, who had scarcely landed before being sued (Aug. 23, 1655) by Heyltie 't Havens for insult. The winter had hardly set in before the sixteen-year-old maiden, Marretie Hendrick, asked legal aid to settle a dispute between herself and her master, Captain Francis Fyn, to whom she had been indentured, " regarding a difference about service rendered and agreement made thereon." The court appointed Sieurs Paulus Leendert van Grift and Govert Loockermans to reconcile the parties. Eight years later the young lady was sued for slander by Pietertje Jans. Tryntje Jans seems to have been comparatively quiescent for six years. At the age of twenty-eight, however, she said disagreeable things about Teuntje Jurriaans, who haled her into court, where she was ordered to prove or eat her words. In the same year, 1661, we learn from a lawsuit that Lysbet Jansen, now twenty-four years of age, was the widow of Dancker Cornelissen.

The youngest of the consignment, Catalyntje Jans, had to wait fifteen years before she found a husband.

On June 28, 1670, her banns of marriage with Claes Cornelissen, of Schoonhoven, are recorded. Her senior by three years, Marritje Hendrik, had to be content with a widower, in 1671, when her banns were published. Barent Gerritsen von Swol, widower of Grietie Dirx, was the happy bridegroom.

Of the boys, Hendrick Thomassen and Francis Leigh (1674) make countercharges of theft and violence. On Oct. 30, 1666, Otto Jansen was prosecuted for stealing and selling at Albany a horse. He declared that "Jan Hendricksen had sett him uppon it wch beinge alledged to the said Jan Hendrickx he denyed the same." Otto "confessed in open court that he hath stollen this Summer in New England, twoe horses." Later he became a soldier. In 1664, he petitions to have surgeon Van Imburg's bill paid, for services during illness contracted during the Esopus Campaign.

The lot of the indentured servant was hard enough, but that of the negro slave was harder still. After a certain number of years the white servant became his own master, and, as we have seen, had land allotted for cultivation and animals to stock it, part of the produce and increase of which paid the annual rent. The negro slave, however, had no assurance that he would ever be free, although for good conduct and faithful service manumission was not an uncommon occurrence, even during the owner's lifetime; and the wills show that the masters frequently followed the ancient custom of freeing slaves at their own demise. The terms in which the slaves are referred to often show that there was real attachment between master or mistress and slave. Among many examples the following may be mentioned. Roger Rugg bequeaths to his friend, Mr. Rider, "My negro boy, Mixon. Be kind to him for my sake." William Leath leaves " to my servant, Wan, the Spanish Indian boy, now living with me, his freedom, provided he serves my wife seven years." Anna Medford frees her negro man, Frans, on account of his true services and leaves him a small parcel of ground. Daniel Sayre desires that his negro woman may have liberty to choose her master when she is sold. Jan Francisco was freed at the request of Dominie Megapolensis (1646) " on account of his long and faithful services." In return for the boon, however, he was to pay the Company ten *schepels* of wheat a year. Nathaniel Pearsall provides: "If my negro, Francis, shall grow unruly, my son, Thomas, may sell him. . . . If he is sold, the produce of him shall go to my five daughters." John Ramsden wills that his negro man, John, is to be freed after four years and " he is to have one good suit of clothes, one cow, one horse, and whatsoever else my wife shall see fit."

Negroes did not always earn the approbation of their owners. In 1658, the Fiscal is ordered to sell a man and woman, "the one being lazy and the other a thief."

Negro labor was very important in developing New Amsterdam. Many of the rich merchants and settlers owned small colonies of them. Frederick Philipse, for instance, owned forty. In 1700, more than one fourth of the population of New York consisted of negroes. The Thirtieth Article of the " Freedoms and Exemptions " (1629) stated that the Company would use their endeavors to supply the colonists with as many blacks as they conveniently could.

The West India Company obtained its own negroes from the Spanish Main; but till the middle of the century there was no direct traffic in the slaves by the individual settlers. The need of cheap labor was, however, greatly felt; and on Jan. 20, 1648, the Council resolved to import negroes from Angola. On April 11, the Directors wrote to Stuyvesant approving: "Such as have completed their trade in Angola may carry negroes to your place to be employed in the cultivation of the soil."

It would seem that the Company's negroes had to endure the hardest kind of servitude: many of the more serious crimes committed by the whites were punishable by working in chains with the negroes. For example, on June 6, 1644, Michel Christoffelsen pleaded guilty of stabbing some of the Company's negroes and was sentenced to twelve months' hard labor in chains with the Company's negroes.

The Company's negroes were apparently a savage lot in the early days. On Jan. 17, 1841, Manuel de Gerrit, the Giant, and eight of the Company's other negroes pleaded guilty to having killed Jan Premero, another negro. It would have been too expensive to execute the whole batch, — negroes were too valuable in the little settlement, — so the prisoners were sentenced to draw lots to determine who should suffer death; whereupon, "by God's Providence the lot fell on 'the Giant,'" who was condemned to be hanged, as an example to all such malefactors. It would appear that Manuel was too valuable to be sacrificed, for the proceedings at the gallows look decidedly suspicious. The court minute sets forth that the hangman turned off the ladder the above negro, having two strong halters about his neck, both of which broke, whereupon all the bystanders called out "Mercy!" which was accordingly granted. Two years later Manuel the Giant and ten other negroes were set free on condition of paying the Company annually thirty *schepels* of maize, wheat, peas, or beans, and one fat hog valued at twenty guilders; but their children, born and unborn, were to be slaves.

In 1649, the authors of the "Remonstrance" complain of the authorities here having exploited the negroes for their own profit. They say:

> Even the [Company's] Negroes, which were obtained with Tamanderé were sold for pork and peas; something wonderful was to be performed with this, but they just dripped through the fingers. There are yet sundry other negroes in this country, some of whom have been manumitted on account of their long service; but their children continued slaves, contrary to all public law that anyone born of a free Christian mother should notwithstanding be a slave and obliged so to remain. To this Tienhoven replies that the Company's negroes were set free in return for their long services on condition that the children remain slaves, and the latter are treated the same as Christians. At present (1650) only three of these children are in service; one at the House of the Hope, one at the Company's Bouwerie, and one with Martin Crigier, who, as everybody knows, brought up the girl.

The negroes who were set free received land and stock, like other servants when out of their indentures. Thus, in 1643, Domingo Antony, negro, received a patent of five morgens, and five hundred and five rods on Bouwery No. 5, near the Fresh Water; and Catelina, widow of Jochim Antony, negro, received another of four morgens and ninety-one rods, next the above, a double wagon road between both. The above apparently formed the nucleus of the negro quarter, not far from Stuyvesant's farm.

In 1650, it was recommended to the States General that the inhabitants of New Netherland shall be at liberty to purchase negroes wheresoever they may think necessary, except on the coast of Guinea, and bring them to work on their bouweries on payment of a duty. In April, 1652, the necessary consent was written to Stuyvesant for the colonists to import negroes direct from Africa, excluding, however, the Gold Coast, Cape Verde, Sierra Leone, the Pepper Coast, and Qua Qua Coast. They were also forbidden to go farther west than Popo Sonde. The duty of fifteen guilders a head, however, was too heavy to encourage the colonists to charter their own ships for the trade, which was therefore carried on by Amsterdam merchants chartered by the West India Company. The first direct importation of slaves from Africa into New Amsterdam (1650) was in the ship *Wittepaert,* which the home Directors authorized to be chartered in Amsterdam, to go to Africa for ivory and for slaves or New Netherland " to the increase of population and the advancement of said place." In 1653, the Directors informed Stuyvesant that they have allowed two or three ships to go to Africa for slaves for the West Indies; if they come to New Netherland, he must " assist them in every proper way to clear away all obstacles." In August, 1664, the *Gideon* landed at New Amsterdam two hundred and ninety slaves (one hundred and fifty-three men and one hundred and thirty-seven women) on account of the West India Company.

There was no feeling in the community that slavery was anything but an eminently proper institution. Cornelis Steenwyck bought negroes from William Penn; and in 1691 Colonel Lewis Morris leaves " to my honored friend Wm. Penn my negro man Yoff, provided he come to dwell in America. I leave to Wm. Bickly one negro man and to Samuel Palmer a negro girl. . . . I leave to John Bowne of Flushing one negro girl that is at old Thomas Hunts."

SHOW ROOM, DOLL'S HOUSE
RIJKS MUSEUM, AMSTERDAM

SERVANTS AND SLAVES

The prices of slaves varied in accordance with the natural gifts or acquired knowledge and skill of the individual. In 1655, a negro woman and her little son cost 525 guilders. Colonel Lewis Morris (1691) owned twenty-two negro men, £440; eleven negro women, £165; six boys, £90; two girls, £24; twenty-five children, £125.

CHAPTER VIII
EDUCATION

EDUCATION in Holland, as in other countries of Western Europe, had been taken care of by the Church until the Reformation, when it was transferred to the magistracy of the towns, by whom it was supported and regulated. In the schools which thus supplanted the parochial schools, the elements of Greek, Latin, and German, reading, writing, and arithmetic, were taught. These schools were only for those who wanted to study, education not being compulsory; and pay schools of all grades for boys or girls, or both, were also licensed by the various school boards. It must be remembered that education during the Seventeenth Century was at a very low ebb. The farming-classes of all countries cared nothing for it, and even the lower class of citizens could often neither read nor write. A trading community, however, in a seaport, such as Amsterdam, Rotterdam, or New Amsterdam, found reading, writing, and arithmetic obligatory accomplishments in their business, as well as at least a smattering of the languages of their foreign customers and commercial rivals.

The West India Company recognized the importance of primary education, but, as it would appear, only along the lines of the old church schooling, that is, to teach children their duty towards God and their duty towards their neighbor, and not for the sake of any material benefits to be derived from mundane knowledge. Thus, in 1629, it was provided:

The Patroons and Colonists shall in particular and in the speediest manner, endeavour to find out ways and means whereby they may support a Minister and Schoolmaster, that thus the service of God and zeal for religion may not grow cool and be neglected among them, and they shall, for the first, procure a Comforter of the sick there.

The first schoolmaster sent out by the Company was Adam Roelantsen, who arrived with Director Van Twiller and Dominie Bogardus in 1633. As a character to set a moral standard for the edification of youth, the schoolmaster was on the same plane with the minister and the Director-General. All three seem to have been early and successful apostles of graft on Manhattan Island, and habitual drunkenness was by no means the most serious offense of which they were accused. Roelantsen married Lyntje Martens, who certainly was not a penniless bride, for the first occasion of her husband's appearance in court was in June, 1638, when his brother-in-law, Cors Pietersen, got judgment against him for Pietersen's wife's share of her deceased mother's estate.

He was soon dissatisfied with the rewards of learning, and found it more profitable to establish a laundry, or bleachery, as it was then called, but had trouble in making a success of his new venture.

Adam was manifestly gifted with a malicious and slanderous tongue, and seems to have been a match for any lady in the community. He was also apparently always in hot water with his male neighbors, the officials and others. On Sept. 20, 1640, he sued Gillis de

Voocht for a washing account. It is evident that the "bleachers" contracted to do the washing by the year, for Gillis claimed the year was not yet expired. Adam was therefore ordered to make up the full time and then collect. A year later his garden was damaged by the cattle of his neighbors Jan Damen and Jan Forbus, and he sued them for trespass. His wife's property and his own energies would appear to have resulted in a certain amount of prosperity, for in February, 1642, Jan Teunissen contracted to build a house for him. In August, 1638, he sued Jan Kant for slandering him. Kant had reported to the Council that Adam had declared he did not care for any one in the country. On August 26, he himself was sued for slander by Jan Jansen, gunner, and had to pay fifty-five stivers to the poor. In January, 1639, "Blanch Ael and Adam Roelantsen are ordered to discontinue their slanders against one another on pain of fine." In August, 1640, he was fined for slandering Jochem Heller's wife.

In August in the same year he deeded to Elderich Klein a house occupied by the Company's negroes. A year later he received a patent for a lot next to Philip Gerardy's property. This was adjoining the marsh near the Sheep's Pasture, and was very favorably situated for the drying-ground, or bleachery, of that day, where, after being washed, the linen was laid out on the grass in the open air to whiten.

About this time his activities as a teacher came to an end, for his successor arrived in 1643. He had amply justified the opinion of the home authorities regarding the deteriorating influence of the New Netherland climate on the morals of the Company's servants. It is evident that the court here had no confidence in the treatment his motherless children

EDUCATION

were receiving, for in March, 1646, " Philip Geraerdy Hans Kierstede (surgeon), Jan Stevensen (schoolmaster) and Oloff Stevensen van Cortland (brewer) were appointed curators of the estate and children of Lyntje Martens, late wife of Adam Roelantsen." In July, 1646, the Fiscal prosecuted him for slander.

On Dec. 17, 1646, for attempted rape, he was sentenced to be publicly flogged and then banished; but in consideration of his being burthened with four motherless children, and on account of the approaching cold weather, he was reprieved to a future date, when he was to leave the country.

Apparently he had not yet found the wherewithal for a young man to mend his ways; for in March, 1647, he was sued for debt and pleaded for time to pay. Three months later it is reported that Claes Calff and Adriaen Jansen declared that the unregenerate Adam had been thrown out of the tavern by order of the Fiscal Van Dyck, — doubtless on account of bibulous and riotous excess. Notwithstanding all this, in 1647 he was appointed provost!

Roelantsen's successor was Jan Stevensen, who arrived in 1643 and resigned his position with the Company in 1648.

The first settlers were apparently too busy with the pioneer work of the young colony to care very much about either religion or education; for, five months after his arrival, we find Stuyvesant writing to the Directors (Nov. 11, 1647) to know what provision is to be made for a school, " as there is none in New Amsterdam and the youth are running wild." We also learn that " for want of a proper place, no school has been kept in these three months." Stuyvesant's complaint about the deplorable conditions is fortified by his enemies in their celebrated "Remonstrance" of 1649, wherein they say:

There ought to be a public school provided with at least two good teachers, so that the youth in so wild a country where there are so many dissolute people may first of all be well instructed and indoctrinated not only in reading and writing, but also in the knowledge and fear of the Lord. Now, the school is kept very irregularly, by this one or that, according to his fancy, as long as he thinks proper.

To this Van Tienhoven retorts that a place has been selected for a school of which Jan Cornelissen is the master. The other teachers keep school in hired houses, so that the youth are in no want of schools that fit the needs of the country. "'Tis true that there is no Latin school, nor academy."

Stevensen was succeeded, Oct. 26, 1648, by Peter Van de Linde. In the following year we find Jan Cornelissen, Adriaen Van Ilpendam, and Joost Carelse all teaching here; and in 1650 another schoolmaster was sent out from Holland. In April, 1652, the Company Directors write to Stuyvesant that a schoolmaster from Hoorn named Frederick Alkes is coming on the *Romeyn;* they do not know much about him, but he has been well recommended by a person of quality.

If his habits are as good as his penmanship and a schoolmaster is wanted, you might consider him, but let him first be thoroughly tested, for we have noticed that the climate over there does not improve people's characters, especially when the heads of the administration do not set a good example to the community. We hear a number of complaints from people against the Fiscal and about his drunkenness and other things.

KITCHEN, DOLL'S HOUSE
RIJKS MUSEUM, AMSTERDAM

In 1652, Johannes Momie de la Montagne and Hans Steyn were licensed to keep school. Stuyvesant's representations had borne fruit, for on April 4, 1652, the Directors wrote:

We also agree with your proposition to establish there a public school and believe a beginning might be made with our schoolmaster (*hypodidasculum*), who could be engaged at a yearly salary of 200 to 250 guilders. We recommend for this position Jan de la Montagnie, whom we have provisionally appointed to it, and you may use the building of the City Tavern, if you find it suitable.

The next to petition for leave to keep school was Andries Hudde, whose request was referred to the ministers of the church on Dec. 8, 1654. The official schoolmaster at that time seems to have been William Verstius, for on March 23, 1655, he requested and received his discharge and Harman van Hoboocken was appointed in his stead as schoolmaster and clerk of the church of New Amsterdam. The latter evidently had miserable accommodations for his pupils and his family, for on Nov. 4, 1656, he respectfully requested the authorities to grant him the hall and the side room of the City Hall for the use of the school and as a dwelling, inasmuch as he did not know how to manage for the proper accommodation of the children during winter, for they greatly needed a place adapted for fire and to be warmed, for which their existing quarters were wholly unfit; moreover, being burthened with a wife and children, he was greatly in need of a dwelling for them. The City Fathers refused, on the ground that the rooms requested were not in repair, and were, moreover, required for other purposes; " but in order that the youth, who are here quite numerous, may have the means of instruction as far as possible and as the circumstances of the City permit, the petitioner, for want of other lodgings, is allowed to rent the said house for a school, for which one hundred guilders shall be paid him yearly on account of the City for the present and until further order."

In January, 1658, Jacobus Van Corlaer was ordered to discontinue teaching until he had obtained the proper authority to do so; and in August Jan Lubberts was licensed to teach reading, writing, and ciphering. In 1660, Jan Juriaense Becker and Frans Claessen received similar permission; the latter died within two years.

In the middle of the century, the schoolmasters of the small settlements had various duties to perform: they not only taught the children reading, writing, and arithmetic and the articles of the Christian faith, but on Sunday officiated as *Voorleser* and precentor, read the Creed and Lesson, led the singing and kept the church records of christenings, marriages, and deaths. This was in accordance with the customs of Fatherland.

In May, 1661, Evert Pietersen was commissioned to be comforter of the sick, schoolmaster, and precentor at New Amsterdam; and, Jan. 18, 1661, the inhabitants of Middelburgh (Newtown), Long Island, petitioned that Richard Mills, their schoolmaster and "soul's help on the Lord's Day," be allowed the use of the minister's house and glebe. (Granted.) July 4, 1661, the magistrates of Breuckelen petitioned for aid to pay their court messenger, "who acts also as chorister, schoolmaster, sexton and bell-ringer." (Granted.) Oct. 27, 1661, Harman van Hoboocken was appointed to be cadet and schoolmaster at Stuyvesant's Bouwery. On September 21, also, Johannis van Gelder was licensed to teach school in New Amsterdam. On December 28, Boudewyn Maenhout was appointed schoolmaster and reader (*voorleser*) at Bushwick. In July, 1661, also, Carel de Beauvois was appointed court messenger, precentor, bell-ringer, grave-digger, and schoolmaster in Breuckelen. Other schoolmasters appointed to the various settlements of New Netherland were Johannes La Montagne, Haarlem, 1664; Andries Jansen, Fort Orange, 1650; Andries Van der Sluys, Esopus, 1658; Adriaen Hageman, Midwout, 1659, and Renier ——, Midwout, 1660; Richard Mills, Middelburgh, 1660; Englebert Steenhuysen, Bergen, 1662; and Evert Pietersen and Arent Evertsen Molenaar, New Amstel, 1657 and 1661.

Several petitions are made to the Burgomasters in 1662. In February they are requested for a lot in Brewers Street for a schoolhouse, and a lot without the City Gate for a burying-ground. In September Johannis van Gelder petitions for a license to teach school in New Amsterdam; and this is granted. Finally, in December, the Schout and magistrates pray "that Engelbert Steenhuysen shall perform his contract as schoolmaster. This is ordered by the Court." In March, 1664, the Director-General and Council declare that it is highly necessary for the youth to be instructed from childhood in reading, writing, and arithmetic, but more especially in the principles and fundamentals of the Reformed Religion. In order, therefore, to promote so useful and God-acceptable a work, the schoolmasters are commanded to appear in church with the children in their charge on Wednesdays before the commencement of the sermon in order after the conclusion of Divine Service to catechize them in the presence of the ministers and elders as to what they have committed to memory of the Christian commandments and Catechism. Afterwards the children are to have a holiday.

It is very easy for us to form a clear idea of the schools and the manner in which they were conducted, from the descriptions of travelers, and more particularly from the pictures which the Little Masters so frequently painted of school interiors. At the schoolmaster's door hung a card, describing in his own handwriting the subjects which he was permitted to teach. This was to provide against misrepresentation; and the omission to hang out such a sign was punishable by a fine of two guilders. In front of some schools was also hung a sign on which appeared in large letters, " School, Here Children are Taught."

The schools were mostly low-ceilinged, small rooms on the second floor of the house, looking on a dirty little street or back yard. Sometimes they were damp mouldy basements of some old public building. In summer school was frequently held under an awning outside the house. The children of the prosperous and poor were separately taught in the front and back part of the same room. In one of the corners stood the *pultrum* (reading-desk) with the Bible, and in the center a *catheder* with a desk, at which the master sat, and on which were placed the *plak* and a willow rod, its companion, besides the books of writing texts, an inkhorn, sandboxes, and a sharp penknife, a tile with a smooth pebble on which to mix inks of all colors, shells and horns large and small to hold the different kinds of ink, a vase full of black ink, goosequills, parchment, a seal, green wax, slates and copybooks, the book in which the names of the scholars were written, a horn-book, hymn-book, New Testament, and other school requisites. Inside the *catheder* also

From old prints

OLD DUTCH SCHOOL SCENES

stood a chair, on the right side of which hung the
A B C board, and beside it an iron comb with a wooden
handle, the mere sight of which is enough to make us
shiver when we remember that it was used to curry
unclean scalps. A single stroke was enough to make
the blood trickle down the face. On the left hung the
dunce's or ass's board, which was hung over the chest
of the scholar who was too stupid or too lazy. Behind
the raised desk hung calculating-boards, and specimens
of fine penmanship that had gained prizes for the
scholars, the Ten Commandments, the Lord's Prayer,
and other samples of the schoolmaster's calligraphy,
the school ordinance regarding the pupils' behavior
on the street, at home, and in church; how they had
to sit down, stand up, bow, nod, not to shuffle their
feet, scratch themselves, blow their noses too loud,
quarrel, fight, strike, kick, hurt, or abuse others. According to some ordinances, the children had to pay
homage to the master, bowing subserviently and saying "Your Health!" when he sneezed. For the
smaller children very small benches which were called
A B benches were used.

Doors and windows were left open for ventilation.
When it grew dark, tallow candles on wooden blocks
or in iron candlesticks were lighted. In these low, dark,
and damp rooms, and in an atmosphere reeking with
the flicker of the tallow candles, children were kept
sometimes from seven in the morning until seven at
night. School was opened in summer at six and in winter at seven in the morning. The children kept their
hats and caps on, removing them only at prayers and
when they said their lessons.

Not only was the master's rule over his pupils despotic, but he also took precedence over the parents at
public dinners. At the appointed hour he arose from

his seat, said the prayer, or made one of the scholars say it, read a chapter from the Bible, and sang a hymn, after which the school work began. At eleven in the morning school was closed with prayer. Most of the children left; but some of them stayed and ate their lunch which they had brought with them. From one until four and from five until seven were the afternoon sessions, both opening and closing with prayer, Bible reading, and singing. On Wednesday afternoon school closed an hour earlier, and on Saturday afternoon there was no school. Five days a week the children were instructed in singing and in the Catechism. Sundays and holidays, the dog-days, the afternoons after the writing for the prize and the paying of the quarterly dues, and market days, were holidays. Pupils tried to coax the teacher for extra days off. The schoolmasters were often easily persuaded, but any bad behavior was punished severely.

Punishment consisted in striking the palm of the hand with the *plak* (a flat piece of wood on a handle) and flogging with the rod or switch. Neither the one nor the other was lacking in any school of proper "discipline," and they hardly ever were out of the schoolmaster's hands. The *plak* was often an instrument of horrible torture, of different makes and sizes. Some *plaks* were finely made with a twisted handle; some coarse and unfinished, — a round piece of board with a handle. There were round and oval *plaks*, thick and thin of blade, some with a smooth surface and some carved in diamonds; *plaks* with twisted copper wire, and with sharp points or with pin points, which tore the flesh of the palm. He who had misbehaved at school or was guilty of only a minor offense was punished with the plain *plak* and light strokes; but the thief, or the fighter, or the incorrigible, got the hard *plak* and heavy strokes. The punishment with the rod was even more severe. According to the gravity of the offense this was administered on the naked body, or with the clothes on. In some schools boys were strapped with leathern belts. In the yards of some others, principally the poor and orphan schools, there were whipping-posts where boys and girls were whipped; and in the school of the poorhouse in Amsterdam a bench whereon the small malefactor was put with his head through a board, fastened down, and smartly punished. In another school a block was fastened to the leg of the culprit and had to be dragged home through the streets and to church on Sundays. Nobody blamed the master if he beat or kicked the boys, or if he made them stand on a table and hold two or three heavy school boards above their heads during the lesson. We also read of leather cushions with tacks pointed upwards on which unruly girls were placed; and of girls being beaten, kicked, and bruised. In some cases the schoolmasters were veritable tyrants, but fortunately they were the exceptions.

The schools in most of the cities were under the supervision of the curators of the Latin or principal school. These appointed the teachers, who after having signed the canons and articles of uniformity and taken the oath at the City Hall, were considered sufficiently licensed. Little attention was paid to them afterwards and the schools were never inspected, although they always had to be kept with unlocked doors, so that the curators could visit them when they desired. They were summoned by the beadle to appear before the curators only in case the parents complained of lack of discipline, or insubordination of the children, or too severe punishment, or the neglect of the school on account of the master's drunkenness; and from the curators' sentence there was no appeal. There certainly was no lack of capable teachers, ornaments to their profession, but in general the condition of the schools was deplorable.

The girls' schools were just as bad. In the better class of schools the mistress sat before a little *pultrum* on which were a book, a willow rod, and a wooden *plak*. She had also a long stick with which she could reach the rear benches. The children sat with their caps and bonnets on; in a corner of the room was the common toilet. The mistress also dealt in sweatmeats, for which the children spent their school pennies. The schoolroom generally served the mistress as bedroom, living-room, and kitchen. If the mistress was able to read (which was not always the case), a chapter and a Sunday lesson were droned into the children's ears; if not, the instruction was limited to repeating the alphabet, the Lord's Prayer, the Ten Commandments, and the Articles of the Faith, till the children knew all that by heart, without being able to read or write. Some mistresses held these lessons in the forenoon, and taught sewing, knitting, and needlework in the afternoon, in summer, on the stoop.

These dame's schools were common in New Netherland, especially in the outlying small communities. We have a record of one in 1685, when John Rodes leaves to his son John some land " and ye little house Goodey Davis keeps schoole in," which he is to remove for a shop.

The teaching was dull, aimless, and monotonous. The alphabet was taught without any attention being paid to the form, shape, difference, or proper sound of the letters. Words were spelled without significance or sense in a droning tone, and were often mispronounced. The sound produced by twenty children reading or spelling at the same time was so nerve-racking that the neighbors complained, and would rather live next to a smithy than a school. The schoolmasters excelled in penmanship; samples exist that are hard to distinguish from copperplate. The texts they set in running and Roman hands were generally short proverbs, such as "To know God is the highest good," "He that lives well dies well," "We are all mortal," "Always do that which has to be done well," "Obedience is pleasing to the Deity," "Reason has to govern everywhere," etc. There was a quarterly writing competition for prizes, and the winner was rewarded variously with a silver pen, a Breda *étui*, a writing-desk, a penknife, a hymn-book, or a New Testament. The winning handwriting was exhibited on the wall of the schoolhouse. Many teachers were as good at arithmetic as in penmanship, and some were employed to make up the accounts of the city treasurer and keep the ledgers for some of the mercantile houses. Ciphering was taught first on the arithmetic board, where the children began by adding penny to penny, advancing with the aid of the books of the various authorities on the subject. Later in the century, other books were used for the education of the scholars, such as "The Destruction of Jerusalem," "The Four Heem's Children," "The Beautiful Story of Fortunatus' Purse," etc. There were also introduced the Epistles and the Acts of the Apostles, the History of David and Joseph, the Proverbs of Solomon after the version of Carel de Gelliers, schoolmaster of Leeuwarden. Picture books with stories arranged for children were not yet known.

Schoolmasters complained not only of the wildness and insubordination of youth, but that their doting mothers encouraged them in their mischief, as they were always more or less elated over their sons' pranks; and also that they were taken from school too soon to learn a craft or to be trained for the office or the shop. The curators of Dordrecht asked the city government to prohibit boys leaving school too soon, as the custom deprived the schools of their incomes.

The material benefits of linguistic knowledge being so apparent, the original settlers were anxious that their children should have the advantages of which they evidently had been denied. Anneke Jans's own daughter, Sara Roelofs, the wife of Hans Kierstede, for example, was probably more learned in the native Indian tongues than any one in the province, and received a grant of land for services rendered to the province in acting as interpreter with the Indians.

The early settlers in New Netherland, as a rule, were exceedingly illiterate, the women particularly. It is astonishing to see how many wills, deeds, etc., were signed merely "her mark." As shining examples we may cite Anneke Jans and Sarah Ooort (Kidd, Cox). Cornelis Beeckman and his wife, in their joint will, 1669, both sign with a mark; so also do many others who were in prosperous circumstances.

In the early days of the Dutch Republic the United Provinces were overrun with refugees of the Reformed Religion who were expelled from Brabant and Flanders. Many of these were people of good character and education, and well fitted for the instruction of youth; and consequently they opened French schools as a means of livelihood, and were highly esteemed. Towards the middle of the Seventeenth Century the number of these had greatly diminished; but after the Revocation of the Edict of Nantes the numbers increased greatly with the Huguenot immigration, and

GENERAL VIEW OF DOLL'S HOUSE
RIJKS MUSEUM, AMSTERDAM

EDUCATION

the resulting competition reduced the livelihood almost to the starvation point. The masters and mistresses of these French schools were subject to the same rules and regulations as the native Dutch teachers. They had to submit their textbooks to the approval of the local church board, and satisfy the latter that their teaching had no taint of Roman Catholicism. These schools were frequented by the children of the well-to-do burghers, who afterwards finished their education with travel, visiting foreign capitals and making a particularly long stay in Paris.

Strange to say, there seem to have been no schools in which High German was taught; nor were there any English schools, although a knowledge of English was very desirable for the merchants. English, however, seems to have been little known here, for on Feb. 25, 1656, Jan Peecq was appointed to be broker to the merchants of New Amsterdam, "as he speaks Dutch and English."

As we approach the end of the century numerous wills testify to parental provision for their children's education. For example, Evert Wessels's children, 1683, are to be sent to school to learn to write and read. Daniel Veenvos, 1695, and Gerritt Roos, 1697, make similar stipulations. Henry Coyler, 1690, wills that his wife "shall be obliged to cause the under-aged children to learn reading and writing decently." Hendricks Boelen's son, 1691, "is to be instructed to read and write and afterwards to learn a trade by which he shall live in the future." Thomas Foster, 1663, wills: "My children are to be taught to read English well, and my son to write, when they do come of age, and if my wife should marry and not teach ye children as aforesayd, then my will is that two cows more be layed out for yt end, to give ye children learning." Sylvandt van Schaick's children, 1683, are to be "exercised in the fear of the Lord and instructed in reading writing and arithmetic, and such art or trade that they in time may decently live in the world." Christian Teller, 1696, orders that his executors shall put his daughter to board with "Mr. Geestie Dethys or at my brother De Reimer's, and she is to be instructed in such arts, sciences or tongues convenient for her, as can be learned in this province."

Latin was the diplomatic language of the Middle Ages, and was a common accomplishment with every Dutchman whose studies extended beyond reading, writing, and arithmetic. The student of the history of New Netherland cannot help being struck with the Latin forms of the Christian names and even surnames of many of the Dutch here. It is evident that the average prosperous burgher here was not satisfied with the Three R's, but wanted his children to have the advantages of a Latin school, as in Fatherland. In September, 1658, the Burgomasters lay before the Lords Directors the increase of the youth of the province, now very numerous, and "though many of them can read and write, the burghers are nevertheless anxious to have their children instructed in the most useful languages, the chief of which is Latin." They humbly request that a suitable person for master of a Latin school may be sent, "hoping that, increasing yearly, it may finally attain to an Academy."

The home authorities promptly responded; but they had a great deal of trouble to find a Latin schoolmaster. Finally Alexander Carolus Curtius, late Professor in Lithuania, was engaged at a yearly salary of five hundred florins, "board money included, and also a present of 100 florins in merchandise to be used by him upon his arrival there." One of the two ships, the

Bever or the *Moesman*, carried the schoolmaster, but we learn that "The books required by the schoolmaster now coming over for the instruction of the young people in Latin, could not be procured in the short time before the sailing of these ships; they will be sent by the next opportunity."

The Director-General was instructed to give Mr. Curtius "a piece of land convenient for a garden or orchard," and he was to be "allowed to give private instructions, as far as this can be done without prejudice to the duties for which he is engaged." In 1660, he resigned and returned to Holland. His successors were Jan Juriaense Becker, Frans Claessen, and on May 2, 1661, Evert Pietersen. The next to come, on July 30, 1663, was Ægidius Luyck, rector of the Greek and Latin school,[1] who petitioned for a salary and was engaged at one thousand guilders ($400) a year in wampum. He returned to Holland in 1664 to study theology, and after his ordination to the ministry he came back to Manhattan to assist Van Nieuwenhuysen. In 1673, he became a schepen. His school attained such fame that pupils came to him from Albany, Delaware, and Virginia. The next name on the list is Johannes van Gelder.

On Feb. 2, 1662, we learn that part of the old Burying Ground is granted to the Burgomasters for the purpose of erecting a public schoolhouse.

At the head of the Latin schools were curators, nominated partly by the government and partly by the College of Preachers. The curators met once a fortnight or once a month, and with the sanction of the rectors appointed or discharged teachers, looked after the welfare of the school, and determined the promo-

---

[1] This school still survives as the Collegiate Reformed School of New York.

tion of pupils to higher classes, the fines and dues that had to be paid, and the prizes to be distributed. They also settled the differences between teachers, or, in case their good offices were unsuccessful, they were called in finally to decide. At first each school had its individual laws, but in 1625 the States General passed a school law, which by their order was drawn up by the Leyden professors in consultation with the principal rectors and was put in effect in all the schools throughout the land. The schoolrooms were mostly somber, damp, cellar-like chambers, with high windows and stone floors, heated in winter and furnished almost as barely as the schools already described. They were generally parts of the old convents, the other parts of which were used as living-rooms for the teachers and boarding-pupils. The courtyard of the building served as a playground, while the garden proper was reserved for the rector. In summer the porch bell tolled at eight A. M. for morning school and in winter at nine, and at one or two P. M. for afternoon school. After the teacher had called the " horn," or roll, the pupils went to their classes, where the lessons began with prayers in Latin and Greek, and closed with thanksgiving after lessons. In some places, parts of the Holy Scriptures were read in these languages, and psalms were sung. After this the regular work began in the various classes. Some schools had four classes, others six, which were divided again into grades. The two highest classes were taught by the rector and co-rector; the lower ones were directed by preceptors. In the lowest reading and writing were taught, and arithmetic in the next. The third class translated Cæsar and Cicero's Orations and were taught to speak pure Latin and Greek. The second class were taught to expound those works and to compose essays on the classics. The first class had to translate the New Testament and the Tragedies of Euripedes or Sophocles, and translate Sallust, Livy, Tacitus, or Curtius from Greek into Latin, explain the Odes of Horace, and make Latin verses. If the Latin school was an "Illustrious" school, the pupils had also to take part in the professors' classes. In some schools Hebrew was also taught. Each pupil of both the highest classes had to keep a "liber carminum" in which he wrote Latin poems. He composed these for every special occasion and for every family festival. After the annual examination there was a solemn distribution of prizes to those promoted. In the vacations the pupils presented a school play in Latin, the cost of production being defrayed by the city government. These were generally representations of scenes from the Old and the New Testament, legends of the saints, etc., on platforms in front of the town halls, or sometimes on bridges or in open squares.

When the splendor of the French court, under the young King Louis XIV, outshone all the other capitals of Europe, French became the language of fashion and diplomacy and supplanted Latin, and everything in the education of the upper classes of Holland became à la française. The French schools attracted all the youth who did not study for the liberal professions. Those who could afford it employed French private tutors for their children, and these accompanied their pupils when of age to make the European tour.

One of the accomplishments necessitated by the French taste was dancing, which had been a bone of contention in the community ever since the Reformation. The church authorities generally disapproved of it. Those who indulged in it were severely censured. When a wedding was to take place, the members of the church council went to bridegroom and bride with the request to abstain from having dances. This was even done at the wedding of William I. with Charlotte of Bourbon. After a time they asked the municipalities to close the dancing-schools. The preachers warned the congregation against the "abominable and God teasing sin of dancing, dancing was against the Word of God, dancing was not an act of wisdom or carefulness, but of carelessness and folly, the cause of much lightheadedness, frivolity, sinful love, unseemly acts and shame. They were foolish parents that allowed their children to learn how to dance." Dancing-schools were put in the same class as disorderly houses; but in spite of all this opposition, the young people of the period learned how to dance the "courante," the "sarabande," the "pazzamezzo," the "galliard," and the "round" dance. When the followers of Voet became powerful, the dancing-schools were closed. The French dancing-master then put his kit under his arm and went to private residences to teach the young. Though objections were made to dancing, singing-schools and dramatic art were strongly encouraged; and if the authorities tried to prevent the use of organs at the public gospel services, they did not forbid the lessons in music. Singing was taught in all the schools; even in the Latin schools translated psalms were sung, and hours were set apart for lessons. In several of the larger cities were singing-schools under direction of clever composers.

Dancing does not seem to have been taught in New Amsterdam. When it became New York, however, the dancing-master soon made his appearance concurrently with the fencing-master, presumably under the patronage of the pleasure-loving English officers of the Fort. The dancing-master, however, was regarded on much the same plane as "play-actors, and other vaga-

PORCELAIN AND EARTHENWARE
RIJKS MUSEUM, AMSTERDAM

bonds." For instance, on Jan. 3, 1687, an order in council required Francis Stepney, dancing-master, to give security that he would not become a public charge. On Dec. 18, 1675, Thomas Smith, fencing-master, was licensed to open a school to teach the use and exercise of arms.

The Dutch were essentially a God-fearing nation. Religious observances formed an important feature of home life. No bread was broken without the head of the house first invoking a blessing from above, and the meal was also ended with grace. The father also began and ended the day with prayer, reading the Scriptures, and singing a psalm. In some homes an afternoon was devoted to religious meditation and reading — usually the works of prominent preachers. Even the baby in its mother's arms was present, and the first thing the mother taught it was how to pray. As soon as the baby could walk, it toddled to church at its father's and mother's side.

There was no period when the religious education of a child was of more importance than during the Seventeenth Century. Church and State took the matter greatly to heart. Rectors, masters, mistresses, and teachers were ordered to give the children their instruction in the Gospel. Not only the Wednesday and Saturday afternoons were devoted to this, but at every *fête* or holiday some Bible texts had to be learned by heart, and recited at the head of the class. On Sundays children were required to go to school dressed in their best, mornings and afternoons, and from there to church, escorted by their teachers, who after the service would ask them about it, to see that they had paid proper attention. In many families, while the various members occupied themselves in the evening with some kind of hand or fancy work, the father would read from the Bible or some religious book, varied occasionally with selections from the voyages of the early navigators.

Slates and pencils are frequently found among the shop goods. Peter Marius, 1702, has eighty-eight English primers. John Spratt, 1697, has among his shop goods school books valued at three pounds ten shillings.

The libraries at this period contained no light literature. They consisted chiefly of Bibles, Testaments, hymn and psalm books, travels, historical works, and occasionally a few Dutch poets. Somewhat unusual is the collection of Dominie Nicholas Van Rensselaer in Albany in 1679, consisting of "about two hundred bookes, quarto and octavo, the most of them in strange languages," which, with "a brass pocket-watch out of order," are worth two hundred guilders. Mrs. Van Varick had "a parcel of printed books, most of them in High German and foreign languages, and so little value here, wherefore they are packed up to be kept for the use of the children when of age."

In many houses the great Bible, mounted with silver or brass corners and heavy clasps, rested on a reading-desk to which it was attached by a chain. This was the family record for births, marriages, and deaths, as well as the book from which the head of the family read morning and evening.

The inventories contain innumerable examples of such Bibles, among which we may note that Derick Clausen had a turtleshell-covered Bible plated with silver and silver clasps and a Psalm-book with silver clasps (£3); Cornelis Dericksen had a Dutch Bible (£1 16s. 0d.); Mrs. Van Varick, a Testament with gold clasps and a Bible, clasps tipped with gold; and among Dr. De Lange's shop goods we find:

	£	s	d
One Bible bound in carret and tipt with silver	1	6	0
One Testament with gilt hooks and gold hangers and a gold chain	14	0	0
One Testament with silver hooks	0	7	0
One Testament bound in printed gold leather	0	6	0
One small Bible bound in printed gold leather	0	9	0
One Psalm-book bound in printed leather	0	4	0
One small Testament bound in black cloth	0	4	0
One Book tractating of the Lord's Supper bound in printed leather	0	2	0

Mr. Van Exween, who died in 1690, had "a great Bible with brass clasps and a Bible, silver." Abraham De Lanoy, 1702, had six books of Evangelists, £2 3s. 0d.; nine Historical school books, £3 4s. 0d.; ten books of Cortimus, 3s. 9d.; fourteen Catechism books, £3 6s. 0d.; thirty-two song books, £4 6s. 0d.; thirteen books of Golden Trumpets, £2 6s. 0d. Judah Samuel, 1702, had a Hebrew Bible and five Hebrew books; and Henry Pierson, 1681, books, £6 19s. 0d.

Rich women wore their Testaments or Psalm-books on a chain at their side when they went to church. Some of these were very handsome. For instance, Cristina Cappoens had "a church book with silver clasps and chain," which was valued at £1 16s. 0d.

CHAPTER IX

RELIGION, PERSECUTION, AND SUPERSTITION

THE West India Company, recognizing the authority of the Established Church of Holland, intrusted the care of the colonies to the Classis of Amsterdam, by which body all the colonial clergy were approved and commissioned. The Directors immediately sent out two *Krank-besoeckers* (consolers and visitors of the sick), Sebastian Jansen Crol and Jan Huyck, or Huyghen, brother-in-law of Peter Minuit. Their duties were to visit the sick and conduct religious services. At first religious meetings were held on Sundays in the upper floor of the horse-mill, and consisted of reading the Commandments, creed, and, occasionally, a printed sermon, and the singing of hymns. Two years later, the Directors sent out a regular minister, the Rev. Jonas Michiels, or Michaëlius, a graduate of the Leyden University, who had ministered to the Dutch in San Salvador, Brazil, and had served as chaplain of the West India Company's Fort in Guinea. He sailed from Amsterdam on Jan. 24, 1628, with his wife and three children. The Dominie was received with "love and respect" by the Dutch and Walloons, and was able to organize a church of fifty communicants. To aid him and to form a consistory, two elders were chosen, Director Minuit and Huygen. The other "Consoler of the Sick," Crol, was sent to Fort Orange. The

RELIGION

Dominie's knowledge of French made him popular with the Walloons; and in order to qualify himself for missionary work among the Indians, he began to study their language. It is thought that he returned to Holland with Peter Minuit in 1633.

The next minister was the Rev. Everardus Bogardus, who arrived with Director Van Twiller. Bogardus was a widower; but in 1638 he married the rich Anneke Jans, widow of Roelof Jans, to whom had been granted in 1636 the Company's Farm No. 1, a tract of sixty-two acres on Broadway.

It was at this juncture that the question of a church was agitated. But where was the money to come from? It happened about this time that Everardus Bogardus gave in marriage to Hans Kierstede, the surgeon, a daughter of Anneke Jans. The director thought this a good time for his purpose, and set to work after the fifth or sixth drink; and he himself setting a liberal example, let the wedding guests sign whatever they were disposed to give towards the church. Each then with a light head subscribed at a handsome rate, one competing with the other; and although some heartily repented it when they recovered their senses, they were obliged to pay. The subscription list amounted to eighteen hundred florins.

De Vries, writing in 1642, claims credit for the idea, and tells the story as follows:

As I was every day with Commander Kieft, dining generally at his house, when I happened to be at the Fort, he told me one day that he had now built a fine tavern of stone for the English who, passing continually there with their vessels, in going from New England to Virginia, occasioned him much inconvenience and could now take lodgings there. I told him this was excellent for travellers, but that we wanted very sadly a church for our people. It was a shame when the English passed there, and saw only a mean barn in which we performed our worship. In New England, on the contrary, the first thing that they did when they had built some dwellings, was to erect a fine church. We ought to do the same. Kief asked me then who would like to superintend this building? I replied, the friends of the reformed religion. He told me that he supposed that I myself was one of them as I made the proposition, and he supposed I would contribute a hundred guilders? I replied that I agreed to do so; and that as he was Governor he should be the first.

We then elected Jochem Peterzen Knyter, who having a good set of hands, and being also a devout Calvinist, would soon procure good timber. We also elected Damen, because he lived near the Fort; and thus we four formed the first consistory to superintend the building of the church. The Governor should furnish a few thousand guilders of the Company's money, and we would try to raise the remainder by subscription.

In 1649, the Director's enemies complained that Kieft "insisted that the Church should be located in the Fort, the location being as suitable as a fifth wheel to a coach. The Church, which ought to belong to the people who paid for it, intercepts the south-east wind from the grist-mill, and this is why there is frequently a scarcity of bread in summer for want of grinding." In 1642, the new church was built. This was of stone, with a roof of oak shingles, a tower and a weathercock, and a peaked roof. It was seventy feet long, fifty-two feet wide, and sixteen feet high, and on the front was a stone tablet with the words:

An. Dom. MDCXLII.
W. Kieft Die. Gen. Heeft de Gemeente dese Tempel Doen Bouwen

[A. D. 1642. W. Kieft being Director General, has caused the Congregation to build this Temple.]

DRINKING-GLASSES
RIJKS MUSEUM, AMSTERDAM

RELIGION

The bell bore the legend:

Dulcior E. nostris tinnitibus resonat aer. P. Hemony me fecit 1674.

[The air resounds sweeter for our ringing. P. Hemony made me.]

Bogardus was not an ideal pastor; he quarreled with Van Twiller, and his successor, Kieft, denouncing the latter from the pulpit as a tyrant, and trying to stir up the people against him. When summoned to answer for his conduct before the authorities here, he defied them. Kieft charged him with habitual drunkenness, even at the communion table, and absented himself from public worship conducted by the turbulent priest. For this the Director's enemies bitterly denounced him as follows:

What religion could men expect to find in a person [Kieft] who from the 3d of January, 1644, to the 11th of May, 1647, would never hear God's word, nor partake of the Christian sacraments, doing all he could to estrange from the Church all those who depended upon him. His ungodly example was followed, in like manner, by his fiscal Cornelis van der Hoyckens; his counselor, Jan de la Montaigne, who was formerly an elder; the ensign, Gysbert de Leeuw; his secretary, Cornelis van Tienhoven; Oloff Stevenson (Van Cortlandt) [1] deacon; and Gysbrecht van Dyck; besides various inferior officers and servants of the company, to the soldiers inclusive. During the sermon he allowed the officers and soldiers to practice all kinds of noisy amusements near and about the church, such as nine-pins, bowls, dancing, singing, leaping, and all other profane exercises; yea, even to such extent that the communicants, who came into the fort to celebrate the Lord's Supper, were scoffed at by these blackguards. . . . During the prefatory service

[1] The Breeden Raedt (1649).

(*proef-pedicatie*), the Director Kieft several times allowed the drums to be beat. The cannon was discharged several times during the service, as if he had ordered it out a-Maying; so that for the purpose of interrupting the audience, a wretched villany happened against God's church.

Kieft, however irreligious he may have been, was tolerant in some respects. He afforded protection to the Jesuit missionaries, Father Jogues and Father Bressani, rescued them from the Indians, and gave them a free passage to Holland. He also welcomed many Anabaptists, who, being persecuted in New England, sought the more tolerant rule of the Dutch. Among these were two ladies, Mrs. Anne Hutchinson and Lady Deborah Moody. The former settled at Pelham Neck, the latter at Gravesend, Long Island. In 1643, John Throgmorton and thirty-five Anabaptist families received permission to settle at a spot in the Bronx subsequently called Throgg's Neck.

In 1647, Bogardus sailed for Holland in the *Princess* to defend his conduct before his ecclesiastical superiors. It was a strange fate that led the ex-Director, Kieft, to take passage on the same boat, for these two bitter enemies both suffered death by shipwreck in the Bristol Channel.

In 1654, the Company being evidently troubled by the dissensions, made the following wise regulations:

No person shall take the name of the Lord in vain, whether by cursing, swearing, or blaspheming, in jest or otherwise, upon the penalty of ten stivers, and arbitrary correction, according to the degree of profanity and blasphemy which shall be uttered and expressed.

Also shall no man presume to rebuke, to contemptuously treat, disturb, or in any wise obstruct the Minister

RELIGION

or exhorter of God's Holy Word, in the performance of his office or calling.

Further, whenever, early in the morning or after supper in the evening, prayers shall be said, or God's word read, by any one thereto commissioned, every person, of what quality soever he may be, shall repair to hear it with becoming reverence.

No man shall raise or bring forward any question or argument on the subject of religion, on pain of being placed on bread and water three days in the ship's galley. And if any difficulties should arise out of the said disputes, the author thereof shall be arbitrarily punished.

Stuyvesant was accompanied from Curaçao by the Rev. Johannes Backerus, who remained only a year in New Amsterdam. On his departure the Rev. Johannes Megapolensis was transferred from Fort Orange to New Amsterdam, where he remained until his death in 1669. In 1652, the Rev. Samuel Drisius, a bachelor of forty, was sent out, "a fit assistant to the old gentleman, Do. Megapolensis." They worked together in amity, but the results of their work among the Indians was not altogether satisfactory. In 1659, they wrote to Amsterdam a report of the religious conditions of the colony, from which we learn:

We have had one Indian here with us full two years, so that he could read and write good Dutch; we instructed him in the grounds of Religion; he also answered publicly in the church and repeated the prayers. We likewise presented him with a Bible in order to work through him some good among the Indians. But it all resulted in nothing. He has taken to drinking of Brandy; he pawned the Bible and became a real beast who is doing more harm than good among the Indians.

About eighteen miles up the North River lies Esopus. It is an exceedingly beautiful Land. There some Dutch Inhabitants have settled themselves, and prosper especially well. They hold Sunday meetings, and then one among them reads something out for a postille.

The Dutch on Long Island were without a church or minister of their own until the middle of the century, and in order to attend public worship were obliged to visit New Amsterdam. Occasionally, however, the Dominie visited the outlying towns and held services in private houses. In December, 1654, the Director and Council having endeavored to remedy this want, sanctioned the erection of a small church at Midwout (Flatbush), by the joint effort of three towns; and the Rev. Johannes Theodorus Polhemus from Brazil was installed as pastor. Here services were held on Sunday mornings and at Breuckelen and Amersfoort on alternate Sunday afternoons. Drisius reports:

It took three hours for these devout people to get to the church in the Fort, so when De Polhemus arrived from Brasils, they requested that he might be appointed their preacher which was granted. The four other villages on Long Island, viz., Gravesend Middelburgh, Vlissingen and Heemstede were established by the English. At Gravesend there were Mennonists; at Flushing, Presbyterians, who after a time absented themselves from church and refused to pay the preacher, who fled to Virginia. . . . Last year a fomentor of error came there. He was a cobbler from Rhode Island and stated that he was commissioned by Christ. He began to preach at Flushing and then went with the people into the river and dipped them. This becoming known here, he was banished the province.

At Middelburgh (Newtown) there were mostly Independents, led by one Johannes Moor, and at Heemstede some Independents Presbyterians under the charge of Richard Denton, an honest, pious and learned man.

On the west side of the East River about one mile through Hellgate another English village has been begun over two years. It was named Oostdorp. The inhabitants are also Puritains *alias* Independents. They have no preacher. They hold Sunday meetings reading from an English book, a sermon and making a prayer.

Lutherans, Quakers, and Anabaptists gave the Directors and Dominies much trouble. A few examples will suffice to show how difficult it was for alien sects to flourish while Dominie Megapolensis was Father of the Flock. In 1652, he requested that Anna Smits, an Anabaptist, should be restrained from using slanderous and calumniating expressions against God's Word and his servants; and the Director-General and Council ordered

that Anna Smits shall appear on the following Wednesday at the school of David Provoost, where the Nine Men usually meet and that the Director and Council together with the complainant and the consistory shall assemble there also, to hear what the said Anna Smits has to say against the teachings of the complainant.

Also, on Nov. 8, 1656, William Hallet, Sheriff of Flushing, for allowing Baptist conventicles in his house, was sentenced to pay a fine of £50 Flemish, to be banished, with costs, and to remain in prison till the fine was paid. William Wickendam was fined £100 and other penalties as above for officiating as a gospel minister; but three days later the fine was graciously remitted "as nothing can be got from him."

No sect, however, alarmed the good Dominies more than the Lutherans, who showed at an early period symptoms of growth. On Oct. 24, 1656, they petitioned that they might not be prevented continuing their religious exercises, as they "expect a regular clergyman next Spring." It was ordered that the petition be forwarded to the West India Company; "meanwhile the laws will be enforced against Conventicles and public meetings of any but those belonging to the Reformed Dutch church."

The Directors were not pleased at this persecution. They wrote (1656):

We would also have been better pleased if you had not published the placat against the Lutherans, a copy of which you sent us, and committed them to prison, for it has always been our intention to treat them quietly and leniently. Hereafter you will therefore not publish such or similar placats without our knowledge, but you must pass it over quietly and let them have free religious exercises in their houses.

Stuyvesant (1656), however, supported Drisius and Megapolensis with the following proclamation:

Whereas the Director General and Council are credibly informed that not only Conventicles and Meetings are held within this Province, but also that in such gatherings some unqualified persons have assumed unto themselves the office of teaching; announcing and declaring God's Holy Word, without being called or appointed thereto by authority either of Church or State, which is in direct contradiction and opposition to the General policy and Church government of our Fatherland, because from such manner of gatherings divers mischiefs, heresies and schisms are to be expected, which to prevent, the Director General and aforesaid Council do hereby, therefore, absolutely and expressly forbid all such Conventicles or Gatherings, whether publick or private, except the usual and lawful ones in which God's reformed word and the ordained assemblies of God's Reformed worship are observed and conducted conformably to those of the Synod of Dordrecht, here, in our Fatherland and in other Reformed Churches of Europe, under the penalty of One Hundred Pounds Flemish, to be forfeited by all who assume any unqualified office whether of preaching read-

PORCELAIN, EARTHENWARE ORNAMENT AND GLASS TUMBLER
IN THE VAN CORTLANDT MANOR HOUSE

ing or singing, whether on Sunday or any other day in such Gatherings whether private or publick. Without intending, hereby, however, any violence to Conscience to the prejudice of the Patents formerly granted, or to prohibit the reading of God's Holy Word, family prayers and Worship, each in his own house.

Attendants at any unlawful meeting were also to be fined £25 each.

It is astonishing to find how very soon after Fox began to preach his followers became active on this side of the Atlantic. Naturally, Quakers first made their appearance among the English settlers on Long Island. It was not likely that Stuyvesant and his Dominies would be indulgent to this new heresy. On Jan. 10, 1658, John Tilton was fined £12 Flemish and costs for harboring some of "the abominable sect of Quakers." Henry Towsen (Jan. 15) was fined three hundred guilders for the same offense.

In January, 1661, Stuyvesant was again troubled with the pestilential Quakers. One Henry Townsend was reported to have entertained members of the sect at Jamaica, Long Island. The Director wrote to the magistrates and sent the Rev. Samuel Drisius to officiate there, and a deputy sheriff to inquire into the holding of conventicles. A search for Quakers followed on Long Island, and the arrest of a Quaker's cloak and of Sam Spicer; names were also given of those who attended the preaching of George Wilson. Henry Townsend was fined £25, and Slicer £12. John Townsend and John Tilton were banished from the province. On January 24, Stuyvesant notified Jamaica of the appointment of new magistrates, and the quartering of soldiers on the inhabitants on account of their heresy. On Aug. 24, 1662, the Flushing magistrates lodged information against John Bowne for holding meetings every Sunday of "that abominable sect called Quakers, of which the majority of the inhabitants are followers." John Bowne was fined £25 and costs, and finally banished.

On Sept. 14, 1662, Stuyvesant issued a proclamation declaring that the public exercise of any religion but the Reformed " in houses, barns, ships, woods or fields, would be punished by a fine of fifty guilders; double, for a second offense; and quadruple, for the third with arbitrary correction." In April, 1663, however, the Lords Directors censure Stuyvesant " for banishing John Bowne, the Quaker."

It is hard to understand the hatred aroused by the proverbially harmless Quakers. It appears, however, that in the early days their enthusiasm in proselytizing sometimes led them into aggressive missionary methods. For example, in 1677, the town of Huntington, Long Island, petitioned Governor Andros that the Quakers "be not permitted to come into the meeting-house (as they frequently do) in time of worship, to disturb the congregation." " Samuel Forman of Oyster bay, came to the City, where he lodged at the house of Anthony Jansen from Salee, and, by inspiration from Christ Jesus intended to repair to the church during divine service and exclaim: 'O cry what shall I cry, all flesh is grass, grass is the flower of the field, the flower falls and the grass withers, but the word of God obeids forever.'" Two days later, he was sentenced to be publicly whipped and then banished, for having disturbed public worship in the church at New Orange.

The Dutch church service was simple. The foresinger, or clerk, standing at a desk beneath the pulpit, or in the deacons' pew, began the service by the command: "Hear with reverence the Word of the Lord"; then he read the Ten Commandments and announced the Psalm. While this was being sung, the Minister entered, stood for a few minutes at the foot of the pulpit stairs; and, after a silent prayer, ascended the pulpit. He preached with an hour-glass before him. At the end of the sermon the clerk inserted in the end of his staff the public notices to be read and handed them to the Minister. This duty ended, the Minister delivered a short homily on charity, and the deacons walked through the church to take up a collection, each having a long pole, at the end of which was a black velvet bag for the offerings.

There was great difference of sentiment regarding the Quakers. Sometimes we find special bequests to them, as in the case of Colonel Lewis Morris, who, in 1691, gives "to the meetings of Friends called Quakers £5 per annum." In quite another mood, William Hollyoake, of Southold, Long Island, makes his will in which he emphatically orders:

If my sons Thomas, Peter or William, or any of their succeeding heirs, whether sons or daughters, whom I doe constitute my heirs, shall Apostate from the Protestant Doctrine of faith of the Church of England as it is now by law established, and if they or any of them shall at any time hereafter, take upon him or them, any profession of such Doctrines or faith whereby they shall be drawn away from attendance upon the Publick Worship of God, practiced in this place, and warranted by the Holy Scriptures; and if they shall neglect or contemn the said publick Worship; and if the said Thomas or any of them shall at any time espouse and contract marriage with any Quaker, or to the son or daughter of any Quaker as they are now called; It is my positive Will that they shall be utterly disinherited and disowned. And I bequeath the lands so forfeited by such wicked practices to the next lawful heir. . . . I leave to my son John who as an obstinate Apostate I doe reject and deprive of all other parts of my estate, yet I doe hereby give him my Second lot at the Wading Creek.

In 1658, Megapolensis and Drisius petitioned the Classis to send out "good Dutch clergymen"; and a young candidate for the ministry, Hendricus Blom, was induced to come out. He soon received a call to Esopus (Kingston) and went home to be ordained. On Dec. 22, 1659, the Directors of the West India Company wrote to Stuyvesant a letter disapproving of the narrow views of himself (for he was a good deal of a bigot) and his subordinates. They regarded themselves as a trading corporation, not a body of sectarian propagandists, and therefore discouraged intolerance.

We intend to send over two or three young preachers on the same conditions as Domine Blom, and have been looking about for them; it is not sufficient that they lead a good moral life, they must be of a peaceable and moderate temperament, which depends a good deal on the place of their studies, and not be infected with scruples about unnecessary forms, which cause more divisions than edification. The preachers there, Des. Megapolensis and Drisius, do not seem to be free from this kind of leaven, for they make difficulties in regard to the use of the old formula of baptism without order from the Classis here, pretending that they might be accused of innovations, although the name of innovators could be better applied to those who have made changes in it without the order of the Church generally, or of a Classis. The most moderate preachers here understand this and consider it an insignificant ceremony, which may be performed or omitted according to circumstances and without hurting one's conscience. We had expected that the above-mentioned preachers and brothers would hold the same opinion after our too friendly letter to them. We are told, it is true, that the Lutherans come to church now and that every thing goes on quietly and peaceably, but care must be taken that this state of affairs continue; that is uncertain, as long as such precise forms and offensive expressions are not avoided. It is absolutely necessary that they be avoided in a church, which is so weak and only beginning to grow, especially when we consider the difficulties liable to arise, which might result in the permission to conduct a separate divine service there, for the Lutherans would very easily obtain the consent of the authorities here upon a complaint, and we would have no means of preventing it. We find it therefore highly necessary to direct herewith, that you communicate all this to the aforesaid preachers there and seriously admonish them to adopt our advice and use the old formula of baptism without waiting for further orders from here. That will allay the dissensions in the state and of the church there.

On Blom's return, he was accompanied by the Rev. Henricus Selyns, to become pastor of the Breuckelen congregation. Mr. Selyns was installed on Sept. 7, 1660. As the people were unable to pay his salary, the Council was petitioned for aid. Stuyvesant agreed to contribute personally two hundred and fifty guilders if Mr. Selyns would preach every Sunday afternoon at his Bowery. Writing to the Classis, Oct. 4, 1660, Mr. Selyns says:

When we arrived, we repaired forthwith to the Manhattans; but the negotiations for peace at the Esopus necessarily retarded our progress thus long. We preached meanwhile, here, and at the Esopus and Fort Orange; during our stay were provided with board and Lodging. Esopus needs more people; but Breucklen more wealth; wherefore I officiate Sunday afternoons at the General's Bouwerye at the Noble General's private expense. I was suitably received (in Brooklyn) by the Magistrate and consistory and De Polhemus was forthwith discharged. We do not preach in any church, but in a barn (*Koren-*

schuur), and shall, God willing, erect a church in the winter by the co-operation of the people. The congregation is passable. The attendance is augmented from Middelwout, New Amersfoort and frequently Gravesande, but most from the Manhattans. To Breuckelen appertains also the Ferry, the Walebocht and Gujanus. There can be no Catechising before the winter, but this shall be introduced either on week days or when there is no preaching at the Bowery. Christmas, Easter, Whitsuntide and September will be most suitable, as Thanksgiving is observed on these festivals. . . .

There is preaching in the morning at Breuckelen but, towards the conclusion of the Catechismal exercises of New Amsterdam, at the Bowery which is a continuation and the place of recreation of the Manhattans, where people also come from the city to Evening Service. In addition to the household there are over forty negroes whose location is the Negro quarter. There is no consistory here, but the deacons of New Amsterdam provisionally receive the alms offerings, and there are to be neither elders nor deacons there. Besides me there are in New Netherlands DD Johannes Megapolensis and Samuel Drisius in New Amsterdam; D. Gideon Schaets at Fort Orange; D. Joannes Polemius at Middelwout and N. Amersfort and Hermanus Blom at the Esopus.

In 1664, he returned to Holland in the *Beaver* to visit his aged father; and, after his departure, Charles Debevoise, schoolmaster and sexton, conducted the services. During his ministry Selyns married in New Amsterdam, in 1662, Machtelt Specht, daughter of Herman Specht, of Utrecht, "a young lady of rare personal beauty and worth," to whom he wrote a poem that has been much admired. Soon after he left, Dominie Drisius wrote of him to Amsterdam in warm terms of admiration of his preaching and pastoral work:

FLOWERS
JAN VAN HUYSAM

He has attached very many unto him, among them a number of the negroes, who are greatly grieved by his departure. But considering the fact that he owes filial obedience to his parents it is the will of God that he should leave us.

He thinks it probable that the recently arrived son of Dom. Megapolensis will take charge of Brooklyn and the Bouwerie; and adds that the French on Staten Island would gladly have a preacher, but cannot afford to support one. Governor Stuyvesant allows Drisius to go there and preach every two months and administer the Lord's Supper, but " in the winter season it is troublesome on account of the great water of bay, which must be crossed, and the showers and storms, which occur."

The English conquest put an end to the exclusive sway of the Dutch Reformed Church. Freedom of worship was allowed to all congregations who cared to pay their own ministers.

In 1669, Megapolensis wrote to the Classis of Amsterdam complaining that the West India Company had " unrighteously withheld about 2000 guilders salary " from him, having falsely accused him of having had a hand in delivering the town to the English. Though the people took a great interest in the preaching, and the church was filled on Sundays, still they showed " little interest in contributing to the support of the Gospel and in paying our salary." When the Governor was appealed to for aid, his reply was: " As the Dutch enjoy their freedom of worship, they should provide for the support of their minister."

Samuel Megapolensis, who had been his father's assistant since 1664, resigned and went to Holland; and the old Dominie, who had now spent twenty-seven years in the New World, was full of grief to think that when he and Dominie Drisius should pass away their congregation would probably scatter. Nothing seems to have given him more distress than the fact that the Lutherans had recently received a minister from Amsterdam.

In 1669, Megapolensis the Elder died; and as Samuel Drisius was growing old and unable to shoulder all the duties of his charge, a new minister was needed. As no one seemed willing to come, Governor Lovelace in 1670 sent word to the Classis of Amsterdam that he would give any "scholarly and godly minister a hundred guilders a year, a dwelling rent free and firewood." The Rev. William Nieuwenhuys accepted the terms, and in 1671 became sole pastor of the Dutch church on the death of Drisius.

On his death, in 1681, Selyns returned and was received with open arms by his old friends. Doubtless he was well acquainted with the widow of Cornelis Steenwyck, whom he very promptly married, she conveniently inheriting the taste of her mother, Vrouw Drisius, for divines. Selyns wrote enthusiastic letters home, informing the authorities that the people were building a parsonage of brick (or stone), three stories high, and that he had four hundred families on his list; but he complained that there was too much work for one man.

Selyns was minister during the usurpation of Jacob Leisler, and at one time was the only Dutch minister in the province; for Delius escaped to Boston; Van Varick, minister of the four Dutch towns of Kings County, was convicted of treason and imprisoned; Tesschenmaker was massacred at Schenectady in 1690; and Van der Bosch deposed at Kingston. Selyns himself was accused of harboring Bayard, and his house was searched by public officers.

RELIGION

Dominie Rudolphus Van Varick was dragged from his home in Flatbush, imprisoned and heavily fined. He had arrived from Holland in 1685, and succeeded the Rev. Casparus Van Zuren as minister of the Long Island churches. He became deeply involved in the Leisler troubles. His wife, Margarita Visboom, had many valuable and beautiful possessions.

Governor Andros wrote in 1678:

There are religions of all sorts, one Church of England, several Presbyterians and Independents, Quakers and Anabaptists of several sects, some Jews, but Presbyterians and Independents most numerous and substantial.

Governor Dongan, who was a Roman Catholic, and who brought over with him a Jesuit priest who celebrated Mass in the Governor's private apartments in the Fort on Sundays, to which the Roman Catholics of the town were admitted, wrote home the following:

New York has a chaplain belonging to the Fort of the Church of England; secondly a Dutch Calvinist; third, a French Calvinist; and fourth, a Dutch Lutheran. There be not many of England; a few Roman Catholics; abundance of Quaker preachers, men and women; singing Quakers, ranting Quakers, Sabbatarians, anti Sabbatarians some Anabaptists, some Independents, some Jews; in short, of all sorts of opinions there are some, and the most part of none at all.

In 1865, William Byrd, of *Westover,* Virginia, noted on his trip to Albany:

They have as many Sects of religion there as att Amsterdam, all being tolerated, yet the people seem not concerned what religion their Neighbour is of, or whether hee hath any or none.

Miller, also in 1695, remarked upon the condition of religion in not very complimentary terms. He said:

The number of the inhabitants in this province are about 3000 families, whereof almost one-half are naturally Dutch, a great part English and the rest French. As to their religion, they are very much divided; few of them intelligent and sincere, but the most part ignorant and conceited, fickle and regardless.

Finally, Madam Knight observed in 1702:

They are generally of the Church of England and have a New England Gentleman for their minister and a very fine church set out with all Customary requisites. There are also a Dutch and Divers Conventicles as they call them, viz., Baptist, Quakers, etc. They are not strict in keeping the Sabbath as in Boston and other places where I had bin, But seem to deal with great exactness as farr as I see or Deall with. They are sociable to one another and fare well in their houses.

Under Stuyvesant and Drisius, people were compelled to observe the Sabbath in the strict Mosaic fashion. The Director and Council issued several ordinances for the better observance of the Sabbath. The first of these, dated April 29, 1648, runs as follows:

On the Lord's day of rest, usually called Sunday, no person shall be allowed to do the ordinary and customary labors of his calling, such as Sowing, Mowing, Building, Sawing Wood, Smithing, Bleeching, Hunting, Fishing, or any works allowable on other days, under the penalty of One Pound Flemish, for each person so offending; much less any idle or unallowed exercises and sports, such as Drinking to excess, frequenting Inns or Taphouses, Dancing, Card-playing, Tick-tacking, Playing at ball, Playing at bowls, Playing at nine-pins, taking jaunts in Boats, Wagons, or Carriages, before, between, or during Divine Service, under the penalty of a double fine (Two Pounds, Flemish); and in order to prevent all such accidents and injuries, there shall be a fine of Twelve Guilders for the first offence; Twenty-four Guilders for the second offence; and arbitrary correction for the third offence; the One-third for the Officers; One-third for the Poor; and the remaining One-third for the Prosecutor.

Many were the cases brought into court for breaking the Sunday laws, and many were the excuses of the defendants. Sometimes they plead ignorance of the law, and sometimes they break the law and pay the fines with callous indifference. Let us glance at the wickedness of a few of the sinners. Hendrick de Backer, of Fort Orange, 1660, was fined twelve guilders for bringing in a load of hay on Sunday, about the third tolling of the bell. In 1664, Manuel Sanderson, a negro, was fined six guilders and costs because his son had been found shooting pigeons in the woods on Manhattan Island on Sunday. Tiebout Wessels was fined for the same misdemeanor, and a certain Jan de Noper was complained of for resisting an officer who wanted to arrest him at the same time. Jan Bockholt, a herdsman, prayed for forgiveness, pleading ignorance of the law, but was fined twelve guilders and costs. The Fiscal also complained against Dame Gerritse, "who is famous for being a scold," for abusing the officer who had seized her son's gun while shooting pigeons on Sunday; and she was fined twelve guilders and costs. On the same court day an ordinance was issued "for the better and more careful instruction of youth in the principles of the Christian religion."

In 1667, the Schout says that Claes Dietlofs and Jan, the cake-baker, "rolled a barrel with maize along the street on last Sunday." He demands the fine according to Placard. "Defendants answer that they first came in the morning with a canoe, and that they durst not trust it the whole day in a canoe." In 1663, Jacob Stoffels, Ide van Vorst, and other farmers were fined six guilders each for working on Sunday.

Judging by the ordinance of 1667, Sabbath breaking was deplorably common:

> Whereas we experience to our grief, that the previously enacted and frequently renewed Placards and Ordinances against the desecration of the Sabbath of the Lord, the unlawful and unseasonable tapping on the same and after setting of the watch or drum beat, are not observed, but that many of the inhabitants almost make it a custom, in place of observing the Sabbath, as it ought to be observed, to frequent the taverns more than on other days and to take their delight in illegal exercises, to prevent and obviate which hereafter as much as possible for the future, the Schout, Burgomasters and Schepens renew the aforesaid Placards, enacted on that subject and hereby interdict and forbid within this City of N: Orange and the jurisdiction thereof from sunrise to sundown on Sunday all sorts of handicraft, trade and traffick, gaming, boat-racing or running with carts or wagons, fishing, fowling, running and picking nuts, strawberries, etc., all riotous racing, calling and shouting of children in the streets, together with all unlawful exercises and games, drunkenness, frequenting taverns or taphouses, dancing, card-playing, ball playing, rolling nine pins or bowls, etc., which is more in vogue on this than on any other day; to prohibit and prevent which, all tavern keepers and tapsters are strictly enjoined to entertain no clubs on this day from sunrise to sunset, nor permit nor suffer any games in their houses or places, on pain for the tavern keeper, who shall be found to suffer such in his house, of forfeiting for the first offence 25 gl. for the second offence 50 gl. and for the 3^d offence he shall no longer be allowed to tap and moreover forfeit a fine of one hundred guilders zeawant; and each person found on Sunday in a club or gaming house shall forfeit three guilders

THE PARROT CAGE
JAN STEEN

zeawant; and if any children be caught on the street playing, racing and shouting, previous to the termination of the last preaching, the officers of the law may take their hat or upper garment, which shall not be restored to the parents, until they have paid a fine of two guilders.

The intention of the above prohibition is not, that a stranger or citizen shall not buy a drink of wine or beer for the assuaging of his thirst, but only to prevent the sitting of clubs on the Sabbath, whereby many are hindered resorting to Divine Worship.

Further no tapsters, nor tavernkeepers shall tap, present or sell any wines, brandies, beer, etc., nor set any clubs on Sunday, nor on the night of any other day after setting of the watch or ringing of the bell, under the penalty and fine as above.

Special days of fasting and thanksgiving were frequently set apart. The first seems to have occurred during Director Kieft's rule, when a Fast Day was appointed, March 4, 1643, in consequence of the Indian troubles, and a Thanksgiving Day on Sept. 6, 1645. His proclamation of Aug. 31, 1645, reads:

Whereas God Almighty has been pleased, by his grace and mercy, and in addition to the numerous blessings that we have enjoyed, to bestow on this country that long desired peace with the savages — so it has been deemed becoming to proclaim this good tidings throughout the New Netherlands, with the intention that in all places where there are any English or Dutch churches, God Almighty shall be thanked and praised, on the sixth day of September next in the forenoon. The words of the text must be applicable to the occasion and the sermon likewise.

Another day of special sanctity was the New Year, especially during Stuyvesant's administration, and on

March 24, 1653, the first Wednesday of each month was appointed a fast and prayer day.

Superstition was general in all creeds and classes. People believed in omens, signs, and prognostications, and in such antidotes as charms, amulets, and scapularies. Comets and eclipses of the sun and moon filled every one with fear, for they predicted war and other calamities, while earthquakes and thunderclaps were thought to be utterances of God's wrath. In every house was found The Wheel of Adventure, or the Spiritual Truth Sayer, Planet books, and the works of Ludeman. There were also fortune-tellers, who predicted the future by means of cards, reading the palm, coffee and tea grounds, etc. A very favorite method of divination was by turning the Bible. On April 6, 1662, George Hewel, Dr. Clarke, John Too, and Daniel East of Mespath, Long Island, were prosecuted for having had recourse to turning the Bible in order to discover who had stolen tobacco from William Britton. It would seem that they were led astray by a false prophet, for the individual accused by their investigations later brought an action for slander against them.

People believed in ghosts, in haunted places, in changelings, and, above all, in witches. No old women with wrinkled faces and no women of fascinating charms were safe from the accusation of witchcraft. Storms, barrenness of the land, disease of people and cattle, — in short, every disaster, great and small, was attributed to witchcraft. If anybody wanted to know whether a sick person was ill or bewitched, the only thing to do was to cut open the pillow from under the head. If the feathers were changed into flowers or ferns, there was no doubt that he was touched by the evil hand. If one wanted to find out who had done the evil act, all that was necessary was to put a live black hen or cock in a pot of boiling water, and the person who passed the door while the bird was crying was the witch. In early youth the children were already taught to believe in witchcraft, as appears from the following Dutch catechism:

Q. What is the second capital-sin? *A.* Witchcraft. *Q.* Does Witchcraft appear in God's Word? *A.* Yes. *Q.* Prove it. *A.* Exodus xii. vers. 22, and xxii. v. 18. Deuteronomy xviii. v. 10. Acts viii. v. 9. *Q.* Are there any people who say that there is no witchcraft? *A.* Yes. *Q.* Who are they? *A.* The "Sadducees" of this day and the Libertines amongst the so-called Christians, who believe that all that is said of Satan and his work are fables and that everything that takes place is perfectly natural.

Witches were, of course, in league with Satan, changed themselves into cats, rode on broomsticks, and cast evil spells on man and beast; it was unsafe to take an apple or any other dainty from the hands of a witch, for, just as likely as not, it would turn into a toad.

It seems somewhat strange that from the middle of the Seventeenth Century and during the Long Parliament (1640–1660), when the terrible "witchfinders" sent three thousand witches to death, and while the English settlements on South Hampton and East Hampton were sending their supposed witches to Connecticut for trial, no witches were persecuted in New Amsterdam. The Dutch and French churches of New Amsterdam protested, asserting that "the apparition of a person afflicting another is very insufficient proof of a witch, and that a good name, obtained by a good life, should not be lost by mere '*spectral accusation.*'" The only witchcraft trial ever held on the island was that of Ralph Hall and his wife of Seatalcott, Long Island, under Governor Nichols in October, 1665. It took place at the City Hall, and both parties were discharged.

The authorities of New England, however, did not respect their more enlightened neighbors. No less a personage than Governor Stuyvesant's sister-in-law, the attractive Judith Varleth, was tried and held as a witch in Connecticut in 1662. This circumstance brought forth the following letter from Stuyvesant to the Deputy-Governor of the Court of Magistrates at Hartford in 1662:

Honoured and worthy sirs: By this occasion of my brother-in-law being necessitated to make a second voyage to ayd a distressed sister, Judith Varlet, imprisoned, as we are informed upon pretended accusation of witchery, we really believe, and out of her well-known education, life, conversation and profession of faith, we dare assure, that she is innocent of such a horrible *crimen*, and, wherefore, I doubt not he will now, as formerly, finde your honour's favour and ayde for the innocent.

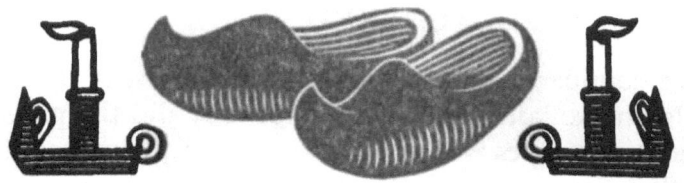

CHAPTER X

COURTSHIP AND MARRIAGE

TWO festivals were particularly honored among the Dutch, — the christening and the wedding. Parents began to provide for the future from the very birth of the child, and betrothals sometimes took place while the babies were lying in the cradle; sometimes even alliances were determined before birth. Gold coins and medals were accumulated for dowry, silver and jewels were collected, and coffers and chests filled with linen; and, as she grew up, the maiden spun and collected her linen, and made the lace collar and cuffs, her bridal gift to her future husband.

This custom of infant betrothal was naturally most prevalent in the upper classes, where wealthy alliances were of importance for political or business reasons; but in the family of the average burgher considerable latitude of choice was allowed, and, as long as the prospective bride, or groom, was not absolutely objectionable to the parents on either side, the course of true love ran fairly smoothly. The custom known in this country as "bundling" prevailed in Holland as well as in England and Wales. As a rule, the more humble the class, the greater was the freedom of intercourse between the Dutch youth. Female virtue was a question of the highest solicitude with the Church, and the average morality of the Dutch housewife was very high. The mother set a good example and reposed almost entire confidence in the daughter. This was the case in North Holland especially. Not only did the parents absent themselves when the lover visited their daughter, but they even allowed the lovers a separate room for courtship. These visits sometimes lasted five or six hours, and sometimes even until daybreak, without attracting the slightest attention. Not only did the parents allow this, but they even encouraged it. No girl was respected that did not have an honest *queester* (night visitor), and even widows received these visits. The laws of propriety were seldom transgressed, and assistance was always at hand at need. Sometimes the visitor was received in the parents' bedroom.

In South Holland, the daughters were strictly watched, and the church or a visit was the only means of forming an acquaintance. Lovers often had to resort to ruse to meet one another. The first meeting was generally effected by bribing the maidservant, or if there was no servant the girl's attention was attracted by fastening a flower, bouquet, or wreath on the front door. If this lay in the street the next morning, the lover was not disheartened, but replaced the flower by another with a ribbon tied round it, and sometimes he added a verse or motto. Later he would place on one of the window-sills of his sweetheart's room a prettily decorated basket filled with candy, or he would fasten this to a branch of a May-tree near the window. These baskets were followed by others with choice fruit and flowers, and rhymes and sonnets in which the lover expressed his feelings, and these were followed again by serenades. If upon a first visit the girl stood up, arranged her bonnet, and smoothed out her dress so as to make herself attractive, the lover knew he was welcome, but if she went to

COUNTRY HOUSE
PIETER DE HOOCH

the fireplace and gripped the tongs, he had to try his luck elsewhere.

To effect an introduction matchmakers were often hired. These were often the wet-nurses or the midwives. They had, according to the popular saying, to put "the door on the latch," and effect the first meeting, generally on Sundays at six o'clock. Each young man then chose his girl, at whose door he knocked at nine o'clock. If he came before nine, the door was not opened to him; if later, then it was thought that he had been disappointed at another girl's house; but the door was opened and the regular conversation followed, as is described in hundreds of Dutch books on love. On entering, the meeting at the church was discussed, and shortly after the lover left to tell the news to his comrades. Custom demanded that the young man should propose to the girl on three successive Sundays. In case he did not please, he received his refusal on the third Sunday, otherwise his visits were encouraged, and he then called earlier. The accepted lover was also allowed to call on Wednesdays, to take his sweetheart to Whitsuntide *fêtes* and to the *kermis*.

On examining the court records of New Amsterdam, we must conclude that many of the inhabitants were extremely lax in their compliance with and observation of the laws of Fatherland. Several of those who described the customs of the province notice the loose ties among a large class of the inhabitants. The evil was evidently a serious one, because the following law was passed on Jan. 15, 1658:

Persons whose banns have been published must marry within one month, or show cause to the contrary, under a penalty of 10 guilders for the first week and 20 guilders for each succeeding week.

No man or woman shall be at liberty to keep house as

married persons, before they are legally married, on pain of forfeiting 100 guilders, more or less, as their quality shall be found to warrant, and all such persons may be amerced anew therefor every month, according to the order and custom of our Fatherland.

The binding nature of the betrothal in the eye of the law is evident from many entries in the records. A promise of marriage, given in the presence of others with the exchange of a pledge, generally in the form of a ring or a coin, was regarded as being as sacred as the marriage ceremony itself; and many suits for breach of promise of marriage were tried in the courts here. Thus, on May 17, 1644, Elsje Jans, widow of Jan Petersen, sued William Harlo for breach of promise, producing a shilling which she had received from the fickle William, as a pledge of his troth. After hearing what he had to say, the court ordered him to bring proof that the lady had acted unbecomingly since the betrothal.

The offense in the eyes of the law was a very serious one in the case of the breaking of the engagement after the publication of the banns. For example, on April 5, 1658, Nicholas Albertsen, for deserting his ship and betrothed bride after publication of the banns, was sentenced to have his head shaved, then to be flogged, and have his ears bored, and to work two years with the negroes. Even when there would seem to be good cause for the non-fulfilment of the contract, the authorities were extremely unwilling to consent to its abrogation. Thus, in 1654, we read:

A suit has been instituted before the Court of the City of New Amsterdam by Pieter Kock, bachelor, against Anna van Vorst, spinster living at Ahasimus,[1] respecting

[1] In New Jersey.

a marriage contract, or an oral promise of marriage, mutually entered into between said Pieter Kock and Anna van Vorst, and in confirmation thereof certain gifts and presents were made by plaintiff to the aforesaid defendant; however, it appears by the documents exhibited by parties, that defendant, in consequence of certain misbehaviour, is in no wise disposed to marry said Pieter Kock, and also proves by two witnesses that Pieter Cock had released her, with promise to give her a written acquittal to that effect, therefore Burgomasters and Schepens of this City, adjudge, that the promise of marriage having been made and given before the Eyes of God, shall remain in force, so that neither plaintiff nor defendant shall be at liberty without the knowledge and approbation of the Worshipful Magistrates and the other one of the interested parties to enter into matrimony with any other person, whether single man or single woman. Also that all the presents made in confirmation of the promise of marriage shall remain in the possession of defendant, until parties with the pleasure, good will, contentment and inclination of both, shall marry together, or with the knowledge of the Magistracy shall release and set each other free.

Still more serious is a case in 1662:

Maria Besems made a written demand on the property of Boudewyn van Nieulant, absconded from here. "Whereas the said Boudewyn has acknowledged before this court to have given the aforesaid Maria Besems a written promise of marriage, the Burgomasters decree that she shall enter on all that the aforesaid Boudewyn has in this country, nothing excepted, for the payment of childbed expenses and the support of the child.

Parental consent was necessary for the publication of the banns and to render the marriage legal. This is evident from a case which occurred in 1648; when William Harck, Sheriff of Flushing, having married

Joan Smith, without her parents' consent, to Thomas Nuton, widower, was fined six hundred guilders and dismissed from office; the marriage was annulled. Nuton was fined three hundred guilders, and the marriage had to be again solemnized after three proclamations. The second ceremony was performed thirteen days later.

Quite a romantic story is that of Maria Verleth and Johannes Van Beeck. It seems that there was great opposition on the part of the young man's father, and consequently they went into Connecticut and published their banns in Gravesend. This occasioned great excitement, for on Jan. 26, 1654, the "Schout appeared in Court and made a complaint of the illegal proceedings of the Court of Gravesend in setting up and affixing the bans of matrimony between Johan Van Beeck and Maria Verleth both of whom lived in New Amsterdam. This if allowed to pass might establish a precedent and prepare a way, whereby hereafter some sons and daughters unwilling to obey their parents and guardians, will, contrary to their wishes, secretly go and get married in such villages or elsewhere." A fortnight later, the Gravesend magistrates received a letter informing them that Johannes Van Beeck had presented a petition to the New Amsterdam Court to enter and properly proclaim his banns with Maria Verleth, who had previously made proclamation through the court at Gravesend, which was contrary to the style and laws of the Fatherland. In order to prevent future improprieties therefore they were informed that, "according to the custom of our Fatherland every one shall have three publications at the place where his domicile is, and then he may go and be married wherever he pleases." On February 16, Casper Verleth, the bride's father, and Johannes van

Beeck appeared in court and prayed most earnestly that disposal should be made of the petitions and remonstrance concerning the marriage. Three days later, the court decided:

Regarding the bans of matrimony between Joh. van Beeck and Maria Verleth, therefore it being noted

First, Who in the beginning instituted marriage; also what the Apostle of the Gentiles teaches therein.

Secondly, The proper and attained ages of Johannes van Beeck and Marya Verleth.

Thirdly, The consent of the father and mother on the daughter's side.

Fourthly, the distance and remoteness of places between this and our Fatherland together with the difficulty between Holland and England.

Fifthly, The danger that in such circumstances matters by long delay might come to be disclosed between these aforesaid young people, which would bring disgrace on both families, as well on one side as on the other

'T is true that our Theologians say, and that correctly, that we must not tolerate or permit lesser sins, in order thereby to avoid greater ones. Therefore we think (with due submission) that by a proper solemnization of marriage (for the Apostle to the Hebrews calls the marriage bed honorable) the lesser and greater sins are prevented.

Therefore the Burgomasters and Schepens of this City are of opinion that the proper ecclesiastical proclamations of these aforesaid young people ought to be made at the earliest opportunity to be followed afterwards by their marriage.

Evidently the course of true love did not run smooth even yet; and so, after waiting weary months, the young couple took matters into their own hands and we hear that on Sept. 14, 1654, Maria Verleth ran away with Johannes van Beeck and was married at Greenwich, Connecticut by an unauthorized farmer, Goodman

Crab. Immediately the marriage was declared unlawful, and the couple ordered to live apart. Maria Verleth came of a race of ladies who were strong of mind and strong of fist as well. Her mother, Judith Verleth (Mrs. Nicholas Bayard), was held for a witch in Connecticut after her husband's death. Maria had to fight her father-in-law in various lawsuits. In 1658, she was again married to P. Schrick, and for her third husband took William Teller, in 1664.

Even after divorce, the unoffending party could not marry again without permission from the authorities. In 1655, for example, John Hicks, of Flushing, received permission to remarry.

Judging from the numerous cases in the records, we must conclude that the marriage state in New Amsterdam was by no means a uniformly happy one, even among those in authority. Thus, in 1659, the Schout, Nicasius de Sille, petitioned for divorce and separation of marriage from Catharina Croegers on account of " her unbecoming and careless life, both by her wasting of property without his knowledge, as by her public habitual drunkenness."

The court's sympathy did not always go out towards the plaintiff. When, in 1652, Jacob Claessen demanded of his wife, Aeltje Dirrick, why she remained away from and would not live with him, " To prevent all trouble it was ordered that plaintiff remain imprisoned until the ships sail for Fatherland."

When a separation was granted for good cause, punishment was frequently inflicted on the offending party, as was the case in 1658:

Whereas Geertje Jans, wife of Jan Hendrickzen, glazier, has, in consequence of her committed offences and faults been banished by the Court, from this City's jurisdiction; but having for a time absented herself therefrom, and coming in acknowledgement and sorrow for her perpetrated offences and through much intercession made by worthy Burghers and inhabitants to the Burgomasters of this City, therefore is it that the Heeren abovenamed, partly from especial consideration and moreover in censequence of the continual importunity and intercession, hereby pardon the above-named Geertje Jans and consent and allow her to live again with her husband within this City's jurisdiction, under her promise of amendment and a return from her previous faults and misdemeanors, and to behave herself as an honest and virtuous woman ought to do, so that no worse may happen to her.

Once being married, it was impossible for husband or wife to have the bonds of matrimony broken except on the ground of unfaithfulness. Even a separation was difficult to obtain except for persistent cruelty. An occasional wife-beating, and even an assault on the husband by his spouse, was common enough; and, if brought into court, the judges would turn the case over to the good offices of the Ministers of the Gospel with instructions to do all they could to reconcile the parties. Thus, in 1673, when Arent Lantsman's wife, Beletie Jacobson, asked for a divorce on the ground of cruelty, their Worships authorized some honorable and fitting person to reconcile, if possible, the parties to love and friendship, and report to the court. The ministers appointed could not reconcile the parties, and the court agreed with the husband's contention that it was a case of too much father and mother-in-law, and ordered the parents not to harbor their daughter beyond fourteen days, at the same time warning Arent to treat his wife kindly. Shortly afterwards Beletie's father, Lodowyk Pot, again complains that Arent has beaten her, and asks to be allowed to take his daughter under his protection. Arent was bound over to good behavior, and ordered to pay four guilders weekly to his wife for the maintenance of the children. Later, he pleaded to have his wife back, promising to give no discontent to the Worshipful Court. Two years later, however, by order of the Mayor, the following order was sent to Lantsman:

> Whereas complaint has been made of the unbecoming and improper treatment of your wife, yea, so that the neighbourhood suffers great disturbance by the noise and uproar, caused principally by you, all which is in direct opposition to the orders and warnings given from time to time by this W. Court, you are therefore hereby again strictly charged to comport yourself towards your wife in such wise that no further complaint come to us.

Arent, two years later, "aggravated his evil behaviour by blasphemy," and received a final warning on pain of banishment.

New Amsterdam, being essentially a trading-port, it was only natural that some of the scum of the sea should float ashore. There is plenty of evidence that bigamists were not uncommon here. Mr. Tienhoven, the Schout, himself was accused of bigamist practices. In 1664, one Anneke Adriaen prays for divorce from A. P. Tack, "who has married another woman in Holland." In November, 1658, Laurens Duyts, who had sold his wife, Ytie Jansen, to John Parcell, an Englishman, was sentenced to have a rope tied around his neck, then to be severely flogged, to have his right ear cut off, and to be banished for fifty years. Ytie was whipped and banished. Her successor in her husband's affections was Geesze Jansen, who was publicly stripped naked, conducted outside the city gates, and banished for fifty years. On December 12, on the petition of John Parcel and Ytie, "two sorrowful

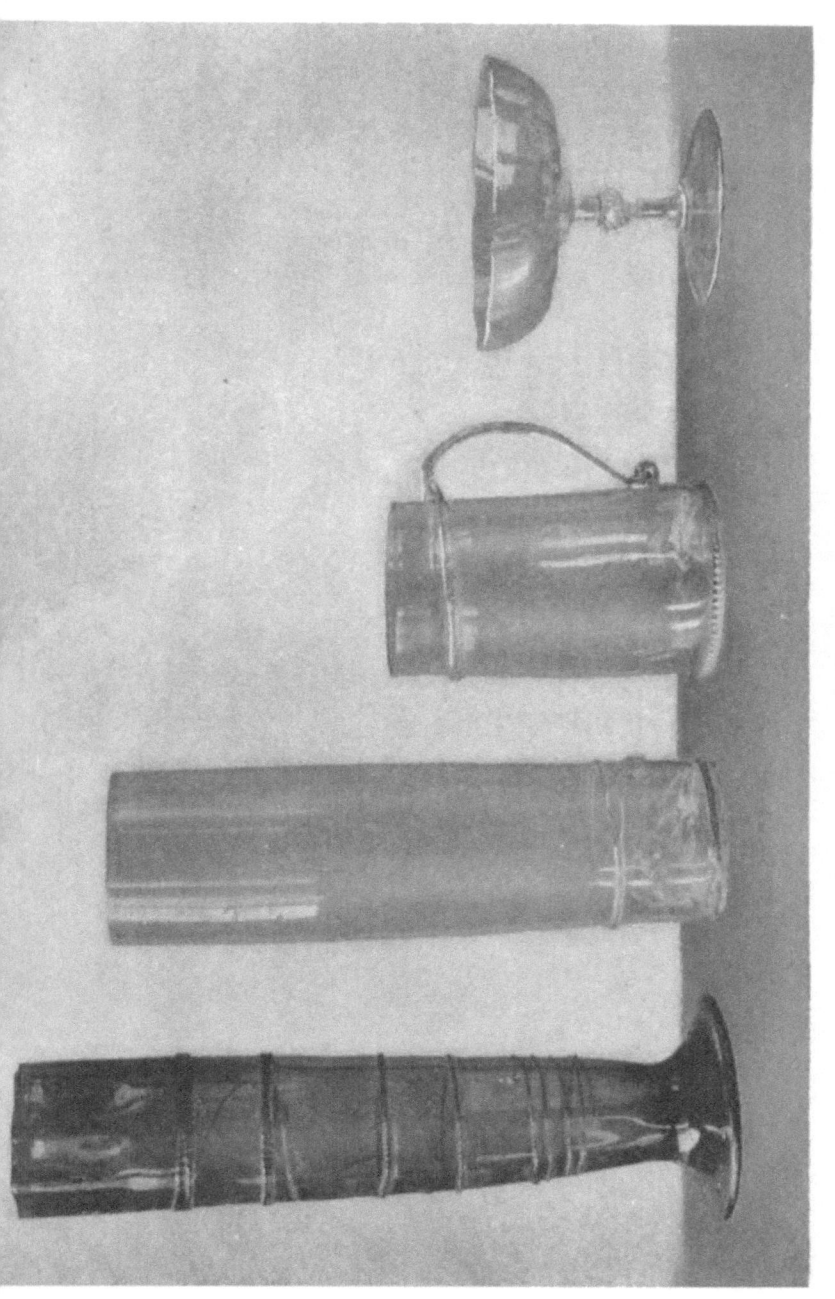

GLASS DRINKING VESSELS
RIJKS MUSEUM, AMSTERDAM

sinners," for pardon and leave to marry, it was ordered that they might remain three months to settle their affairs, but must separate from each other at once.

It was the custom among the wealthier classes, after consent had been given, to invite all relations and friends, to the betrothal. As soon as the contract was signed in presence of a notary, the young people received congratulations; and then the betrothal took place, that is, the rings were exchanged. Sometimes these rings were made to order and consisted of two hoops that fitted together. In addition to the rings, the betrothed gave each other the halves of a coin broken in two. Like the Indians, they confirmed their marriage sometimes by drinking the blood from a wound made in their arms. Sometimes the betrothed would sign the wedding contract with their blood, and sometimes it was entirely written in blood. Such contracts, "pact-pence," and rings were often taken to the church council when one of the betrothed had broken faith, on which the unfaithful one was summoned before that tribunal, and exhorted to repair the breach. Where no contracts were made or rings exchanged, the love letters were shown. The father-in-law of the bride gave her a *châtelaine* of silver, leather, or filigree, with various articles hanging from silver chains, among which were a pair of scissors, a small knife in leather sheath, finely mounted, a needle-case, a silver-bound pincushion, a scent-ball, and sometimes a small mirror. These *châtelaines*, sometimes made of gold and of exquisite workmanship, were a sign that the young lady was engaged or betrothed, and it was considered an honor to wear them. They often appear in the New Amsterdam wills and inventories; for example, in 1679, Mary Jansen left to Margaret Van der Veen "a silver chain with keys," and to Susannah Leisler, "a silver chain with a case and cushion." "A silver girdle with hanging keys," and "a silver girdle with three chains with hooks" are found among Asser Levy's belongings in 1682; and in 1694, Annetie van Brommell had "a set of silver chains about the middle." William Richardson (1692) leaves to Mary Cock "a pair of silver hilted knives and a pair of scissors with a silver chain to them."

It was customary for a lover to present his sweetheart with a muffler of the finest cambric, embroidered in red silk with the name and date, and with acorns in the corners; a pledge of love, and the "wedding pence, or God's pence, sometimes made up of one hundred new shillings ($12 of our money), with a rhyme, "if you will, there is the muffler and the pence; if you won't, you can return it." Instead of a muffler a silver wedding casket, filled with "pot pieces," was sometimes presented. The betrothal was always celebrated by a dinner to which the immediate families and intimate friends were invited. The wedding-day was settled and the bridesmaids ("play-mates") selected, also two *speeljonkers* (play-youths) and two *spellmeisjes* (play-girls) appointed. Their duty was to decorate the house, to regulate the various entertainments, and to serve the bride and bridegroom. They had a bride's servant under them, who remained near the bride during these "brides-days" and on the wedding-day. She could always depend on a good present from the bride. The duties of the bridesmaids were numerous. Some of them introduced the guests, while others arranged the seating of the guests at the table and showed them their places. It was their duty to be merry and entertaining, and make everybody else gay and light-hearted. The playmates also decorated the bridegroom's pipe with garlands and ribbons. This was so highly prized that it was kept in the china or curio cabinet after the wedding, and very often reappeared at the silver-wedding.

Another duty was to arrange the bride's basket, filling it with green garlands and flowers with the initials, or monogram, or names of the happy couple picked out in pretty blossoms. In another basket, not less richly decorated, were laid the lace collar and cuffs, the bride's presents to the bridegroom. Both baskets were exhibited beside the bride's throne until the wedding-day. From the flower basket the bride's attendants, both men and maidens, scattered flowers and palms upon the path of the couple on their walk to the registry and the church.

On their return from the Court House, the couple, preceded by the playmates, all dressed in their best, the men wearing the colors of the bride and the girls the colors of the groom, were received in state at the house of the bridegroom, and the bride was introduced to his family. In a shower of flowers, maiden-palm, and garlands, the young couple was led into the "state" room, where, after the presentation of the guests by the playmates, they were presented with a silver bowl and spoon containing the "Bride's Tears" and the "Show" pipe. The "Bride's Tears" was the well-known Hippocras, and also called "spiced" or "sugared" wine. Later, Hippocras was replaced by other wines, or by red wine and sugar, or brandy and sugar and raisins; sometimes, indeed, gin and syrup was decanted, called *klongel-eul*, or girls' beer. Besides the "Bride's Tears," sugared peas or sugared almonds called "bride's sugar" were served, which, like the Hippocras, was made by the apothecary. With the poorer classes, *bemste, beguine, Deventer* cake and other sweetmeats were served, and while the silver platter passed amongst the playmates, the finely decorated green-painted "Sleigh coach," filled with small bottles of wine in straw covers, and boxes filled with candy tied with silver and gold ribbons, passed through the streets drawn by a gayly decked horse, and the Hippocras and sweets were sent to the houses of the friends and acquaintances. In the evening the invited guests met at a more or less elaborate meal called the "commissary's" meal; but this was more solemn than gay. It often ended without music or dance, and sometimes one of the guests would read aloud from *De Trouwring* (*The Wedding-ring*) of Jacob Cats.

It was not considered good form to go to church when the banns were published.

The days preceding the wedding were spent in festivity and general merrymaking. The bride and bridegroom were both busy making arrangements for the banquet and in the preparation of their costumes, especially with people of moderate means, who, as a rule, superintended everything themselves. The playmates in this case came only "to make the green." The bride and bridegroom also wrote the announcements of the wedding themselves on perfumed gilt-edged paper, and these were sent out after the reading of the first banns. De Vry gives a lively picture of the bustle and preparations:

The bride's dress has to be made, and the materials, laces, linings, trimmings, gimps and cords, to be purchased. Who knows the end of all this business. One material is too light another too dark, the third too dull, without gloss, and the worst is that while they are deliberating, examining and ordering, you are constantly interrupted by trade solicitors who are eternally knocking at the door, this one to ask to supply the banquet; a second, the decorations; a third, to do the cooking; the next to make the pastry, who all want to ask the bride for her custom, and do not give her any time to attend to her other work. "Oh," she says, "the time is so terribly short. And the seamstresses, the lace-mounter, and the ironer have to be ordered, for Jeanie has promised to send the linen brought home, and Antoinette, the laces, and neither has come. Now run, boys and girls, remember that a brave bride's gift will pay you for your work."

Meanwhile the bridegroom is running all over town to engage humorists to entertain the wedding guests. He is also ordering Rhine, French and Spanish wines, to treat those who come to congratulate bride and bridegroom.

The homes of both bride and groom were beautifully decorated during the period between the betrothal and the wedding ceremonies, and nearly every day a dinner was given in honor of the couple by relatives or friends. These "bann dinners" were returned by the bride and groom's "ante-nuptial dinner." The bride also received in state during these days. (See illustration facing page 224.) The walls were draped with tapestry or other hangings, and hung with garlands. Among the flowers, palms, and wreaths, two seats were placed underneath a large crown of flowers, trimmed with colored ribbons and gold and silver braid. In the centre of the crown were two silver hands clasped, and two silver hearts pierced by an arrow. Sometimes the initials of the couple were also formed of flowers. Under this dais, on a kind of throne, bride and groom, surrounded by the playmates, awaited the arrival of the relations and friends who came with congratulations and wedding-gifts. In front of the throne in a circle were placed rows of chairs, and in the centre was a table covered with rich and well-filled dishes of silver and crystal, beakers and flagons, drinking horns and cups, decorated with leaves and ribbons, festoons and garlands. The playmates sometimes handed round small cakes with comfits.

The bride had not worn her crown as yet, but her hair was finely braided and scented. On her neck sparkled a diamond brooch, and diamond or pearl earrings in her ears. On her costly stomacher glittered a "pendant," and around her neck hung necklaces of gold or pearls. The bride was not dressed in her "wedding," but in her "bride's," dress. The very wealthy had more than one. Some in the bride's days changed their dress two or three times a day. Sometimes these bride's dresses were not less costly than that worn on the wedding-day. On her finger the bride wore the "hoop," and on her wrists gold bracelets set with pearls, or silver bracelets with jewels. The groom was no less richly dressed.

Presents were universally given. Nobody congratulated the couple without an offering; and those who could not present a piece of furniture, jewelry, china, or handsome gift, left a kitchen utensil or small piece of money. The lovers exchanged jewels or gold, or, if they could afford nothing better, a small article of trifling value. However poor the bride and groom might be, crowns and green were never lacking, even if the neighbors had to defray the cost.

At Fort Orange, in 1658, Abraham Vosborch's wife sued Annetie Lievens, wife of Goosen Gerritsen, for payment of some "coronets," which she loaned defendant. Annetie pleaded that she and Maria Wesselsen being bridesmaids had borrowed the articles in common. They were ordered to pay the bill between them. Annetie Lievens also figured in court again soon after her wedding, for, on July 19, 1657, her husband, Goosen, sued Jurriaen Jansen for having circulated a report that he was betrothed to Annetie

Lievens. Jansen acknowledged having circulated the false report, but pleaded that he had been instigated to it by Cornelis Teunissen. On confessing the falsehood of his statement, and asking pardon of bridegroom, God, and the court, Jurriaen was pardoned.

Seated before her large mirror and toilet-table, on which stood one of those small cabinets of costly wood, inlaid with ivory, with numerous small drawers for powder, perfume, patches, hairpins, tweezers, small scissors, brushes, and everything belonging to the toilette of a lady of the period, sat the bride. On the table were also the standing mirror and the gilded leather comb and brush case. The costly wedding-basket had been unpacked, and the rich garments were lying about. Near the bride stood the bridesmaids, superintending the dressing of her hair. Notwithstanding the sermons against curling hair and powdered and false wigs, lion's manes, loose braids and ribbons, hanging locks, corals and pearls, much attention was paid to the coiffure. The head-dressing finished, the magnificent dress, of the French style, was put on. The bride's dress was as costly as her parents could afford. In Holland, the richest brides wore bodices and skirts of heavy Lyons silk, white or violet velvet, or cloth of silver or of gold, sometimes costing from $40 to $80 a yard, trimmed with gold or silver fringe and glittering with pearl or diamond buttons. Her stomacher was covered with magnificent lace, and her cuffs and ruff were also of lace. The latter sometimes contained as much as sixty or eighty yards of deftly plaited cambric edged with lace. Instead of a ruff the bride sometimes wore a turned down French collar cut in points and which fell halfway down her back. A pearl necklace with jeweled clasp was placed over this. Her shoes were of velvet or satin; her stockings blue, yellow, or cardinal; her gloves perfumed; and her fan of mother-of-pearl handle was painted with exotic flowers and birds. When her hair was dressed and perfumed, the veil was arranged and fastened with jeweled or golden pins.

A bride of less wealth and fashion wore a Lyons silk; but although she preferred white as a rule, black was sometimes chosen, and this was put away after the wedding, and used for mourning when occasion demanded. Brides of humbler station in life dispensed with the fan and perfumed gloves, but never with the veil, unless they were of the very poorest. With the ordinary citizens this was of cambric, embroidered with acorns in the corners, and plaited around the face. The rich bride always wore a lace veil fixed to the headdress above the forehead, and descending in wide folds to her feet. Sometimes she was hidden in a cloud of lace. The veil was generally worn only when the wedding was "consecrated"; but sometimes the bride wore it all day; this was called, "standing in the white." "They rig themselves up nicely," writes J. Buckman, an Englishman; "they load their fingers with such heavy gold and silver rings that they crack. They rather go hungry, so that they be able to cover themselves with silver ornaments on both sides of their bodies, until they wabble like a fatted goose. The clothes they wear, are that wide, that their fat stomachs can hardly be noticed. And their particular pride is in their hands that they are whiter than they ought to be."

The women of New Netherland were in no wise behind their sisters in Fatherland of the same station in life in their love of jewelry and rich clothes; and the wills and inventories of the period show that the mothers were able to start their daughters in life some-

From an old print

A DUTCH BRIDE IN STATE
SEVENTEENTH CENTURY

times with considerable luxury in this respect. Gold jewelry, enamels, pearls, emeralds, and diamonds were by no means rare in New Amsterdam. The patroons, too, were opulent and elegant in their tastes. William Van Rensselaer was a pearl merchant, and it was to him that the Earl of Bellomont applied when he wanted to satisfy his youthful bride's craving for a pearl necklace. If any independent evidence were necessary to prove the existence here of the display of wealth and taste in the latest style of the day, we have only to turn to Madam Knight, who tells us:

The English go very fashionable in their dress. But the Dutch, especially the middling sort, differ from our women, in their habitt go loose, were French muches wch are like a Capp and a head band in one, leaving their ears bare, which are set out with Jewells of a large size and many in number. And their fingers hoop't with Rings, some with large stones in them of many Coullers as were their pendants in their ears, which you should see very old women wear as well as young.

While the bride was being dressed at her home, the groom's best man was busy helping him dress at the home of one of his bosom friends. The groom's clothes were also costly and in keeping with his social position. Men of modest means wore waistcoat and trousers of cloth, wool, or serge, and the favorite costume was a heavy durable " Leyden cloth." Sometimes the wedding costume was handed down from generation to generation, and worn by children and grandchildren, the cut being altered to suit the fashion. A handsome black suit is found in the wardrobe of nearly every Dutch gentleman in New Amsterdam. What the average bridegroom received from his parents, we learn from a will dated 1698, in which

Catharine Blanck, widow of Jurian Blanck, left to her son, Symon Barentsen, 30 shillings in full for all pretence he may have to my estate, real and personal; he having been sufficiently provided for during the life of my husband Jurian Blanck; having received one half of a sloop, a wedding dinner, two wedding suits, a cloak, a fine red broadcloth waistcoat with silver thread buttons, one half dozen fine holland shirts, one half-dozen striped Calico neck cloths, an ozenbrig feather bed, two new blankets and had his diett for two years after he was married.

The toilets of both bride and groom being completed, the bride, preceded by her playmates, enters the reception-room, where nothing has been changed since the day of the formal betrothal. She takes her place on the throne, and is soon joined by the bridegroom. Now the doors are opened to admit the guests, who enter to see the bouquet given to the bride and the crown put on her head. The bouquet was of real or artificial flowers ornamented with a Cupid; the cipher of the betrothed; or two pierced hearts or clasped hands made of silver or gold. It was pinned by the groom on the bride's bosom. The little crowns in the bouquet differed according to the rank of the groom. Citizens made crowns of palm, majoram, and flowers, while more important people wrapped a ribbon with jewels and pearls around it or placed a velvet band studded with diamonds around the stem. After this ceremony the guests attacked the pyramids of food on the table and drank "the Bride's Tears" with many blessings. A couple of boys then took up the bride's costly train, and threw the veil over her face; and now upon a path strewn with roses and through a decorated arch the couple went to the church. There everything had been prepared beforehand; a handsome carpet was laid in the nave, where two armchairs wreathed in green and two footstools were placed for the bride and groom. Behind these were placed the chairs for the family and playmates. Sometimes the choir arch was also wreathed in green, or an arch of honor was built. Marrying with closed doors was not known then. The ceremony was performed in public, and began by the reading of parts of the epistles of Saint Paul, with psalm-singing between the lessons. While this was going on, the bridal party entered the church, the bride and bridegroom being solemnly escorted by their parents. Then the pastor entered the pulpit, read the formulas of marriage, took the oath, and ordered the singing of a psalm, and also a collection to be taken up for the poor, after which the company, preceded by the bride and groom, left the church, their pathway being strewn with palms and flowers, and proceeded to the bride's home.

The wedding-procession here was not always devoid of excitement. On one occasion at least, a bride was insulted as she passed on her way leaning on the arm of her newly made husband, who promptly sued the offender. We learn, in June, 1658, that Philip Schoof brought a case against Anneke Sibouts, who insulted his bride, Jannetje Teunis Kray, as they were coming out of church from the wedding. She said the bride did not deserve to have palms strewed before her. Very rarely, indeed, was a wedding performed at the City Hall or Court House. On the return of the wedding-party to the bride's home, a collation was served in the reception-room. This consisted of sugared cake, marchpane, sugared almonds, chaptersticks, sugared beans, Hippocras, and many kinds of sweet cordials. Sometimes, immediately after the ceremony, the guests would all view the sleeping-room of the young couple. From there they went to the wedding-dinner. Unless this was given in the reception-room, an adjoining room was also decorated with green, with garlands of maiden-palm and flowers. The fine porcelains on the mantel were filled with flowers, and everything, even the buffet, was wreathed in green and decorated with ribbons. The buffet was resplendent with fine porcelain, family silver, and sometimes a gold table service, beakers, glasses, etc., which were beautifully engraved and many of which had belonged to grandparents and great-grandparents. Generally the crown descended from the ceiling over the heads of the young couple, in the centre of which emblems of love were hung. Around the table were placed chairs, with embroidered cushions for the guests, the number of which was decided by permit, and in Amsterdam was not allowed to exceed fifty; but this was not always respected, for a rich entertainer would rather pay the heavy fines than that anybody should be absent — heedless of pulpit denunciations. The tables were horseshoe shaped. At the head sat the bride and groom, and the other guests according to their relationship, rank, and age. This placing of guests was of supreme importance and those who felt themselves not sufficiently honored often left the table; thus serious family quarrels often had their origin from the breach of etiquette. The playmates served the happy couple. According to some rules, the dinner had to consist of two courses: a "fore" and "dinner" course. The first consisted of fifty or more different dishes served on large round or oval dishes of pewter, porcelain, and earthenware for meats, and deep large plates for soup; and these dishes and plates stood between garlands, flowers, and palms, which so completely covered the table that the costly damask table-cloth could hardly be seen. Even the plates were surrounded by green, and flowers and tulips filled the many flower-vases on the table. The food was piled in pyramids on the dishes, — the beef and mutton in large pieces; the wild boar and venison in quarters; the partridges, capons, and ducks in numbers from twelve to twenty-four. At rich weddings whole sheep, young goats, sucking lambs, and pigs were served, roasted on the spit, and stuffed, while poultry and venison, hares and rabbits were served by the dozen on one platter. The centre-piece or principal dish was always a beautifully dressed peacock with spread plumage or a turkey. Between the plates and platters were pyramids of fruit. According to an ordinance in 1655, it was forbidden to put fine candy on the table under a fine of $40, but no notice was taken of this. At many wedding-dinners there were piles of patties of hares, chicken, salmon, cheese, and fruit; flat apple, brown, and wine tarts. The centre of this course was marchpane. The smaller candies were made in mythological figures, hunts, or allegorical subjects, sometimes emblematic of the trade or position of the groom, or the arms of the couple. The larger pieces of sugar work represented scenes of Leda, Danæ, Noah's Ark, etc. At some weddings all kinds of comfits were seen, for the most part French, such as candied peel of oranges, ginger, comfits of sugar, Spanish comfits of cherries, sweet and delicate melons, pears, pomegranates, etc. The wines were Ay-Frontenac, Chablis, Portuguese, Italian, and Spanish, and Malmsey that cost two hundred ducats a barrel. Delft, Breda, Dordt, and Limburg beer were also drunk. Both wine and beer were poured out of cans with lids or spouts, some of great antiquity and strange inscriptions, which stood on the buffet or side tables, and from which the liquid was poured into the various drinking-vessels on the table and presented to the company. After the grace was said by a clergyman or, in his absence, by the father of the groom, the table-laws were read by the table-master. They were mostly in rhyme, and ended to the effect that anybody transgressing them would have to empty a large glass (pipe or whistle) as a fine.

The Dutch were generally considered as wasteful and lavish at *fêtes* and holidays as they were economical and staid in daily life. At the beginning of the feast everything was conducted with ceremony, but hardly were the official healths propounded when the drinking-vessels were brought on the table, and the merriment knew no bounds; people began with the smaller and ended with the larger bumpers (*fluiten*). Then were drunk the "clover-leaf" (see page 272), or rather the "clover leaf with the tail," the "friendship's beaker," and "the Arminian drink," the "drink on the country's prosperity," the "triple-drink," the "little mill," the "ship's sails," the "great and small fisheries," "Hans in the cellar," "the abbot and his monks," "Alva was tolled out" (a reminiscence of the Spanish War), or "St. Gertrude's health," all with the accompaniment of the songs belonging to the various drinks. At important weddings it was the custom to present the guest with silver or golden wedding medals, struck for the occasion, all on the subject of love and increase of family. These medals later were replaced by silver shields, on which the names of the couple were engraved, with the usual emblems.

The wedding generally wound up with a dance for which a band of music was hired by the families. The farmers were satisfied with a fiddler and a bag-piper (*doedel-zak*).

There the bride was danced to bed, that is, she was

brought to the bedroom where the mother and bridesmaids were awaiting her.

Before going away the green was torn off the walls and mirrors and a dance round the bride's crown was held. This crown, under which the bride had been seated was placed on a chair or on the floor, and the guests danced around it, after which it was declared forfeited, torn to pieces, and all who could get any flower or ribbon from it would pin it to his or her dress as a trophy of the wedding, and wear it home. Sometimes the bride was blindfolded, and the little crown that she wore was taken from her head before she retired. The lucky one who had grabbed the crown was supposed to be the first to get married. The bride did not only part with her little crown, but she also gave away her garters. These were sometimes very costly, and were given away by her in her bedroom; for it was the custom for her escort to remain until she had loosened her garters or had one of her friends loosen them for her. The young man who had the good fortune to get them fastened them as a trophy to his waistcoat.

The groom's nightdress was generally kept hidden until he had promised to give a pleasure-party, which was held shortly after the wedding. Sometimes, to escape the annoyance of the friends and guests, the bedroom was prepared in the house of a relative or friend. If the guests discovered this, they would march thither in state, carrying a torch of burning candles. Then followed the couples with clanging shovels and tongs. When near the house the torch was laid on the ground. and a dance was held around it until the couple appeared.

The morning after the wedding, the young wife received from her husband the "morning gift," generally a jeweled ring, a costly fur, or an ornament for the home. The parents on both sides also gave them "morning gifts." The remnants of the wedding-feast were given to the playmates unless they did not want them; in that case they were given to the poor or to the orphan-house. The "after-fun" (*Napret*), consisting of excursions and parties, was kept up for three weeks after the wedding.

Poorer people were often married in numbers on the appointed days, and went on foot, sometimes preceded by the strewers, who continually strewed flowers and green from a basket. So accompanied by a crowd of people they would walk to the church and back again.

With even a greater abundance of fish, flesh, and fowl in New Amsterdam, the colonists lavishly entertained on such occasions as weddings and ceremonial dinners. Oysters, crabs, lobsters, and game of all kinds were plentiful, fruit was abundant, and bakers and pastry-cooks numerous and efficient. In 1654, Jacob Stoffelsen went to court with Ide Van Vorst because she laid claim to "half a negro whom he received from Captain Geurt Tysen and his company in return for a feast given to him at which two sheep were eaten, and Ide van Vorst had also two sheep at her wedding." Ide insisted that the cost of the sheep was to be shared by both sides.

The same ostentation and extravagant expenditure, often far beyond the means of the hosts, prevailed here as in the Fatherland. The bride received from her parents a generous trousseau, and it was customary for the bridegroom's parents also to dress him handsomely; for instance, Mrs Anna Cuyler (1702) leaves to her daughter Mary £200 and to Eve £120, " it being my custom to give so much to each of my daughters

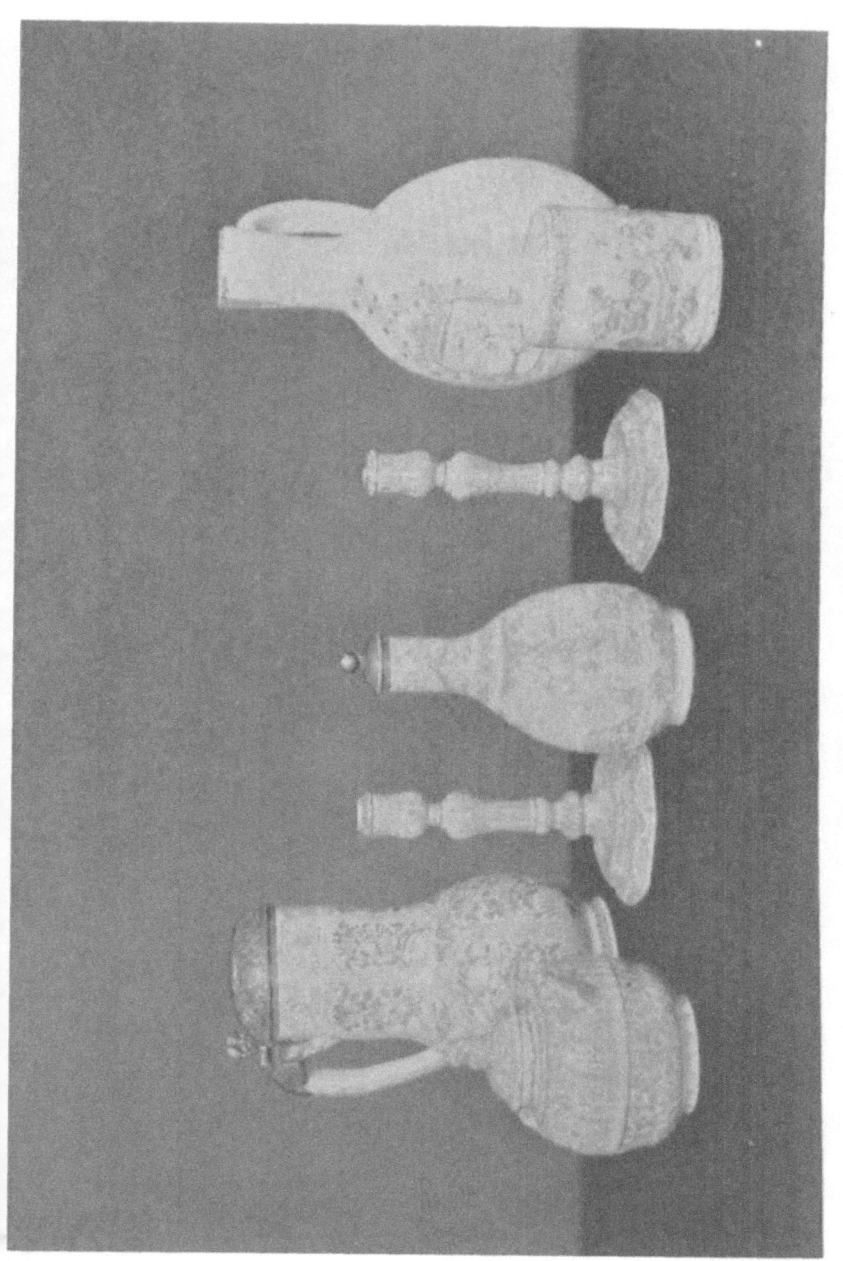

PORCELAIN AND EARTHENWARE
RIJKS MUSEUM, AMSTERDAM

at their marriage for their wedding, which they have had." Also, in 1684, Jacob Delany leaves to his daughter, Cornelia, " 200 guilders Holland money for her outsetting, before any division."

On the wedding-day, open house was kept, and in the small city of New Amsterdam practically everybody was welcomed. The amount of liquor consumed at the wedding of an ordinary burgher's daughter was considerable. This we gather from more than one entry in the records, which show that the parents were not over-particular in paying the excise when making provision for the entertainment. Thus, on Jan. 2, 1660, Peter Pia was sued for excise on beer laid in for his daughter's wedding; and on Jan. 4, 1661, Marten de Werft laid in three barrels of beer for his wedding and paid excise on only five half-barrels.

It will be remembered that it was at the wedding-breakfast of Sara Roeloffse, daughter of Anneke Jans to Hans Kiersted, the surgeon, that Director-General Kieft, taking advantage of the general merriment after the first four or five drinks, induced the guests to subscribe liberally towards the funds for building the new church in the Fort.

It was by no means unusual for the merry-making to end in a drunken orgy, as was frequently the case at funerals, christenings, and the fairs and festivals. For example, on July 5, 1655, Borger Jorisen, being lately at the wedding of Nicolaes de Meyer, insulted Burgomaster Allart Anthony in presence of several friends. Jorisen acknowledged the fault, but pleaded that the words were spoken in drunkenness.

Sometimes practical jokes were played, and if for any reason the bride and groom were unpopular they were insulted. For instance, on Feb. 6, 1663, Johannes La Montagne, sheriff of New Haerlem, complains of divers persons for riot, in planting a May-pole decorated with rags before the door of a newly married couple and assembling around the house, horning, etc. The couple were Pieter Jansen Slot, son of the ex-schepen, and Marritie van Winckel of Ahasimus. The banns were published on February 2, and the villagers indulged in horse-play to the great annoyance of the young couple. Also, on Apr. 23, 1678, we learn that William Loveridge writes to Captain Brockholls, complaining of a fine imposed on him for setting up a tree in Albany before Mr. Thompson's door when he was married, the same being the manner and custom of the place. Loveridge was sent to jail for the offense, but was released on giving bonds for good behavior.

CHAPTER XI

PHYSICIANS AND SURGEONS — BIRTHS AND DEATHS

WHILE the Dutch clergy in general belonged to the poorer classes, the doctors, on the contrary, belonged to the higher burgher class and sometimes even to the nobility. They were educated first in the Greek and Latin schools of their native towns, and then proceeded to one of the universities. Later they went abroad to become acquainted with the celebrities of their profession in the principal cities of Europe and to complete their education under their tuition and to attain the dignity of Doctor of Medicine. Some settled abroad, others were called to a professorship or were appointed personal physicians to royalties or other dignitaries, and returned laden with honors and fame to their Fatherland, where they were appointed to positions of honor. Sometimes they even became burgomasters. Like the clergy, many doctors were learned in a variety of sciences. There were astronomers, lawyers, and able writers among them. The doctors were ranked among the notables of the cities, and were generally held in high esteem. On great occasions they were honored with presents from the cities, and the municipal doctors were presented with "tabbard cloth" (cloth to make a cloak) every year. At the civic dinner they yielded precedence to the clergy; but the dinners they themselves gave were sometimes so splendid that the Burgomasters became jealous and they were consequently fined by the "Schouts."

The salaries of the city doctors varied from four hundred to twelve hundred florins; and besides this they charged the burghers a fee of twelve cents and poor patients eight cents (four stivers). Those who were unable to pay were treated free of charge. The preachers, city lawyers, and apothecaries were also treated at the city's expense. Like the apothecaries, the doctors had the name of the place from where they had their diploma mentioned on their name-plate on the door. Doctors of the Seventeenth Century followed their own theories and disputed as ardently among themselves as did the clergy. Like the preacher, the doctor always had his "study." This was generally arranged with an eye to effect. Contemporary prints and paintings usually show him in a sort of cavernous room, seated at a table surrounded by quartos and folios. He wears a fur-lined coat, has a skullcap on his head, and is writing a prescription, although this was generally done at the counter in the apothecary's shop. Before him stand a pewter inkstand, an hour-glass and a skull, and at his feet sit two cats. In the back are a bookcase and a table with all kinds of surgical instruments. Patients are crowding in at the door.

The physician of the period is a well-known figure in the pictures of the Little Dutch Masters, particularly Jan Steen, who represents him in all the gravity and sometimes pretentious pose he so often assumed. He always appears in a black costume with pointed hat like that worn by Sganarelle in Molière's *Médecin malgré lui.*

There were many quack doctors in this age, who had

various elixirs and could even remove "stones from the head," and who professed to be able to make gold and to lengthen life. Other "wonder doctors" could "read off" fevers and drive out devils. Many also sold blessed images, pennies, and scapularies.

In the Seventeenth Century the barber was not yet separated from the surgeon. Phlebotomy was still regarded as a cure for fever and many other diseases, and the barber did the necessary cupping and bleeding. His calling was far more dignified than at present, both in Holland and England. In the latter country the barbers and surgeons did not part company to form separate corporations till 1742. In 1627, we find that one of the officers of a London charitable foundation was "One chirurgeon barber who shall cut and pole the hair of all the scholars of the hospital; and also look to the cure of all those within the hospital who anyway shall stand in need of his art." Similarly, in New Netherlánd, in 1664, Sybrandt Cornelissen from Flensburgh was appointed assistant surgeon, to be employed in shaving, bleeding, and administering medicines to the soldiers. Dr. Jacob De Lange was one of these barber surgeons, who had attained to wealth at the end of the century. His inventory contains an "iron stick to put out to hang the barber's bason."

As in so many other fields, the practice of medicine was almost identical in England and Holland; charlatanism was rampant, and the barber was the surgeon. The first doctors sent to New Netherland were those who ministered to the ills of the crews and passengers in the West India Company's ships, and those who were hired to stay here and heal the sick among the Company's servants. The resident doctors appointed by the Company charged the independent settlers for their services. Sometimes they charged a lump sum for an accident case or an illness, but it was more usual to contract with a family or an individual for an annual payment. The duties of the ship's surgeon are plainly set forth in the regulations of 1656:

> The barbers, whether on board a ship or ships or on land, shall be bound to give their services cheerfully, and to use all diligence to restore the patients to health, without receiving therefor any compensation except their monthly pay, and, in case any of them receive any money or promise of payment, they shall be obliged to restore what they received, and the promise shall be null and void.

The Company moreover gave an express promise that

> the wounded shall be properly taken care of by means of good Surgeons; and if any persons in the employment of the City, and in the execution of their command, office, or service, happen to be maimed, lamed, or otherwise be deprived of their health, they shall be remunerated as follows, To wit:
>
> | | |
> |---|---|
> | For the loss of the right arm | fl. 333 |
> | " " " " left arm | 266 |
> | " " " " a leg | 240 |
> | " " " " both legs | 533 |
> | " " " " one eye | 240 |
> | " " " " both eyes | 1066 |
> | " " " " the left hand | 240 |
> | " " " " the right hand | 266 |
> | " " " " both hands | 933 |
>
> For the loss of all other members and lameness, whereof any person being fully cured and healed, yet may not be restored to his former health, or may be maimed or thereby disabled from the use which he previously had of his limbs, he shall therefor be proportionally indemnified at the discretion of the Commissioners or Directors, according to previous inspection of the Doctors, Surgeons, or other competent judges. *Provided*, always, that he show and

PHYSICIANS AND SURGEONS

produce a certificate from his superior officer, who, at the time of his being wounded and maimed had the command, and of the entire Ship's Council, that he had received the wound in the execution of his office and employment in the service of the City.

In 1652, the surgeons petitioned that nobody but they shall be allowed to shave others. To this the director and Council replied that shaving was properly not in the province of the surgeons, but only an appendix to their calling; that nobody could be prevented from pleasing himself in that matter, or serving anybody else for friendship's sake or out of courtesy, without receiving payment for it or keeping a shop to do it in, which was expressly forbidden. The authorities added:

Whereas we are informed that last summer two or three grave mistakes have been made by the inexperience of some ships' barbers, therefore the Director and Council order herewith that such ships' barbers shall not dress any wounds or prescribe for any one on land, without the knowledge and special request of the above petitioners or at least Doctor La Montagne.

The names of the petitioning surgeons were

Jan Croon,
Van der Bogaert,
Aldart Swartout,

Hans Kierstede,
Jacob Hendricksen,
Varre Vanger,
Jacob Hughes.

The following is a list of doctors appointed by the West India Company to practice in New Netherland:

1630. Herman Mynderts van den Bogaert.
1637. Johannes La Montagne: Member of the Supreme Council and Vice Director of Fort Orange.
1638. Hans Kierstede (died in 1671).
   Peter van der Linde.

Gerrit Schut.
Jan Pietersen van Essendelft (died in 1640).
1644. Paulus van der Beeck from Bremen.
(He had served in Curaçao and on board the Company's ships: settled in Breuckelen.)
1647. William Hays of Barry's Court, Ireland (served since 1641 as chief surgeon in Curaçao).
Peter Vreucht.
1649. Jacob Hendricksen Varrevanger (entered the Company's service in 1646, discharged June, 1662).
Isaac Jansen (ship).
Jacob Mollenaer (ship).
Jan Pauw (ship).
1652. Jan Herwy (Hervey).
William Noble (ship).
Gysbert van Imbroch.
Jacobus Hugues.
Johannes Megapolensis, jr (returned to Holland about 1656).
M. Cornelis Clock.
Nov. 18, 1658. Peter Jansen van den Bergh.
Jacob L'Oragne.
1659. Alexander Carolus Curtius.
1660. Harmen Wessels.
1662. Jan du Parck (military).
Samuel Megapolensis.
Cornelis van Dyck (died 1687).
1673. Henry Taylor.

Fort Orange

1642. Abraham Staets.
1655. Jacob d'Hinse.

Esopus

1660. Gysbert van Imbroch.
1664. Sybrandt Cornelissen van Flensburgh.
1662. James Clark.
Folcks Mespath.
1663. William Leverich.

DUTCH CLOCK IN THE VAN CORTLANDT
MANOR HOUSE

PHYSICIANS AND SURGEONS

Dr. Hans Kierstede arrived with Governor Kieft in 1638, and married, in 1642, Sara Roelofs, the daughter of Roelof Jansen and Anneke Jans.

When Mr. Kierstede sued the estate of Solomon La Chair for services, an important precedent was established, for the court held: " Mr. Hans is to be preferred before the other creditors as the same is for surgeon's service." Again, on Sept. 29, 1670, the court ordered the curators of the estate of Jan Steelman " to pay 388 gl. 4 st. in zeewan for burial and to Mr. Hans Kierstede for medicines 27 gl. in zeewan as preferred funeral expenses before all others from the first effects."

The surgeons did not limit their activities to practising medicine, but engaged in trade and various kinds of business like the other burghers. Thus, in 1656, we find a report on the repairs done to the Company's house by Surgeon Varrevanger. In June, 1654, we read:

> Jacob Hendricksen Varrevanger showed by his petition that the term of his engagement had expired and that for some years he had imported at his own expense from Holland all his medicines. He requested that some compensation should be given to him for the use of his medicaments.

The Commissary ordered "to credit to the said Mr. Jacob 12 fl. per month from 1 July, 1652 in his account for use of his medicines and to increase his salary."

The clergy were sometimes curers of bodies as well as of souls. A supply of drugs was sent from Holland in the spring of 1663 for " an English clergyman versed in the art of Physick and willing to serve in the capacity of Physician." It is supposed that this was the Rev. William Leverich, who sailed in October, 1660, in *The Spotted Cow* from Amsterdam, and who returned in 1662. In 1661, the Rector, Alexander Carolus Curtius, appeared in court setting forth that the Farmer had spoken to him about payment of the excise; "and whereas Professors, Preachers and Rectors are exempt from excise in Holland, he maintains he also is exempt, the rather as the Director General has granted him free excise." The court, however, decided against him.

The expenses of a serious illness are shown in the following itemized bill:

Robert Hammon Esq. Dr. 1689			
To his chamber 4 months	1	5	0
To firewood in time of his sickness night and day	1	4	0
To candles		9	0
To cash lent and paid for him		5	3
To diet when he retired himself from town		15	0
To his attendance and extraordinary trouble during his sickness	2	10	0
To washing his bedding and linen several times a week during his sickness	1	10	0
To strong drink and rum at several times to the watchers		7	6
To John Jewett for watching several times		6	0
To a woman to clean the house		3	0
To paid for him at old Mr. Davenport		10	6
Katharin Coleman	£9	5	3

The surgeons frequently took payment in shop goods. Thus, on Oct. 31, 1656, Aldart Swartwout demands delivery of a kettle promised for curing Jacob Scheltinger's leg. The latter acknowledges the promise but not the cure. Both parties acknowledge to have agreed to a perfect cure or no pay, so the matter is referred to Mr. Hans Kierstede and Mr. Jacob Varrevanger, "both old and experienced surgeons," to investigate and report. On Feb. 11, 1662, the curators of the bankrupt estate of Dirck Houthuyzen sued Mr. Jacob Huges for 6 gl. 11 st. The doctor said he attended Dirck one year; and the court set the one off against the other. In 1674, Jan de Forest sued Jannettie Cregier for medical attendance after an accident: he had overcharged and had to pay back twelve pounds of butter. Gerrit Huygen married Herman Wesselsen's widow. In August, 1673, he sued Manuel Sanders, a negro, for 26½ schepels of wheat, being the yearly salary of his deceased predecessor.

The Court Records supply ample evidence that the doctors of the day supplied their professional services to private families or individuals by the year, and often had trouble to collect their annual stipend. In October, 1661, for example, Mr. Jacob Huges sued five patients for unpaid fees. First came Jan Janzen van de Lange Straat, who was ordered to pay the doctor "six guilders for labour." Then Ludowyck Post was ordered to deposit "twenty guilders for services" with the Secretary of this City. Pelgrum Clock, who owed "nine guilders yearly salary," received a similar judgment. Martin Clazen denied owing eight guilders for service rendered, saying that his wife lay with a severe accident and agreed with the surgeon for a year, but that Mr. Jacob did not once come to see after his wife, and therefore he had been obliged to call in Mr. Hans Kierstede to whom he must pay three times as much.

From Josentje Virhage the doctor demanded ten guilders yearly money for account of her husband. Josentje says she is married only two years to her husband and cannot know what that is for, and he is long since gone to dwell at Fort Orange, and has sent the doctor a beaver. The latter acknowledges having received the beaver, but the bill is more. Josentje says she has not the money now, but promises to send it at the next hunt; with which the doctor is content. In 1660, Gysbert van Imburch, surgeon at Fort Orange, treated a soldier who had eighteen wounds, sued the Company for payment, and got judgment for fifty guilders in beavers. On Sept. 9, 1659, Jacob Huges had to sue Hendrick the Spaniard for half a beaver in payment for some medicaments. Hendrick pleaded that the doctor did not tell him how often he should take them!

On June 22, 1660, Harmen Wessels sued William Bredenbent for thirty florins in zeewan or twenty florins in beaver, or fifteen florins in silver money, for curing a sore in Mrs. Bredebent's shoulder, and says that defendant allows him only six guilders in zeewan. William pleads that it is quite enough, as he can hire the doctor a whole year for twelve guilders. The case was referred to Messrs. Kierstede and Varrevanger for arbitration. On March 18, 1664, Harmen Wessels sued Hendrick Arenzen for seven beavers or one hundred and forty guilders in seawant for surgeon's fees. June 18, 1667, he got judgment against Mme. van Leeuwen for two hundred and twenty-nine orins zeawant, refusing to wait for payment till her husband's arrival. Dr. Henry Tailor (1672) recovered one hundred and fourteen florins wampum from Egbert Mynders, on Dr. Jacob Varrevanger's award.

In New Amsterdam the doctors found plenty to do, not only in curing disease, but in healing wounds gained in tavern brawls, stabbing and slashing affrays, and the frequent fights and quarrels. Sometimes the doctors themselves were violent characters and supplied work for fellow members of their profession. The above Dr. Henry Taylor was irascible, to say the least. In 1673, Else Manning complained that her master, Dr. Henry Taylor, "hath assaulted en battered hur in the fease" and claimed eighty florins for wages due. The Schout prosecuted the doctor, and wanted him

PHYSICIANS AND SURGEONS

fined " 100 fl. above the smart and surgeon's fee, with costs, for he had struck his late maid on the head so that the blood ran out her nose and she lay blind the whole 24 hours." The doctor admitted having struck one blow in haste and had to pay the eighty florins as well as twenty-five florins and costs. Two weeks later, Dr. Harmen Wessels recovered twenty-five florins and costs from his brother surgeon " for curing his maid and for her board and drink."

At the request of Surgeon Hendricksen Varrevanger, a hospital for sick soldiers who had been billeted on private families, and the Company's negroes, was established on Dec. 23, 1638. The first town midwives were (163-) Hilletje Wilburgh, and Tyron Jansen or Jonas, mother of Anneke Jans.

Regarding medicinal plants, Van der Donck says:

No reasonable person will doubt that there are not many medicinal and healing plants in the New Netherlands. A certain chirurgeon, who was also a botanist, had a beautiful garden there, wherein a great variety of medicinal wild plants were collected, but the owner has removed and the garden lies neglected. Because sickness does not prevail much, I suppose the subject has received less attention. The plants which are known to us are the following: Capilli veneris, scholopendria, angelica, polypodium, verbascum album, calteus sacerdotis, atriplex hortensis and marina, chortium, turrites, calamus aromaticus, sassafras, rois Virginianum, ranunculus, plantago, bursa pastoris, malva, origænum, geranicum, althea, cinoroton pseudo, daphine, viola, ireas, indigo silvestris, sigillum salamonis, sanguis, draconum, consolidæ, millefolium, noli me tangere, cardo benedictus, agrimonium, serpentariæ, coriander, leeks, wild leeks, Spanish figs, elatine, camperfolie, petum male and female, and many other plants. The land is full of different kinds of herbs and trees besides those enumerated, among which there undoubtedly are good *simplicia,* with which discreet persons would do much good; for we know that the Indians with roots, bulbs, leaves, etc., cure dangerous wounds and old sores, of which we have seen many instances.

And again, in the *Representation of New Netherland* (1650), we read:

The medicinal plants found in New Netherland in a day, by a little search, as far as they have come to our knowledge, consist principally of Venus's hair, hart's tongue, lingwort, polypody, white mullein, priest's shoe, garden and sea beach orach, water germander, tower-mustard, sweet flag, sassafras, crowfoot, plantain, shepherd's purse, mallows, wild majoram, crane's bill, marshmallows, false eglantine, laurel, violet, blue flag, wild indigo, solomon's seal, dragon's blood, comfrey, milfoil, many sorts of fern, wild lilies of different kinds, agrimony, wild leek, blessed thistle, snake-root, Spanish figs, which grow out of the leaves, tarragon and numerous other plants and flowers. . . . It is certain that the *Indigo Silvestris* grows here spontaneously without human aid. It could be easily cultivated if there were people who would undertake it.

Van der Donck says that Kilian van Rensselaer sent seeds of the *Indigo Silvestris* to his colony and that it was sown on Bear Island; and that Augustin Heerman, "a curious man and lover of the country, made an experiment near New Amsterdam, where he planted indigo seed, which grew well and yielded much. Samples of this indigo were sent over to the Netherlands, which were found to be better than common." Minuit sowed canary seed, which grew and yielded well, but he thought that the "time of the cultivators should not be spent on such experiments but to the raising of the necessaries of life."

Writing to the West India Company on Sept. 17,

OLD CHEST, LINEN PRESS, AND TWO WARMING-PANS
OWNED BY MR. FRANS MIDDELKOOP, NEW YORK

1659, Governor Stuyvesant requests that "medicinal seeds " be sent, and instructs his correspondents to have each package of seeds placed in a separate linen bag and these small bags in a great linen bag to be hung up during the voyage so as to receive light and air. On Dec. 22, 1659, the Directors inform him that the seeds requested have been sent, and also that they have sent some silkworm seeds as well.

The arrival of a new member of the family was an event of great delight to the Dutch household. Great preparations were made for the comfort of the new-comer, and in rich homes presents poured in. Many of these were silver, such as the cup, the pap-bowl, the cinnamon-bowl, spoons, etc. A handsome basket lined with silk, preferably yellow, and draped with lace, was filled with toilet articles, and was generally the gift of the husband's mother, or aunt, to the young mother. Another and larger basket contained the linen. The cradle was also tastefully and comfortably draped, and stood near the fire, from which it was protected by a screen. Special drinks and sweet cakes, or biscuits, were offered to visitors. In 1662, a case comes into the New Amsterdam Court regarding these special breads, for we read:

Pursuant to the order of this, W. court, the defendant produces a declaration of Hieletje Jans, wife of Yde Cornelis, passed before the Notary Salomon La Chair, 23 August, 1662, to the effect that she had agreed with defendant in the presence of her husband's sister and Trijntje Walings, to bake a quantity of biscuit for her lying-in. Burgomasters and Schepens, having read and considered the declaration, find that defendant has not baked the rolls with a design to sell them; but for biscuit; therefore dismiss the Officer's entered demand and deduced conclusion.

It was usual for the mother to be churched six weeks after the birth of the child. It would have been considered bad manners if she had gone out of doors, or appeared in society, or in the street before this ceremony, and it would have been against all customs if at her return no "churchtrip meal" (*kerkgangsmaal*) had been prepared. According to the old Dutch custom at those dinners, there was "hearty fare and plenty of good cheer." As this was being carried to excess, an ordinance from the church was published that at a christening-dinner, no more than a specified number of neighbors were allowed to be present. This number differed in the various towns. Although, according to the resolutions of the church, the child had to be baptized, as soon as possible after birth, it became customary among the richer classes to put off the baptism until after the mother had made her first visit to the church. The baptism took place in the church, sometimes before, and sometimes after the sermon, but generally during the afternoon service, rarely at the morning or evening service. The compulsory baptism, performed in case of illness by the nurse was not considered legal. Sick children were sometimes baptized before the service. Natural children, the birth of whom had to be sworn to by the nurse before the church council, were christened in some places in the forenoon. The father had to be present at the baptism, and it was left to him to bring brothers or sisters or friends as witnesses, provided these were members of the Reformed Church and did not stand under "censure" or excommunication. Prominent burghers wore on such an occasion a special suit of clothes, called the "Lord's Supper Suit" (*avondmaalpak*), or he appeared in a solemn black suit and white collar. Many, however, wore their wedding-suit or had one made for the occasion.

The laws of New Amsterdam were very strict regarding any irregular baptisms. In 1674, Schout De Mill, against Jannettie de Kleuse, said that she baptized a child of Reformed parents on the 18th of April, "when the father was from home, which is a thing which can never be tolerated by those of the Reformed religion; he concludes therefore that the defendant shall be imprisoned and moreover be condemned in a fine of one hundred guilders zeawant, with costs. Defendant admits she baptized the child through ignorance; and requests forgiveness if she did wrong. The W. Court having considered the matter and likewise weighed the evil consequences and other inconveniences, which might result and arise therefrom, condemn the defendant for her profanation and disrespect of the Holy Sacrament of Baptism that she shall be imprisoned and remain there until further order." At Heemstede there was, in 1657, a Presbyterian colony and preacher named Richard Denton, who was liked by the Dutch because he conformed in all things to the Dutch Church. We learn from Megapolensis and Drisius that the Independents of the place listened attentively to his preaching, "but when he began to baptise the children of such parents as are not members of the church, they sometimes burst out of the church."

As in the case of the bride's dress, the christening robe was as costly as the parents' means would allow. Rich families wrapped the baby in a handsome lace shawl. The little bonnet showed the sex of the child, — six plaits were made for a boy and three for a girl. The bows of ribbon also gave evidence of the sex, both regarding color and the way they were tied. In case the mother had died or the parents happened to be in mourning, the baby was dressed in white with black bows. After the baby was swaddled and dressed, neighbors and friends were invited to come and have a look at it, and light refreshments were offered. Then the christening-party started for the church. On this day the best pincushion, on which the child's name was picked out in pins, was uncovered. The baby was laid on a pillow and wrapped in a "christening-cloth" of white silk, satin, or Marseilles embroidery, and the long skirt of the child's robe was arranged in folds over the nurse's shoulder to be held by one of the witnesses. If there was no font in the church, an urn of gold or silver gilt was used, and this was filled with lukewarm water. In some places the elder children of seven, eight, or nine would carry the baby.

When the christening-party returned from church, the child was blessed by the father, and then undressed and dressed afresh by the nurse in a presentation robe to be presented to the friends and relatives who were invited to the christening-dinner. In the meantime the *berkemeyer*, or large glass goblet with a cover, filled with sugared Rhine wine, or the silver brandy bowl, was passed around merrily.

The christening-dinner was a very costly and elaborate affair and differed little from the wedding-feast. During the progress of the dinner the child was again presented to the guests, when songs were sung and speeches and toasts were made. All the family silver and porcelain was set upon the table, which was also decorated with fruits and flowers, fine pastries and cakes. To these delicacies belonged the *suikerdelbol gaan*, or sugared roll, *kraamvetjes*, cakes made hollow and filled with sugar. Aniseeds covered with a coating of white sugar, rough for boys and smooth for girls, were also served. The *kandeel pot* (caudle cup or cinnamon cup) was never missing. This was a tall drinking-cup filled with Rhine wine sweetened with sugar. In it was placed a stick of cinnamon, — a long one if the child were a boy and a short one if a girl. When this was handed, the sugar was stirred in the cup by the cinnamon stick by the person who presented it.

The fact of having been present at a christening was long remembered, and in after years people often remarked to a young man or woman, " Old friend, I had a sugar piece with you " ("Oude Kennis, ik heb bij je nog een stik met suiker gehad ").

On the return from the baptismal font of the *peter* or *meter* (godfather or godmother), the christening-gifts were presented or promised. As a rule, these were of gold or silver, such as porringers, pap-bowls with spoons, a silver whistle, a silver mounted bag, if the godfathers and godmothers were of the rich burgher class; but the farmers presented the child with silver shoe buckles or coat buttons or some trifle. It was also the custom to give a *luyer korf* (napkin basket) completely furnished, or a gold or silver rattle. The latter had an ebony or a silver handle and a ring on which hung a number of silver bells or coins. The top was surmounted by a baby's head or a fool's head, and in the bottom of the handle was a whistle. These were hung round the baby's neck by a silver chain.

Sometimes the christening-presents were made on the day of the birth, or a few days afterwards, on which occasion a dinner or *kinderbier* (baby beer) was given. Uninvited guests sometimes entered the house on the sly on such occasions, for the more merriment and drinking the more honor for the baby. These festivities sometimes lasted six weeks, one christening-feast following another. The husband in the meantime neglected his business or his work, and an empty purse and debts often resulted. The presents were kept in the " show-cabinet," where also the bride's gifts and the bridegroom's pipe (see page 218) were on exhibition.

The silver was taken to the mint only in dire need; and then it was sometimes discovered that the " gold " presents were often of gilded brass.

When a member of the household became seriously ill, the " Consoler of the Sick " was called in; also the nearest relations, who did not leave the house until the patient had died or was out of danger. The reader and comforter of the sick was very necessary in the new colony, and the West India Company took good care to provide emigrants with his services even on shipboard. Thus, on Aug. 13, 1655, the Company allowed William Brouwer with his wife and three children a free passage on the *Waegh,* on condition of acting as reader and comforter of the sick on board.

The Consoler called frequently to talk to the patient, pray with him, or read to him from the " Consolation of the Sick." Meantime at the church service was held and prayers offered for the invalid's recovery. The members of the household also engaged in religious commune, reading from the Bible or some religious work, and recording the last words and wishes of the dying. If the latter was a prominent personage, his edifying words were sometimes published; and if he was a pastor, then they were repeated at the funeral sermon to the congregation. When the end approached, the family called in the neighbors, who, under penalty of a heavy fine, were obliged to answer the call. Then all kneeled down in the sick-room, while the pastor read the prayers for the dying and spoke some consoling words.. When the last breath had left the body, the nearest blood-relation approached the corpse, closed its eyes, and gave it the parting kiss. Sometimes the pastor did this. After this, a mirror was held before the mouth of the deceased, or smoke was blown into the nostrils. When assured that life was extinct, the wedding-ring was taken off the finger and handed over to the widow, a sheet was spread over the body, the curtains of the bedstead drawn, or the doors of the bedstead closed, and all left the death-room to the "wade" (shroud) neighbors who came to "lay out" the body. They undressed the corpse and put on the "death wade." This was a long shirt with wide pleats and black trimmings and bows of fine homespun linen. This "wade" in some places was made by the bride in the "bridal days" or during the first weeks of marriage; sometimes even it was worn on the wedding-night, and then put away in a special corner of the linen-closet. Generally people were satisfied with merely dressing the body in this burial gown, and covering the head with a linen nightcap with a black plume; but the wealthy dressed the bodies of the dead in rich clothes, and late in the century put the large powdered wigs on the head. The corpse being "wade," that is, washed, shaved, combed, or the hair braided and dressed, was placed on straw or a rolling mat, — the male with the arms extended along the body, the female with the arms crossed or with folded hands, as seen on old monuments. According to law, the corpse had to remain as it was for from twenty-four to forty-eight hours before being placed in the coffin. After the mirrors and pictures had been turned face to the wall, all went into another room to partake of a very liberal but cold collation. Sometimes unseemly scenes followed, but heavy penalties were provided for excesses. Meanwhile all the relations assembled in another room to make the arrangements required by the city authorities on such occasions. These differed not only in the various provinces, but in the various towns and even villages. First, the curtains were taken from the windows, the shutters were closed, and a servant announced the death in the neighborhood and hung a larger or smaller lantern, according to the age of the deceased, with an extinguished candle end, at the front door. In other places, a bunch of straw, or large or small black ribbons, or some blocks of wood with a skull on the top, were placed in front of the door. The wealthy had also their top windows draped with black, and hung their coats-of-arms covered with black over the front door, with the date of death painted underneath; they had the death room draped all in black splashed with silver tears, and lighted with black painted wax candles. The sexton of the church where the body was to be buried or placed in a vault next arrived, followed by the mourners to make out the invitations.

The customs of the poorer classes were naturally simpler; they were helped by their neighbors, who in some instances tolled the parting knell, buried the corpse, and even dug the grave. The wealthy employed " notifiers," who formed a guild, governed by a deacon and officers; women belonged to this also. In some places it was not allowed to bury the dead on Sundays. The dress of these mutes consisted of a long black cloak and white tie, with long mourning streamers of crape from their wide-brimmed hats, and white gloves, which they received at the " death house "; but later they dressed like the pastors and tried to assume equal importance and demand equal respect. They took the upper hand at once, gave their orders, and easily imposed upon the poorer classes, who obeyed them as absolute masters. By the wealthier classes their pretensions were not recognized. They had to notify

DUTCH CRADLE AND CHILD'S CHAIR
ALBANY INSTITUTE AND HISTORICAL AND ART SOCIETY

relations and friends appearing on the list that had been made out, and afterwards invite them to the funeral. The relations were asked to close their window-shutters, but in the case of a sister or cousin one half of the shutter was considered sufficient. The invitation was in printed form.

As soon as the coffin was brought to the house, the "corpse dressers" returned to place the corpse in the coffin. In some places this was required to be done in the presence of two witnesses, strangers to the deceased. The coffin was placed in the front room, on two black trestles, with the feet always towards the door. In some places in North Holland the front room of the houses was never used except for weddings and funerals. In some instances the death robe was not put on till the corpse was placed in the coffin. In some places there were women who made a living by making the "wade" dresses, which sometimes were very elaborate, and in cases of young men or spinsters were tucked and decorated with twigs of green 'and flowers, with a laurel twig or rosemary in the hand.

When a woman died in childbirth, the infant was placed in her arms. In that case the "playmates" (see 218) made the wreaths of flowers and placed them on the head of the departed. This was done when, on the invitation of the parents, they went to the house to take a last look at their friend. Even those who carried the child to the grave had a laurel, myrtle, or rosemary branch in their hand. When the playmates had viewed the body, they were treated to rice-pudding with sugar and cinnamon. In some places the neighbors were called in to see the "dressed corpse," and treated to rolls with wine or beer.

White was the color of innocence and purity; black that of darkness. Black was generally adopted in Holland, except by the Friesland women, who wore the "Hindelopen" dress with blue for mourning, darker or lighter in color acording to close or more distant relationship. In the upper classes mourning was very costly. In the inventories we note fine black cloth "tabbards," black velvet coats, black cloth and satin bodices with black lace, and black velvet trimmed with jet, cambric handkerchiefs and collars with heavy black borders. A bride in mourning wore a black velvet dress, trimmed with pearls, and a long train. Neither gold nor silver was worn, but only white pearls and diamonds. The mourning cloak hung in loose wide folds down to the ground. It was often so long that it trailed on the ground. The bows and rosettes were made of black crape. The collars of men and women had wide pleats, and the hat was surrounded with crape, while the cloaks and sleeves, vests, trousers, stockings, and shoes were all made of black cloth or woolen stuff. People dressed in full, half, and quarter mourning, according to their blood relationship to the deceased. A widow was not permitted to marry during her time of mourning, which lasted one year and six weeks; but in 1656 it was decided that a widow might marry six months after her husband's death. The poorer classes wore black cloth and serge. In some places the women during the first three weeks of their deep mourning were required to pull their black overskirt over their heads; they also wore long black veils. In some places mourning consisted in wearing a cloak with a hood, and putting the hood over the head when following the departed to the grave. Black mourning-hoods were in general use in the Seventeenth Century.

It was the custom to entomb the corpses in family vaults in the church where people worshiped, or to bury in the churchyard when the people were too poor.

BIRTHS AND DEATHS

Everything pertaining to funerals was regulated by law. The wealthy who were fond of great pomp at funerals gladly paid the heavy fines imposed by the sumptuary laws, and buried their dead according to the rank of the deceased. The burghers held their funerals in the daytime, therefore the wealthy generally chose the night, and followed the corpse to the grave escorted by a large following of mourners, torch or lantern bearers, to the tolling of the church bells. This was forbidden in Amsterdam in 1661, unless a permit had been obtained from the court, but was allowed again two years later, upon payment of a fine of twenty-five florins, for a woman who died in childbirth, fifty florins for a child under ten years old, one hundred florins for the burial of a corpse under and one hundred and fifty florins for one above twenty-five years old. Mourning-coaches also came into use at the end of the Seventeenth Century. The churches were paid for the tolling of the bells, the lighting of the church, the cleaning of the vault, and the rent of the litter. In some places this litter was taken to the house of mourning and placed before the door an hour before the funeral; then the undertakers stationed themselves at the door to receive the invited guests. In burgher's homes, the mirrors were taken down or covered with black, but in the wealthier houses the whole room was draped with black cloth and lighted with wax candles. In both instances the relatives stood in rank according to their relationship. In the centre was the coffin, on a pair of black covered trestles. Care was also taken to turn the face eastward in the grave, as it was believed that Christ would come to judgment from the east.

In some towns the women would follow the funeral, in others they did not; but in all places the immediate relatives came first, followed by the others according to consanguinity, and friends next. The body of a preacher was borne by the members of the consistory of the church; of a magistrate, by the members of the court; that of a guild member, by the surviving members of the same; that of a student, by his fellow collegians, followed by the professors and teachers.

The superstition in the Seventeenth Century maintained that the first corpse to be buried in a cemetery could not rest, or was carried away by Satan, and many families took their dead to other cities and villages rather than have them buried in a new churchyard.

The Dutch in New Netherland seem to have soon outgrown this superstition, and in some cases even were not particular about being buried in consecrated ground, but started family cemeteries of their own on their own lands. Thus John Lecount in his will (1697) desires that his body may be buried in the garden of his own house by his sister-in-law. Frederick Philipse also (1700) directs "my body to be interred at my burial place at the upper mill" (near Tarrytown).

The customs observed at the funeral processions differed in nearly every town, village, and hamlet. In one the preachers would precede, in others follow immediately after the coffin; here it was preceded by the orphans and inmates of the poorhouse, at another place it would be followed by them. Sometimes the relatives or friends would carry the coffin, then again the poor.

The pomp and splendor displayed at funerals, notwithstanding the heavy fines imposed by the government, increased so much towards the end of the Seventeenth Century that the consistories of the churches begged the government to take stronger measures. It was all in vain, for the rulers themselves were some of the worst offenders. At many of the funerals of members of that body, not only were the councils and church-members of the places where they had been employed represented, but the very horses were made to go lame, and all the undertakers of the city were present. No funeral (except a State funeral) was more solemn and costly than that of an acting burgomaster. The dinners served at funerals were as brilliant and plentiful as the wedding and christening dinners. Prohibitions and fines were powerless to stop the extravagance. In the middle of the Seventeenth Century, however, these dinners began to be discontinued in the cities, and people were satisfied with serving wine and cakes only on returning from the funeral. The body buried, the company returned home. He who has presided thanks those present for attending and invites them to come into the house. Then refreshments are served. Each drinks what he likes and departs at will. The rich are buried in the churches, and Rhine wine is served; the middle class serve French wine; and the poorer classes, beer. In Groningen this was called "consolation beer," elsewhere "dead beer." Often this wine or beer was taken in excess. The dinners at funerals remained in vogue in the northern provinces for a long time, and although the serving of hot dishes was forbidden, the amount spent on the cold collations often left the relatives in debt for a long time. In burgher families the Bible was placed on the coffin, from which a preacher, a "consoler," or a member of the "church board" read a chapter and afterwards said a prayer. In some places in Friesland a light lunch was also partaken of then. At the appointed hour, — for every hour later, an additional fine had to be paid, — the bells began to toll from the church in which the entombment was to take place, and sometimes also from the churches that were passed on the way. After the undertaker had asked if anybody present wished to take a last look at the dead, the coffin was closed and placed on the bier, feet foremost. This was important, for bodies of those who had committed suicide or who had fallen by the hands of the executioner were carried head first to the grave. Indeed, it was only by special favor that a suicide was buried in consecrated ground, either in Holland or here. Thus, Hendrick Jansen, in 1664, hanged himself and destroyed his life on the branch of a tree on this side of the Fresh Water. The prosecutor therefore demanded " that his goods be forfeit, the corpse drawn on a hurdle as an example and terror to others, and brought to the place where it was found hanging and there shoved under the earth; further that a stake, pole or post shall be set there in token of an accursed deed." However, it was decided that as Jansen had always been an exemplary burgher, and his next neighbors, eight in number, had requested a decent burial, the body should be interred in a corner of the churchyard, after the ringing of the nine o'clock bell.

Dutch and English were alike, both at home and in their colonies, in serving generous quantities of funeral baked meats and entertaining the friends and relatives of the deceased on a scale far beyond their means. Generous provision is frequently made in the wills for their funerals by people of high and low degree. Ouzel Van Swieton (1693) is somewhat exceptional in directing his body " to be buried in a moderate Christian burial." On the other hand, Edward Mann (1702) gives " all his wages now due on board H. M. S. *Jersey* to be employed for the defraying of my funeral expenses." It is evident that even a common soldier's wake was expensive, for we read in 1653 that

Jan Peeck demanded 48 fl. 18 stivers from Jan Gerritsen, for victuals consumed at the funeral of Jan Bronck, a soldier, who had been shot dead, for which defendant had given security. "Defendant says it is true, he has been at the party, consuming the victuals, but as he is no heir nor has received any benefits from deceased, he maintains, he is not bound to pay." It was decided that plaintiff must look for payment to the estate of deceased, or his pay from the Company.

Gloves, rings, scarves, and hatbands were given to the mourners here, as they were in Holland. Many wills contain bequests of this nature. Henry Clark (1679) appoints five friends to carry him to his grave and "to have scarves and gloves according as the custom is." Captain Thos. Exton (1668) leaves seven beavers "to buy wine for the officers and gentlemen who accompany my corpse to the grave." Thomas Pell (1669) gives his body "to a comely burial that it may be decently buried in such a comely manner that God may not be dishonored." Henry Clarke (1679) appoints five friends to carry him to his grave "and to have scarves and gloves according as the usual custom is." Christopher Dean (1689) leaves "to each of those who shall bear up my pall at my funeral, a ring value 15 shillings, and a mourning hat band." Lucas Santen (1692) leaves "to my landlord Capt. John Clopps £10 to buy him a mourning ring, in consideration of the trouble I have given him."

Lawrence Deldyke (1690) leaves £10 "to expend at New York among my friends and acquaintances to be disbursed by Mr. James Mills, my attorney."

The expenses of a funeral at the end of our period are clearly shown in the following examples. Lockerman: Charges for them that carried the body of Maria Lockerman to the grave, 200 guilders; Clerk of the yard, 49 guilders; Mr. Thos. Lovell, for translating the last will of Maria L., 18 guilders; Albert

Bosch, for shrines for the coffin, 16 g. 10 s.; Dr. Lockhart, for medicines, 34 g.; Edward Griffith for two beavers, 48 g.; a carpenter for 2½ days' work, 20 g. William Helcker: "Coffins, £1 0s. 3d.; Angeltie Moll, for undress ye dead, 11s. 9d.; William Portuguese wife for ditto, 5s. 10½d.; candles and rum, 3s.; ½ gross pipes, 2s. 7d.; a place in the church, 9s."

The funeral expenses of John Oort amounted to £30 1s. 6d. "To Johans Von Ekelyn (1697) for beer at his funeral, £1; to the charges of his funeral, £2 – 19 – 9." Justice White for funeral charges, £5; to Daniel Weeks for a coffin, 6 shillings; to John Rogers, for digging the grave, 6 shillings. James Dewsbury: "Paid to nurse, £2 – 8 – 0; for funeral charges, £3 – 15 – 0."

Peter Jacob Marius; funeral:

	£	s.	d.
To 29 gallons of wyne at 6s. 9d. per gallon	9	15	9
To 19 pairs of gloves at 2s. 3d.	2	4	3
For bottles and glass broke, paid	0	3	7
Paid 2 women each 2 days attendance	0	15	0
Paid a suit of mourning for ye negro woman freed by ye testator and making	3	4	7½
Paid for 800 Cokies and 1½ gross of Pipes at 3s. 3d.	6	7	7½
Paid for speys [spice] for ye burnte wyne and sugar	0	1	1
Paid to the Sexton and Bell ringer, for making ye grave and ringing ye bell	2	2	0
Paid for ye Coffin	4	0	0
Paid for gold and making 14 mourning rings	2	16	0
Paid for 3 yards beaver stuff at 7s. 6d., buttons and making it for a suit of mourning	1	14	6
Paid for ½ vat of single Beer	0	7	6
Whole amount of Funeral Charge is	31	6	8½

SAMUEL BAYARD.

As at weddings silver medals were sometimes presented either before or after a funeral. If presented before, they were worn at the funeral. They were in all shapes, round, octagonal, oval, square, etc., sometimes cast, sometimes engraved with the portrait of

SILVER SPOONS
RIJKS MUSEUM, AMSTERDAM

the deceased, or with mythological figures, inscriptions in prose or verse, or sometimes only inscribed with the date of birth and death of the deceased, with or without a verse from the Holy Scriptures. Sometimes the design was a skull and crossbones surrounded by a wreath of laurels, and the dates were added when the medal was required. The memory of the deceased was perpetuated by these medals and by the legacies of the rich to the church and the poor. There were few rich burghers who did not leave generously to both. An enormous amount of money was also spent on the carved tombstones.

CHAPTER XII

TAVERNS AND EXCISE LAWS

IN Holland, during the Seventeenth Century, as well as in England, France, and Germany, the two fashionable as well as low vices were drinking and gambling. The government made stringent laws regulating the opening and closing of taverns, and heavy penalties were imposed for infractions of the liquor laws; but no barriers seemed strong enough to stem the flood of drunkenness. Youth drank as heavily as middle age. The reason for tavern excesses may probably be found in the lack of simple pleasures and sociability in the home circles. When the office hours were over, the shop closed, and the school dismissed, the youth had as a choice for spending his evening the somewhat cold and severe paternal dwelling, the open street with its mischievous and boisterous play, and the tavern. At home there were no entertaining books for youthful perusal, and the atmosphere was lacking in sympathy and companionableness. The tavern, therefore, with its drinking, dicing, cardplaying, and many other games that lent themselves to gambling, offered irresistible attractions. The young men of the day, therefore, in all classes were sadly dissipated.

In New Amsterdam, there was, if possible, even more license than in Fatherland. There are many evidences that, so far from being a crime or a sin, drunkenness was not even a reproach. Weddings and funerals and all occasions of feasts and merry-making were opportunities for hard drinking, of which the guests took full advantage. Drunkenness among women was by no means rare, and the clergy, as a rule, did not set an example of strict sobriety. In fact, habitual drunkenness was charged against more than one of them. It is indeed astonishing to find that drunkenness was frequently treated in the court proceedings as an excuse for having committed serious offenses, such as assault, as we have seen. There are many cases in which men repudiated leases, deeds, contracts, etc., pleading that they were drunk when they entered into the engagements. It is evident that the law allowed a man twenty-four hours to get sober in, because the court would not hold him to his agreement if he could prove that he denounced the transaction on the following day. An instance of a man's readiness to acknowledge drunkenness occurs in 1655, in a case of abuse, in which a certain Christiaen Anthony was called as a witness. He declared that " on the evening the Burghery marched, he came from the Fort sorely fuddled, and does not properly know what passed between Jan van Leyden and Webber's wife."

In Holland the tavern was one of the most important institutions of burgher life. It was the citizen's club, and the most respectable members of the community did not hesitate to spend much of their leisure time there in friendly intercourse and jovial company. The civic governments, which had held their meetings in the large hall of a neighboring abbey or monastery in earlier days, after the Reformation met in the taverns or inns, and were served by the host at the city's expense. If a prince, an ambassador, or any other person of high rank, visited the city, he took up his quarters at the *Peacock,* the *Angel,* the *Pig,* the *Gold Cup,* or at any of the city's inns, where the municipality offered him the "wine of honor," and the city paid his expenses, or some of the highest officials of the city government paid the expenses amongst themselves.

The literary societies also and the various guilds met at the taverns, and entertained there. The notable burghers of Leyden and the professors visited the inns daily and drank their pint of ale or wine. Of Simon Abbes Gobbema it is said that he divided his time between his study and the *Marksmen's Home* in the morning as well as in the afternoon. There were also inns for the "thin beer folks," — people that imbibed all day, characters who were held up to ridicule in all the plays of the period. These inns were often kept by landlords of questionable honesty, who more than once were put in the stocks; but their inns were always scrupulously clean. The hostess saw to it that everything shone brightly, from the cuspidor to the grill, and the tiles on the floor were as clean as the plate that was used at table; even the dice were brightly polished.

In the country, however, inns were not quite so well kept. One of these is described in Van Sauten's *Light Shower.* He says that it was ten times colder inside than outside; that one man had to sit on a pail and another on a turf basket, and that a lump of clay was used as a candle-holder. He adds that a blind horse could not do any damage inside. There is hardly one amongst the hundreds of comedies and farces of the Seventeenth Century in which the most disgusting scenes of drunkenness and vice are not depicted. Usually, when our staid burghers took wine, they drank three glasses. Such was the advice of Bernagin in his

TAVERN SCENE
TENIERS

Wedding-Contractor (1685). The first glass, he said, was for health, the second for taste, and the third for sleep; any more after that might serve as recreation.

There were innumerable kinds of wine, beer, and "hot drinks" that were used in Holland in the Seventeenth Century. In Godewyck's *White Bread's Children,* a young blade says:

> Then I came to the *Lion;* the hostess said "hello Roel! run and give the gentleman a chair with a cushion. What will the gentleman drink? We have some good wines clear in the glass and fine in colour. Do you like Vin d'Anjou, good Bacherach, Neuren, or Vin du Court; or do you like Manebach?" Then when I go to the *Horse* — it is "Sir! go into the room, we have Delé wine; there's none nicer. Or do you like Vin d'Ay, or beautiful Muscadel wine? I will go into the cellar and open a barrel. We have Mentser wine, Elsasger and Rinchouwers; they are silvery fine, much better than Pictou wine. Do you like Bordeaux wine, or good wine of Orleans?" So do I pass the time from sunrise to sunset.

Dordrecht was then the chief wine-market and nearly monopolized the trade. In the Seventeenth Century ice was used to cool the wine, which was kept in barrels, stone jugs, and leather bottles. The wine was drawn from the barrels in jugs which held from a pint to half a gallon, and the customers drank from steins and horns. The beer was drawn in jugs from one quart to one gallon in capacity, and was drunk out of pewter mugs and steins with lids, — in village inns out of wooden bowls. In the smaller inns the host or hostess sold "spare beer," small thin beer, and common beer. In the better class inns the beers used were Dordrecht, Delft, London, English White, Groninger Cluyn, Hamburger, Mentzel, Ipswich, Lubeck brew, and other heavy beers. Much care was given to the beer, and no wonder, for it was the only drink of the ordinary burgher. " Beer is the drink of every man. All that can, drink beer." Caudles, possets, and other hot drinks were common. Gin, called "drinkable fire" by Professor van Genns, was only drunk by the poorer classes, and was called gin-water until 1667. When we first hear of this drink, it is called "clear" and "genever." In the first half of the Seventeenth Century the gin-distilleries were unimportant. In 1672, it was still comparatively unknown, but was used by the army before Alphen. A student who valued his name would not openly call for a glass of genever. A glass of Spanish wine with brandy in winter, and a glass of white wine with spirit of lemon in summer was the strongest drink used. During the Thirty Years' War brandy came into general use in Germany. In the taverns they used Arak, besides Orange, Prince, and Quinjaets essences. Ratafia was also known. After drinking generously of Saint Laurent and Burgundy, people took a mouthful of ratafia to warm the stomach.

The favorite drinks in New Netherland were ale, beer, Rhenish, French, and Spanish wines, wormwood wine, distilled waters, brandy, gin, rum, bitters, cider, and perry. In 1656, a pipe of sack and the excise came to 443.17 florins. In 1659, twenty-four ankers of Annis waters and 7 ankers of bitters (*Borstwater*) cost 350 florins. New drinks occasionally make their appearance, however. In 1653, on a petition of Peter le Feber for leave to sell liquors or waters of a peculiar virtue, he was allowed to sell them in large or small bottles at his own house. In March, 1656, Solomon Lachair was called on to say where he got a flask of *Rosa Solis* he lately drank with some friends.

It was not customary in the Seventeenth Century

for frequenters of alehouses or inns to empty only their one little pint, jug, or mutchkin. They loved company, and oftentimes the host also " joined " in the treat. Then there were dice, cards, or other games; and they drank a round or a " clover leaf." The clover leaf, or the drink round, consisted of three drinks in succession, as the saying was that all good things are three, — three graces, three cardinal virtues, three friend's kisses, three conundrums, three times hurrah, three times to church, three sounds of the bugle, and numberless other three times, but, above all, the thrice clinking of the filled glasses, which, according to tradition, was a custom of the Greeks and Romans.

In the more respectable taverns, where everything was so arranged that the municipality, the guilds, the county judges, and the commissioners of dykes could hold a banquet or large dinner, the china closets were well provided with all kinds of silver mugs and pewter tankards, glass bottles and beakers, cups and saucers and platters in all shapes and sizes, some simply and others artistically cut and engraved, and all made specially for the various beverages. Among them may be mentioned the " handholders," or Frankfort " full holder," the large Rhine wine glasses, then so generally known, always of green glass, blown round, wide, and rather flat, which sometimes held a quart of wine, and which were so heavy that it took both hands to lift them to the lips. According to Van Mander, the painter Frans Floris would drain this glass sixty times against anybody who undertook to drink thirty.

As clubs or missiles, when effectively used, these glasses would often convincingly close an argument about local politics, Quaker baiting, or the relative merits of favorite champions at hockey, bowls, ninepins, or tric-trac. Thus, in 1654, Johannes Withart *v.* Francois Tyn, plaintiff, demands two hundred guilders for the surgeon's bill, pain and smart, as well as loss of time on account of the wound which defendant wilfully inflicted on his face with a glass; demands costs also. Withart finally had to pay the Schout " 50 gl. — half for the poor and half for himself — and 10 guilders to be expended for a treat, and moreover pay the sum of 10 guilders to be laid out at Abram La Nooy's, and a fee of Notary Schelluyne amounting to 24 gl." Johannes Withart seems to have been a truculent character, for about the same time the Schout stated that he had drawn a sword, therewith went to the house of Captain Krigier and elsewhere, and had been guilty of street riot. He was condemned to pay a fine of fifty guilders, ten more for a treat, and ten to be laid out at Abram La Nooy's.

Another familiar drinking-vessel was the birch-beaker, cut from the birch tree, hollowed out, and instead of being carved, left with the original bark, varnished inside with the rosin of the pine tree, and various spices, such as nutmeg, mace, cinnamon, and cloves, leaving these stuck on the inner surface. Then there were *bocals* in the shape of vessels or boats, or of the various emblems belonging to navigation, commerce, and fisheries, engraved on them. In almost every prominent household and in all the large taverns these glasses were to be found, because at every dinner given on special occasions they were used.

The most celebrated drinking-vessel of the day was the " Clover Leaf with the Stem," which is so often referred to in the old Dutch plays (see facing page 272). It was found in every tavern of any importance. A contemporary writer gives the following description of this famous vessel:

On top we see three small round chalices in the shape of a three-leafed clover leaf. Each chalice has its stem, which are joined together, and rest on a globe. Each stem is hollow, and when the chalices are filled, the wine can be seen running down the stems into the ball-shaped bowl underneath, so that when the drinker drinks out of one of the three chalices, or rather sips, the two others empty into the bowl underneath, otherwise it would be impossible to drink without spilling the wine. As the drinkers sip, now from the first, then from the second, and the third, of the chalices, the wine in the bowl would be the last; and this accordingly represents the stem of the clover-leaf. On each of the small chalices hangs a small plate with a coat-of-arms, which is exchanged for the arms of the nobleman giving the banquet or in whose honour it is given. The three chalices, with their bowl underneath, rested on a large trellis-work globe, all hollow, in which a die was to be seen, and according to the number on the die, which came on top when the cup was shaken, the drinks were taken. The whole cup rested on a foot of finely decorated earthenware, with gilt borders. When drinking out of one of the chalices, the drinker said, "Three glasses are three drinks, three makes a 'clover leaf.'" The company would answer, "Hey, he is a man who without spilling can empty a clover leaf and still be thirsty!" Then the cup was passed along to the next.

Hard drinking was the fashion at all family and public entertainments, as we have already seen. In 1605, at the wedding of the preacher Johannes Servatius, a forty-gallon barrel of wine was drunk. For burgomasters' and guild dinners the wine was ordered by the barrel.

In Holland the principal inns were always situated near the city-gates. The principal city-gate of New Amsterdam was the ferry-landing, and there was situated the principal inn of the town. It was originally built by the Company, and was leased to various ferrymen who managed it as a tavern. It also served the purposes of a town hall for the City Fathers, and a room in it was also used as a school. It is a conspicuous landmark on all the old maps of the Dutch towns. The first ferryman mentioned is Cornelis Dircksen. In 1642, he deeded a house, garden, and sixteen to seventeen morgens of land together with the Ferry on Long Island.

The dinners given in the taverns by order of the burgomasters, guilds, or other corporate bodies were usually very elaborate, and consisted principally of roasts, pasties, and sugared fruit. At the installation of the new burgomaster of Dordrecht in 1668, there were brought on the table ten dishes (platters) with mutton, roast beef, and veal, two dishes with boar's heads, ten dishes with rabbits, fowls, and pigeons, eight dishes with pasties of hare, pork, and capons, further soups, salads, horseradish, crackers, cake, waffles, jellies, and marchpane.

In New Amsterdam many a social and civic dinner was given in the City Tavern. These were frequently marred by uninvited revelers, who in their cups invaded the privacy of inoffensive guests. An early instance of this occurs in March, 1644, when declaration was made by Nicholas Coorn, Hans Kierstede, Jan Jacobsen, and Gysbert Opdyck, who with the minister and their wives had been invited to sup with Philip Gerritsen at the City Tavern, concerning an outrageous attack on the party made by Captain John Underhill, Lieutenant George Baxter, and other Englishmen. Captain Underhill was an important personage. Gerritsen petitioned against his unpunished behavior again in May, and the Fiscal was ordered to obtain satisfaction for him on the Captain's return.

CLOVER LEAF DRINKING CUP   OLD DUTCH TANKARD

TAVERNS AND EXCISE LAWS

In 1654, a complimentary dinner was given to Stuyvesant. Unfortunately the *menu* is not on record.

At a meeting in the City Hall, Dec. 12, 1654, where were assembled the Worshipful Heeren Martin Krigier, Allard Anthony, P. L. Vander Grift, Will. Beekman, P. v. Couwenhoven, Oloff Stevensen, Johan Nefius, and Cornelis van Tienhoven, it was unanimously resolved:

Whereas the Rt. Honble Director General intends to depart, the Burgomasters and Schepens shall compliment him before he take his gallant voyage, and for this purpose shall provide a gay repast on next Wednesday noon, at the City Hall in the Council Chamber. Whereupon the list of what was required was made out and what was considered necessary was ordered.

The authorities used the City Tavern for their business meetings and subsequent dinners. On Feb. 26, 1658, Egbert van Borssum was credited with the amount of his bill for wine and liquor furnished the Director and Council and other public officers.

In September of the same year, some of the most important men in the community had a splendid dinner at this hostelry, and some misunderstanding and dispute led the host and his wife to go to court for payment. They exhibited an account demanding a balance of 310.4 florins from Captain Augustyn Beaulieu for entertainment given by him. The Captain wanted to pay only half the amount, because the others shared in the other half. Jacob Huges and Simon Felle declared that they were invited by the Captain, but that they would pay their part. Egbert said that Captain Beaulieu ordered the dishes and agreed for the repast. Captain Beaulieu said there were fourteen of them; half of which he individually was to pay for, and the others the other half. He also offered to pay for the absent. Captain Roselyn declared he assisted in agreeing for the repast. Annetie van Borssum said that Captain Beaulieu alone agreed for the meals, and therefore looks to him. Captain Beaulieu was asked if he had any objection to the account, and answered, " No, except to the fl. 30 for trouble and waiting and fl. 3 for cleaning the things." The court decreed that Captain Beaulieu should have to pay Egbert van Borssum 250 gl. 4 stiv. 8 pence, deducting 20 fl. charged too much for trouble, and that the landlord should collect the remaining money from Adriaan Vincent, Simon Felle, Nicolaas Boot, Mr. Jacob Huges, and Jan Perier, and if the aforesaid persons could prove Captain Beaulieu had invited them, he was then ordered to pay for them. This must have been a very fine dinner to cost fifty dollars a plate, present value!

There were evidently various grades of tap-houses, from the bare cellar where a discharged soldier or old goodwife drew beer for the common laborers to the well-appointed inn. Thus, in 1654, Adriaen Jansen from Leyden received the patent of a lot of land in Albany " north of the highway, on condition that the house to be erected thereon be not an ordinary tippling house, but an inn for travellers." In the same year, Symon Joosten received permission to keep a tavern over the Ferry, in place of Cornelis Dircksen Hoochlant, for the convenience of travelers and there to retail beer and wines. For this he paid one hundred guilders net the first year.

There must have been taverns as well as mere taprooms long before this, however, because in an action for slander in March, 1639, " Cornelis Cool declared that Grietje Reyniers was discharged for improper

TAVERNS AND EXCISE LAWS

conduct when a waiting-girl at Pieter de Winter's tavern in New Amsterdam."

The government was fully alive to the evils of excessive drinking, and early tried to stop it. Thus, in 1638, Kieft and the Council have observed that "much mischief and perversity is daily occasioned by immoderate drinking; therefore, they forbid all persons from now henceforth selling any wine on pain of forfeiting 25 guilders and the wines found in their houses, excepting only the Store, where wine can be procured at a fair price and where it will be issued in moderate quantity."

This did not have the desired effect of stopping the illicit traffic; for, four years later, the Council followed the example of the States General in punishing tavern brawling. The preamble of the law paints a dark picture of prevailing conditions:

We hear daily, God help us, of many accidents, caused for the most part by quarrels, drawing of knives and fighting, and the multitude of taverns and low groggeries, ill conducted, together with the favorable opportunities which all turbulent persons, murderers and other lawless people have for running away and consequently escaping condign punishment; therefore we enact, agreeably to the law passed last year in Holland by the High and Mighty Lords States General that no one shall draw a knife, much less wound any person under penalty of fl. 50, or to work three months with the negroes in chains.

On July 23, 1648, Abraham Pietersen's tavern was closed in consequence of a man, Gerrit Clomp, having been killed there. In 1641, Kieft and his advisers, having received complaints that some of the inhabitants here were " in the habit of tapping beer during Divine Service, and of making use of small foreign

Measures, which tends to the dishonour of Religion and the ruin of this State," forbid the use of any measure but that of Amsterdam, Holland. Tapping was also prohibited after ten P. M.; the *vaen* (four pints) was to cost not exceeding eight stivers. The penalty was twenty-five guilders and forfeiture of the beer, besides three months' exclusion from the privilege of tapping. The officer who was appointed to look after the matter was Adriaen Swits. On Dec. 20, 1642, he declared in court that the beer he got at Jan Snedeker's was short of measure.

There was no excise law in New Netherland till the year 1644. Beer and spirits were imported by the Company and sold at their warehouses, and private individuals received from the Directors the right to brew. On Feb. 16, 1642, Director Kieft leased to Philip Gerritsen the Company's tavern at a rent of three hundred guilders, with the right to retail the Company's wines and brandy, on which he was to be allowed a profit of six stivers the can. A well and a brewhouse were to be constructed in the rear. By this date the bulk of the beer consumed was brewed here; there were already several breweries. Thus, on Aug. 26, 1641, Hendrick Jansen deeded to Maryn Adriaensen a house, barn, and arable land, except the brewhouse and kettles therein.

One of those who evidently sold liquors without the necessary privilege was Jan Schepmoes; for, on June 10, 1638, he was orderd to " entertain no more sailors nor tap wine, hereafter on pain of banishment." Director Kieft would seem to have encroached on the Company's privileges for his own profit for a time; for on Feb. 5, 1650, " William Hendricks swore that Kieft in 1640 engaged him at 25 guilders a month on Staten Island to distil brandy, but after six or seven months Kieft found it expedient to let the Brandy be."

Director Kieft, in the eyes of the majority of the New Amsterdam burghers, was directly responsible for the calamitous Indian war, which brought the province to the verge of ruin. The necessity for raising money to meet the public expenses was the immediate cause of the first excise laws here. In June, 1644, the Council had already raised

as much money as we could obtain on bills of exchange drawn on the Honble. Directors; and Whereas, we are now devoid of all means, and despair of immediately receiving any assistance from Holland, in this our necessity; therefore we are constrained to find out some plan to pay the soldiers, or else must dismiss them, which according to all appearances, will lead to the utter ruin of the country, especially as the harvest is at hand whereby people must live and fodder be procured for the remaining cattle; for neither grain nor hay can be cut without soldiers. These matters being maturely considered, and all things being duly weighed with the advice of the Eight men chosen by the Commonalty, no better nor more suitable means can be found in the premises, than to impose some duties on those articles from which the good inhabitants will experience least inconvenience, as the scarcity of money is sufficiently general.

We have therefore enacted and ordained, and do hereby enact and ordain, that there shall be paid on each half barrel of beer tapt by the tavern keepers, two guilders, one-half payable by the brewer and one-half by the tapster; the burgher who does not retail it, to pay half as much; on each quart of Spanish wine and brandy, four stivers; French wine, two stivers to be paid by the tapsters. On each merchantable beaver purchased within our limits and brought here to the fort, one guilder; the three-quarters and halves in proportion. All on pain of forfeiture of the goods, to be prosecuted by the officer or the collector, to be thereunto appointed; one-third for the informer, one-third for the officer, and the remainder for the Honble Company. All this provisionally, until the good God grant us peace or we receive succor from Holland.

It will be noticed that it was with some trepidation and in an apologetic tone that such an unpopular law was published; and it is intimated that it is only a war tax, and therefore only temporary in character. Once being imposed, however, the source of revenue was too fruitful for the law ever to be repealed. Thenceforward also, for many years, the authorities did not have to worry about illegal tapping, since it was distinctly to the advantage of the officer of the law to be vigilant in hunting for infractions of it, to say nothing of the activities of his casual assistant, the informer. The Fiscal was keen on the scent of the smugglers, as they were called, that is, those who tapped without having paid the excise. He was doubtless soon able to stock quite a respectable cellar of his own with the fines collected. Thus, we read on July 16, 1644:

The Fiscal prosecuted Laurens Cornelissen for smuggling, and the latter was condemned to pay 10 gallons of wine to the Fiscal and his friends.

The law caused great discontent. In 1649, the authors of the "Remonstrance" complained that when Director Kieft forced the eight men to impose a beer excise he promised it should last only till the arrival of a Company's ship, a new Director, or till the end of the war. "The beer belonging to the brewers who would not consent to an excise was distributed among the soldiers as a prize, and so it has continued." To this, Tienhoven replied that the burghers had no cause to complain about the excise, because the trader, burgher, farmer, and all others except the vintners, laid

TAVERNS AND EXCISE LAWS

in as much wine and beer as they pleased, free of excise. They were merely obliged to enter it so that the quantity might be ascertained. The vintners paid three guilders per tun on beer, and one stiver per can on wine; this they received back from their daily customers, and from the traveler from New England, Virginia, and elsewhere.

The authorities next attempted to enforce some degree of decency in the taverns by closing them at nine P. M., and during church hours on Sunday. The immediate cause of this was a serious drunken brawl during the interregnum between Director Kieft's retirement from office and Peter Stuyvesant's arrival. This is fully explained in the ordinance of May 1, 1647:

Whereas we have experienced the insolence of some of our inhabitants when drunk their quarrelling, fighting and hitting each other even on the Lords day of rest of which we have ourselves witnessed the painful example last Sunday in contravention of law, to the contempt and disgrace of our person and office, to the annoyance of our neighbours and to the disregard, nay contempt of Gods holy laws and ordinances, which command us to keep holy in His honor His day of rest, the Sabbath, and forbid all bodily injury and murder, as well as the means and inducements, leading thereto, —

Therefore, by the advice of the late Director-General and of our Council and to the end, that instead of God's curse falling upon us we may receive his blessing, we order all brewers, tapsters and innkeepers, that none of them shall upon the Lord's day of rest by us called Sunday, entertain people, tap or draw any wine, beer or strong waters of any kind and under any pretext before 2 of the clock, in case there is no preaching or else before 4, except only to a traveller and those who are daily customers, fetching the drinks to their own homes, — this under the penalty of being deprived of their occupation and besides a fine of 6 Carolus gilders for each person, who shall be found drinking wine or beer within the stated time. We also forbid all innkeepers, landlords and tapsters to keep their houses open on this day or any other day of the week in the evening after the ringing of the bell, which will be rung about 9 o. c., or to give wine, beer or strong waters to any, except to their family, travellers and table boarders under the like penalty.

The difference between the directorship of Stuyvesant and that of Kieft resembled that between the rule of Solomon and that of Rehoboam over the Children of Israel. Where Kieft chastised them with rods, Stuyvesant chastised them with scorpions. There was a good deal of bigotry and Puritan persecution in the nature of old " Silver Leg "; and on his arrival, among other reforms, he immediately proceeded to carry the regulation of the liquor traffic still further. The new laws of 1648 contained the following provisions: (1) No new taproom, or tavern, should be opened without the consent of the Director and Council. (2) Taverns, taprooms, and inns already established might continue for four consecutive years, but the owners should be obliged to engage in some other honest business with a convenient and decent burgher's dwelling to the ornament of the city, each acording to his condition, social position, and means. (3) The tavern-keepers and tapsters were allowed to continue their business for four years on condition that they should not transfer their business nor let their houses and dwellings without the consent of the Director and Council. (4) The tavern-keepers and tapsters were not allowed to sell beer, wine, brandy or strong waters to Indians, or provide them with it by intermediaries. (5) To prevent all fighting and mishaps they should daily report to the officer whether anybody had been wounded or hurt at their houses. (6) Unseasonable

TAVERNS AND EXCISE LAWS

night tippling and intemperate drinking on Sunday was forbidden, and tavern-keepers and tapsters were prohibited from selling anything by the small measure in the evening after the ringing of the bell, nor should they sell beer or liquor to anybody, travelers and table boarders excepted, on Sunday before three o'clock P. M., when divine service was over. (7) It was necessary to report to the Receiver and obtain a certificate before they could receive beer, wine, or distilled waters into their houses or cellars. (8) All tavern-keepers and tapsters desiring to continue in their business should present themselves to the Director-General and Council eight days after the publication of these rules and promise solemnly to observe them.

The evil of unreasonable and intemperate drinking "to the shame and derision of ourselves and our nation" was fully recognized by the authorities. In the preamble to the above law, the Director and Council speak in an almost despairing tone of the constant and general infraction of their "good orders and well-meant laws." They frankly recognize the reasons, which were

that this way of earning a living and the easily made profits therefrom please many and divert them from their first calling, trade, and occupation, so that they become tapsters, and that one full fourth of the City of New Amsterdam has been turned into taverns for the sale of brandy, tobacco and beer. This causes not only the neglect of honest handicraft and business, but also the debauching of the common man and the Company's servants, and, what is still worse, of the young people from childhood up, who seeing the improper proceedings of their parents and imitating them, leave the path of virtue and become disorderly. Add to this the frauds, smuggling, cheating, the underhand sale of beer and brandy to the Indians, as shown by daily experience, may God better it, which may only lead to new troubles between us and them. If besides these some honest tavernkeepers are licensed and open their places for the service and benefit of the traveller, the stranger and the inhabitant, honestly paying their charges and excise dues and living in convenient houses, either their own, or as tenants, which increases their expenses, they are noticeably injured in their licensed and approved business by such fraudulent innkeepers: this we wish to prevent.

With one house out of every four in the town a beer-shop, we cannot wonder that the authorities should try to devise means to curtail the trade and the disorders arising therefrom.

The burghers of New Amsterdam did not take kindly to any laws that interfered with their pleasures or personal liberties; and therefore the Director-General was forced to issue one year later a new ordinance calling attention to the injury done to the excise farmer and tapsters, who made it their only business:

We hereby order, that no inhabitant, who makes it a business to brew, shall be allowed to tap, sell, or give away beer, wine, or strong water by the small measure excepting at meal times, not even to table boarders, whom they may pretend to board, under which pretext we have seen many frauds perpetrated, we also order that henceforth no beer or wine shall be removed from any brewery, cellar or warehouse nor moved in the houses of the tapsters nor brought into them, unless it is previously reported to the Secretary and his carriers or porters have obtained a certificate of the report, signed by the Secretary's first clerk.

Six years later (1655), the laws were made even more stringent: " Every tavern-keeper had to take out quarterly a license and pay therefor six guilders." The hours of Sunday closing were extended; landlords

TAVERNS AND EXCISE LAWS

were forbidden even to give away liquor or to treat their friends then or after nine o'clock at night on every day of the week; and, in case of a tavern being found open, not only the landlord but the guests were fined. The license was raised the following year by an ordinance dated Oct. 26, 1656:

> Considering that, as well in tapping as in baking, frauds can be introduced, since there is as yet no guild or certain body known, . . . from now henceforth no person shall follow the business unless he first receive a license to trade, which all tavernkeepers and bakers shall renew every quarter, paying each time one pound Flemish, on pain of being suspended from business.

Moreover, the authorities prohibited on Sunday any ordinary work, such as plowing, sowing, mowing, building, wood-cutting, working in iron or tin, hunting, fishing, or any business permitted on other days under a penalty of one pound Flemish; much less any lower or unlawful games or exercises, drunkenness, frequenting taverns or grogshops, dancing, card-playing, backgammon, tennis, ball playing, bowling, ninepins, racing with boats, cars, or wagons, before, during, or between service, under double the fine. More especially no tavern-keepers or tapsters were to allow any clubs to sit during, before, or between the sermons, nor tap, present, give, or sell, directly or indirectly, any brandy, wine, beer, or distilled liquors under the penalty of six guilders, and for each person found drinking, three guilders; on Sundays or other days after setting of the night watch or ringing of the bell under like penalty; the inmates of the family, those attending by order and with consent of magistrates to public business alone excepted.

The city now determined to farm out the excise and

therefore published (Nov. 1, 1656) "Conditions and terms whereon [the City] proposes, according to the laudable custom and order of our Fatherland, to farm to the highest bidder the Burgher Excise of Wine and beer: For one anker of brandy, Spanish wine, distilled waters, or other of such value, 30 stivers. For an anker of French wine, Rhenish wine, Wormwood wine, or other of such value, 15 stivers. For a tun of good beer, one guilder. For a tun of small beer, 6 stivers. Larger and small vessels in proportion." Paulus van der Beeck became Farmer for one year for the sum of 4220 Carolus guilders.

Exceptions were granted in excise payment in certain cases. Thus, in 1673, the Schout, Burgomasters, and Schepens resolved that the tapsters outside the city be allowed to lay in a barrel of strong beer at burgher excise, at harvest, or the Merry Making, and at burials both within and without this city, but all officers belonging to the Fort Willem Hendrick must pay the full excise, as well as the tapsters themselves, if they lay in and consume any wines or beer in tapsters' houses.

In the eye of the law the most serious offense of which a tavern-keeper could be guilty was directly or indirectly selling liquor to the Indians. In 1656, Sander Toursen and wife were convicted of selling brandy to the Indians and sentenced to banishment. In 1658, Paulus Jansen was fined five hundred guilders, and banished for six years for a similar offense.

Even if we had not the official Jeremiads composed over that stiff-necked generation, the Court Records would be sufficiently eloquent of the desecration of the Sabbath by sinners who were sometimes guilty of grave offenses. The breaches of the liquor law were by no means generally so harmless as that of a landlord refreshing a few Sunday afternoon callers with a hospitable draught of beer. Card-playing and games of dice, backgammon, ninepins, etc., were frequently indulged in out of hours on licensed premises; and to any one who has ever perused the police court proceedings in the Monday papers, the excuses given by the tavern-keepers have a curiously familiar flavor. Let us take a few specimens of the charges and the defense offered between the years 1654 and 1664.

On Oct. 19, 1654, the Schout represents that he has found drinking-clubs on various nights at the house of Jan Peck, with dancing and entertainment of disorderly people; "also tapping during Preaching, and that there was great noise made by drunkards, especially on Sunday, at this house, so that he was obliged to remove one to jail in a cart, which was a most scandalous affair." Jan did not appear; so the court decided "on account of his disorderly house-keeping and evil life tippling, dancing, gaming and other irregularities, together with tapping at night and on Sunday during preaching to annul his license." Justice, however, was very tender-hearted at that day in such cases, for when Jan wrote that "he is burthened with a houseful of children and more besides," the court, considering that he was an old burgher, granted permission to resume on condition of future good behavior.

The Schout accused Hans Styn of having tapped on Sunday during divine service, and said that people had been fighting in his house, and wounded each other as appears by the blood which was found there. He requested that Styn's business shall be stopped and he be fined. Defendant acknowledged to have tapped on Sunday, but for none except strangers, who came to eat their usual Sunday meal without having been drunk, or having, to his knowledge, been fighting, or wounded each other.

In 1658, Andrew Vrydach, mason, for being intoxicated and fighting during divine service, was sentenced to lose six months' wages, and to stand sentinel for a like period; Ralph Turner for a similar offense had to stand sentry for six hours a day on six consecutive days with two muskets on his shoulders. Hendrick Assueros was fined for selling liquor to sundry persons, and permitting them to play ninepins during divine service. Paulus Turck was fined one rix-dollar for playing ninepins on Sunday.

Nicasius de Silla prosecutes Dirck Braeck " for that the defendant on last Sunday afternoon during the sermon tapped for and gave drink to 3 or 4 different persons. Defendant denies the same; says he only treated Nicolaes Vareth, Cornelis Aersen and Ide van Vorst and their wives to a drink of beer, through friendship and good neighbourhood without taking a penny therefor, as they did him many favours heretofore when after his cattle." This being a first offense, the defendant was warned and discharged.

It seems that while the masters were being entertained to a drink of beer by Mr. Braeck, their servants were taking advantage of their absence to enjoy themselves also. De Silla sues Cornelis Aersen and Ide van Vorst " For that their servantmen raced on last Sunday evening after the Sermon, within the City with horses and wagons and much noise and singing, from which great damage and disaster might have arisen. Concludes, therefore, that defendants, or their servants be condemned each in the fine of £4 Flemish." The defendants acknowledged that their servants did race on the previous Sunday within the city, but contended that they had no knowledge that any damage was caused thereby, or that the same was forbidden by ordinance. The court, considering the accidents that might have occurred, and the serious consequences of the same unless provision be made against it, fined the defendants, Cornelis Aersen and Ide van Vorst, for the fault committed by their servants, three guilders each; and ordered, further, "that they shall hereafter watch themselves and their people, so that all dangers and irregularities be prevented; else other disposition shall be made therein."

Andrees Rees's wife was accused of having ninepins at her house on Sunday during preaching, and the can and the glass stood on the table. Andrees says he was not at home, but on the watch, and that there were no ninepins at his house, nor can the plaintiff say that he saw drinking at his house during the preaching. Mrs. Rees " denies that there was any nine pins or drinking at her house, saying that some came to her house, who said that Church was out, and that one had a pin and the other a bowl in the hand, but they did not play. The Schout states that defendant's wife said she did not know but Church was out, and offered to compound with the Schout." Perhaps the good-wife did not offer the officer enough. Be that as it may, she was fined six guilders.

Jan Schryver was accused of having tapped half an hour after evening bell ring; he pleaded that it was impossible to drive the people out of the house so precisely, and half an hour passed easily by, before each one had paid his money. Nevertheless, he was fined twelve guilders. When Maria Peck was summoned for having tapped after nine o'clock, she denied it, saying that two sat in her house, who counted their money which she owed them, and she did not tap a drop. Peter Pia was accused of tapping on Sunday after the watch was set and six persons were at his house; the Schout demanded twenty-five florins' fine and six guilders for each person. Peter explained that there were three at his house who were standing up to leave. He was let off.

On June 27, 1661, Hendrik Assueros was fined for selling liquor and permitting ninepins playing during divine service. In 1662, "Andries Joghimsen denies having tapped on Sunday during preaching to negroes; and swears that he gave no drink directly or indirectly, himself or by his wife, at the time when Steenwyck's negro played the Jewsharp at Govert Loockerman's." He was excused.

In many of the low taverns, especially those frequented by the soldiers and sailors, drinking-bouts often terminated in drunken brawls and fighting with fists, knives, cutlasses, and pikes, sometimes with fatal results. Thus, in July, 1648, Abraham Pietersen's tavern was closed by the authorities on account of a man named Gerrit Clomp having been killed there. When closing-time arrived, and the tap-rooms disgorged their drunken patrons, the streets were often the scenes of riotous conduct, such as breaking windows and lamps, breaking into inoffensive citizens' houses to demand drink, and assaulting anybody who objected to their violence. Proceedings against night-brawlers frequently occur in the Court Records.

Even in the better class of taverns quarrels, assaults, and stabbing affrays were not uncommon among the class of citizens who patronized them, — sea-captains, the Company's officers and servants, and burghers who, except when under the influence of liquor, were usually peacefully inclined. The best tavern in the city was not exempt from such scenes, as we have seen. In 1647, a customer named Symon Root, who lost his

A TAVERN BRAWL.
ADRIAEN BROUWER

TAVERNS AND EXCISE LAWS

right ear " in a broil at the great Tavern," applied to the Council, and received a certificate reciting the fact. This was necessary when he traveled abroad, where the loss might have been attributed to a crime, committed here or elsewhere, the punishment of which was ear cropping or boring.

Many examples might be given of the excesses committed by the frequenters of taverns; but the following will suffice. On Aug. 8, 1644, Peter Wolphersen sued three soldiers for cutting his wainscot with their cutlasses. On pleading guilty, two of them were sentenced to ride the Wooden Horse for three hours; and the third, it being his second offense, had to stand three hours under the gallows, with a cutlass in his hand. In 1660, Frans Janzen and Abel Hardenbroeck were fined twenty guilders each because they " at night and at unseasonable hours in company with some soldiers created an uproar and great insolence in the street by breaking windows."

Typical tavern interiors of the period face pages 266 and 288.

CHAPTER XIII

SPORTS, FESTIVALS, AND PASTIMES

IN the Seventeenth Century, the majority of people were fond of games that required violent exercise, such as disc-throwing and all varieties of ball games. Noblemen, burghers, and peasants shared this taste. Games of "short ball," "long ball," balls driven through gates or wickets, balls thrown against a stake, balls struck by the gloved or ungloved hand, racket, stick, club, or mallet, subject to various rules and known under various names, such as tennis, golf, paille-maille, bowls, skittles, ninepins, hockey, etc., were favorite pastimes with the New Netherlanders.

The game of *Kaetsen* was played by striking the ball against a post for the adversary to drive it back after its rebound. Sometimes the ball was solid, filled with horsehair, and struck with a club or racket, and sometimes a soft hollow ball struck by the hand or fist was used. In the early days it was a nobleman's game. The ball court for this game occupied a pretty large square, the larger the space the better. Before the game began, a tree, wall, or post was selected for the goal. The citizens and farmers also enjoyed themselves at these games, but they were so noisy that they were not allowed in churchyards or convent grounds. In Dordrecht there was a city golf-link. In the Seventeenth Century, when golf became a national game, the links were made outside of the cities, in the neighborhood of which gradually taverns were erected, which bought or rented the courts or links. The ball was struck with the bare palm; but those who had tender hands wore thick double gloves, while some persons, in order to strike a still stronger blow, strengthened the inside of the gloves with cord. The women used a kind of racket made of netting with a handle at the end; and a lighter kind of ball was made for their use.

The *Klos,* or *Klootbaan,* was a game of princes in the Middle Ages, but during the Seventeenth Century it was a burgher's game, and finally descended to the farmer class. At the end of a long alley two iron staves or pieces of wood were fastened in the ground and made to join at the top so as to form a sort of gate, and through this gate, from the end of the alley and at a set distance, the player had to throw a round disc. If he missed, he had to take up the disc where it landed and throw until he hit one of the posts, which counted one. Throwing through the gate counted two; and this continued until one of the players had reached the number of twelve, or any other number agreed upon.

Not less primitive, but certainly not less liked, was the kingpin or skittle game, or pin bowling, — called *jeu de quille* in French, and derived, according to Du Cange, from the old Dutch word "bell" or "clock," as the pins were wide at the bottom and more or less in the shape of a bell. In the earliest accounts of the Counts of Holland this game is mentioned, and a number of early authors show how popular it was with knights and nobles. In the Seventeenth Century, there was hardly a tavern without a wooden or stone platform where the game of skittles could be played. Sometimes there were covered alleys with the nine pyramid-shaped pins, one of which was provided with a knob or even a crown which was called the kingpin.

These were often very heavy, and to knock them down with the disc required a strong arm. Children had toy games then as now. The single disc game was also a favorite pastime. This was the rolling of a disc on its rim over a certain space of ground. Cleverly thrown, it would roll a long distance. When it fell, it was thrown again. He who covered the most ground, in a certain number of throws, while the disc rolled upright won the game. This game was generally played in winter on the ice, and also by the fishermen on the sands, where the smooth surface afforded a fine playing-ground.

Prizes were offered for "Clubbing the Cat." This game generally took place on the square in front of the inn, or on the bowling-green, where from two heavy spiles driven into the ground a strong rope was stretched. In the centre of the rope hung a lightly cooped barrel in which was a live cat. At the appointed hour all who wished to throw the club gave their names, and paid an entrance fee. It was also agreed that the winner should pay for three or four bottles of wine, and the landlord gave each of the players a bottle. When a sufficient number of players had entered, the name and number of each was written on a board with chalk, and drawing took place. Then a line was drawn on the ground or a long pole was laid down to show the distance from which the "throwing" was allowed. Now number one stepped forward with his club, which he threw with great force at the barrel. The winner was he who broke the cask and let the cat escape. Sometimes the cat, too dazed or frightened to jump out of the barrel when it was split open, only fell out. In every case the winner was always he whose throw made the cat leave the barrel; and as soon as the cat was out, it was chased, and he who caught it got a bottle

SPORTS, FESTIVALS, AND PASTIMES

of wine as a prize. Sometimes a peacock or goose was used; and sometimes, instead of a barrel, the bird was simply tied to a rope and killed.

Another favorite game was "Pulling the Goose." A goose with its head well greased was fastened to a rope that was stretched across a road, and the sport was for a man to try to catch the bird by the head and carry it off as he rode on horseback at a gallop or drove beneath the bird in a cart going at full speed. This was also called "Riding the Goose." A variation of the game was made by stretching the rope across a ditch or canal or stream, under which a boat was swiftly rowed, and the man, standing on a plank, tried to carry off the bird in the same way, as shown in the illustration facing page 296. If he missed, the plank tipped and he fell into the water; and then he had to swim back to the boat and repeat the attempt. There were always several contestants, and the game was extremely popular. It belonged especially to the Shrove Tuesday pastimes, and was frequently prohibited in New Amsterdam and Albany. Stuyvesant called it "an unprofitable, heathenish and Popish festival and a pernicious custom," and prohibited it, but some people persisted in Pulling the Goose and were fined and imprisoned in consequence, "in order to prevent more sins, debaucheries and calamities." On Feb. 19, 1654, Harmen Smeman and divers farm servants were examined on a charge of "Plucking the Goose," and fines were imposed. Two others were condemned to imprisonment for the same offense and for threatening the Director-General. At the request of the Burgomasters and Schepens, the two prisoners were released from confinement two days later.

The prosecution of these men for Pulling the Goose caused friction between the upper and lower court.

The story is told in the following extract from the records, Feb. 16, 1654:

The Hon. Director General has reported to the Council that both the Burgomasters and the majority of the Schepens appeared before his Honor on the 25th Instant, representing themselves aggrieved by the Director General and Council having without their knowledge interdicted and forbidden certain farmers' servants to ride the goose on the feast of Bacchus at Shrove-tide for reasons the Director General and Council thereunto moving. Besides its never having been practised here in their time, it is moreover altogether unprofitable, unnecessary and censurable for subjects and neighbours to celebrate such pagan and popish feasts and to practise such evil customs in this Country, even though they may be tolerated and looked at through the fingers in some places in Fatherland. Which interdict and prohibition was by the Court Messenger Claes van Elsland served on the farmers' servants the day before the act, who, notwithstanding such service, nevertheless in contempt of the supreme authority, violated the same. Whereupon, some delinquents were legally cited and summoned before the Director General and Council by their Fiscal to be examined and mulcted for their contempt as may be proper. Two or three of them behaving in an insolent and contumacious manner, threatening, cursing, deriding and laughing at the chief magistracy were therefore, as is customary committed to prison, by which the Burgomasters and Schepens esteem themselves particularly aggrieved in their quality, because the Director General and Council have done so without their consent and knowledge; as if we can issue no order or forbid no rabble to celebrate the feast of Bacchus without the knowledge, advice and consent of Burgomasters and Schepens, much less have power to correct such persons as transgress the Christian and Holy Commandment, without the cognizance and consent of an Inferior Court of Justice.

The Director General and Council appreciating their

SPORTS, FESTIVALS, AND PASTIMES

office, authority and commission better than others, hereby notify the Burgomasters and Schepens that the establishing of an Inferior Court of Justice under the name and title of Schout, Burgomasters and Schepens or Commissaries, does in no wise infringe on or diminish the power and authority of the Director General and Council to enact any Ordinances or issue particular interdicts, especially those which tend to the glory of God, the best interests of the inhabitants, or will prevent more sins, scandals, debaucheries and crimes, and properly correct, fine and punish obstinate transgressors. What is solely the qualification of Schout, Burgomasters and Schepens, and for what purpose they are appointed, appear sufficiently from the Instructions given to them, by which they have to abide and conform themselves, without henceforth troubling and tormenting the Inspector General individually about any enacted ordinance, law or order, penalty or punishment issued and executed against and concerning the contraveners thereof by previous resolution of the Director General and Council.

The common people were not inclined tamely to submit to interference with their pleasures, for, on Feb. 8, 1655:

Corn[s] van Tienhoven informed the Court that he had been informed that the country people intended *Riding the Goose* again as they did last year, and enquired therefore if their worships would do anything to oppose it; that it was forbidden by resolution of the Supreme Councillors and prevented. Therefore it was decided that the Fiscal Tienhoven shall, *ex officio*, seasonably declare the same to be illegal.

On Feb. 26, 1658, an order was issued refusing permission to the farmers and their men in the vicinity of New Amsterdam to "pull the goose."

Cats and hares were also used for this cruel sport,

as we learn from a proclamation at Albany in 1677, "prohibiting all misdemeanors which have occurred here on Shrove Tuesday, viz., Riding at a goose, cat, hare, etc., etc., on a penalty of £25 seawan."

Not less popular was the game called "bird cutting." A cock, a duck, or any other bird, was hung head downwards from a rope, and the contestants were blindfolded and placed at a certain distance from the bird. The game was to cut off the bird's head; and whoever was lucky enough to do so, received the bird as a prize.

The fondness of the Dutch for archery and shooting with the crossbow is too well known for detailed description of their shooting-matches and galleries. The sport was a favorite one in New Amsterdam. We learn that on June 16, 1644, Henry Hewit sued Gerrit Jacobson for destroying his eye with an arrow. Jacobson pleaded that more persons than he were shooting arrows at the time; and the next court day he produced two witnesses who were discharging arrows, but they denied having hit the plaintiff.

The vast amount of game afforded the sportsman great opportunity for pleasure. The woods were full of birds and deer, and the marshes of water-fowl. It would seem that birds were plentiful in the city itself, for it is ordered, on Oct. 9, 1652, that guns are not to be fired at partridges or other game within the limits of the city.

The following prohibition on June 12, 1657, shows how fond the New Amsterdam carters were of racing:

> No person shall gallop or race within the gates and walls of this city with any wagon, cart, or sleigh, and no driver shall sit on such, whether drawn by oxen or horses, but walk alongside the same; and if he shall be found sitting or standing thereon, he shall pay a fine of

PULLING THE GOOSE

From an old print

one pound Flemish, and be interdicted six weeks from using such vehicle and the draught cattle thereof.

Cards, chess, backgammon, dice-throwing, were among the pleasures of the age; billiards, too, were not unknown. Francis Hulin has one "old billiard table" (£3) in 1702. Cards appear in many of the inventories and lists of shop-goods. Lawrence Deldyke had three gross and two dozen cards in 1692, and John Coesart one hundred and eighty-seven packs of cards of various qualities in 1700.

Not only were games indulged in at home and at taverns, but there were special gaming-houses. In 1681, for instance, John Tudor was fined by the Mayor's Court for keeping a gaming-house. A picture by Jan Steen and variously known as *The Parrot Cage* and the *Backgammon Players* faces page 202.

A game that was doubtless indulged in, especially in the early days, was one spoken of by De Rasières in 1626, which he saw the Indians play:

They are very fond of a game they call *senneca*, played with some round rushes, similar to the Spanish feather-grass which they understand how to shuffle and deal as though they were playing with cards; and they win from each other all that they possess.

Saint Nicholas was the patron saint of New Amsterdam. The choice was most appropriate, for he was the patron of sailors and all Dutch trading-towns. He was the patron of Amsterdam and other emporiums of Dutch trade. The church in the Fort bore his name, and his festival was celebrated here with as much fervor as at home. Saint Nicholas Eve (December 5) was particularly a children's holiday, and was anticipated by them with feelings of delight and curiosity, for the good children were always rewarded with presents in their shoes, cakes and sweetmeats, while the naughty ones received a rod or switch. Great preparations were made for the festival. Nothing was more important than the Saint Nicholas cake, or bread, sometimes called "Saint Claes baking." Young people assembled at various houses to paste gold and silver leaf on these Saint Nicholas cakes, — an amusement called cake-pasting (*koek-plakken*), after which usually followed a supper, dancing, and a frolic. Many songs were sung on these occasions, among which was the following:

> Sancte Claus goed heijlig Man!
> Trek uw beste tabaert an,
> Reis daer me'e na Amsterdam,
> Van Amsterdam na Spanje,
> Daer appelen van Oranje,
> Daer appelen van Granaten,
> Die rollen door de straten.
> Sancte Claus, mijn goeden vriend,
> Ik heb u allen tijd gediend!
> Wilt u my nu wat geven,
> Dan dien ik u al mijn leven.

> Santa Claus, good holy man!
> Put on your tabard, the best you can,
> Go clad in it to Amsterdam.
> From Amsterdam then go to Spain.
> There golden apples
> And also pomegranates
> Roll through the streets.
> Santa Claus, my dear good friend,
> I have always served you;
> If you will now give me something,
> I will serve you all my life long.

This verse is still sung by the children of Holland. Another ran:

> Saint Nicholas, Bishop, put your tall hat on, give the good children something sweet, and give the bad ones a spanking.

SPORTS, FESTIVALS, AND PASTIMES

Another was:

SINTER KLAAS, BISSCHOP

Zet je hooge muts op;
Trek je langen tabbaard aan,
Rydt er mêe naar Amsterdam;
Amsterdam en Spanje,
Appeltjes van Oranje;
Appeltjes van de boomen.
Ryke, ryke Oome;
Ryke, ryke juffertjes
Dragen lange mouwen;
Hansje willen wy trouwen,
Hansje die sprong over de sloot;
Onze Hans die brak Zijn poot,
    Tien pond suiker!
    Leg de lepel
    Ob de ketel;
Brandewyn met suiker!

SANTA CLAUS, BISHOP

Put your high cap on;
Put your long tabard on,
Ride with it to Amsterdam;
Amsterdam and Spain,
Apples of Orange;
Apples from the trees,
Rich, rich uncle;
Rich, rich damsels
Wearing long sleeves;
Little Hans will you marry me?
Little Hans he jumped over the ditch;
Our Hans he broke his leg.
    Ten pounds of sugar!
    Lay the spoon
    Upon the kettle;
Brandywine with sugar.

Returning to their homes, or when their guests had gone, from the cake-pasting, the children placed their wooden shoes (*klompen*) outside of the bedroom door or by the side of the chimney. Saint Nicholas was supposed to fill these with presents.

Saint Nicholas Eve has always been a favorite subject with the Little Dutch Masters. Jan Steen painted two graphic pictures, one of which faces this page. The painter himself and his family are represented. The interest centres in the little girl, who has a pail full of toys on her left arm while she holds in her hands a doll dressed in the garb of the saint with halo on its head, and her older brother, who is crying because his shoe contains a switch, which his sister is handing to him. His grandmother is beckoning to him in the distance; she may have something hidden behind the curtains of the bed. A younger brother, who is about to ride on his father's stick, points to the unhappy child with heartless derision. Another son is explaining to a baby and a younger brother how Saint Nicholas came down the chimney. By the side of Vrouw Steen is a table filled with sweets and cakes, and a basket of cakes, Saint Nicholas bread, and wafers is standing on the floor. Leaning against the table is a large cake which has been decorated by the cake-pasters with figures of cocks.

Among the special sweets belonging to the Saint Nicholas festival, *marsepein* (marchpane) or almond-paste held a conspicuous place.

A great many confections were undoubtedly imported, but the bakers and cooks in New Amsterdam were skilful, and ceremonial cakes and breads were made here for every festival. That such delicacies were made in rich houses we know from the kitchen utensils mentioned in the inventories; for instance, Cornelis Steenwyck had "tin ware to bake sugar cakes" and a "marsepyn pan" worth £2. Books of gold leaf and boxes of gold leaf are often found in the New Amsterdam inventories, doubtless for the decoration of holiday cakes, Twelfth Night beans, and sugar

ST. NICHOLAS EVE
JAN STEEN

plums. Mrs. Drisius and Mrs. Van Varick, for instance, each had a parcel of leaf gold. Presents were exchanged on Saint Nicholas Eve by the children of the rich; and all the poor of the city — widows, orphans, and helpless old people — were generously remembered by a good meal.

The next festivals to come were Christmas, New Year's Day, and Twelfth Night or Three Kings' Evening. Little business was transacted during the holiday season. From a proclamation issued in December, 1655, we read:

Whereas Christmas is at hand, the Court resolve and order that, according to the custom of our Fatherland, no ordinary Court day, or meeting shall be held for eight days after Christmas.

New Year's Day partook somewhat of the character of Sunday and days of special Thanksgiving. Although visits were exchanged, the day was strictly observed, and the same ordinances were issued in Stuyvesant's time for New Year's and May Day. For instance, that issued in December, 1655, reads:

Whereas experience has manifested and shown us, that on New Year's and May days much drunkenness and other irregularities are committed besides other sorrowful accidents such as woundings frequently arising therefrom, by Firing, May planting, and Carousing, in addition to the unnecessary waste of powder, to prevent which for the future, the Director General and Council expressly forbid that from now henceforward there shall be, within this Province of New Netherland on New Years or May Days, any Firing of Guns, or any Planting of May Poles, or any beating of Drums, or any treating with Brandy, wine or Beer; and all such and greater dangers and mischiefs to prevent, a fine of twelve guilders shall be imposed for the first offence; double for the second, and an arbitrary Correction for the third — to wit one third for the poor, and one third for the Officer and one third for the Informer.

On Jan. 27, 1656, Governor Stuyvesant proclaimed a day of fasting and prayer for God's blessing protection and prosperity in trade and agriculture but principally for a righteous and thankful use of his blessings and benefits. The which the better to observe and practise with greater unanimity, We interdict and forbid, on the aforesaid day of Fasting and Prayer during Divine Service, all labour, Tennis-playing Ball-playing, Hunting, Fishing, Travelling, Ploughing, Sowing, Mowing and other unlawful games as Gambling and Drunkenness, on pain of arbitrary correction and punishment already enacted against the same.

On Dec. 28, 1656, the former prohibition against any person shooting or drumming, etc., on New Year's Day, or planting May-poles on May day, was renewed.

The next festival on the calendar was Twelfth Night, or Three Kings' Night (January 6). On this day young people and children were fond of dancing around three candles placed in the ground, one of which was black, called the "Moor," or "Melkert," from Melchior, according to tradition King of Kranganor. This candle-jumping often occasioned fire and other accidents, and was finally forbidden; but, like all other prohibited games, it was frequently indulged in. While the children were amusing themselves in the streets in this way, the housewives were busy preparing the great Twelfth Night Cake, which neighbors and friends had been invited to share, and in which a gilded bean was placed. He who got the bean in his slice was king of the revels. There were other means employed to elect the king: sometimes three pieces of money were baked in the cake, and he who got the one with a cross on it was the king for the evening. The bean-king was called Beltsasar (Balthazar) and held a mock court, receiving the homage of all present. The evening always ended in merry-making, with plenty of good cheer.

The youths enjoyed a different kind of amusement. They chose three kings, dressed two of them in white and one in black, rubbed the face of the latter with soot, and gave each of them a paper star in their hands with a lighted candle behind it (see facing page 304). Then they accompanied the trio, singing songs to fit the occasion, to the taverns, where they treated each other to beer with sugar and oil-fritters.

Although the Dutch Reformed Church effaced everything that savored of Roman Catholicism, it was hard to suppress festivals that having had their origin in pagan celebrations were seasons beloved of the people. Among these was Shrove Tuesday, which supplanted the heathen *Lupercalia,* known later under the name of *Spurcalia in Februario.* Known in Holland and her colonies by the name *Vasten avond* (evening before fasting), Shrove Tuesday was celebrated, not as a religious feast, but as an evening of wild extravagance. It was the merriest evening in the year. In Holland on this day men of wealth and rank received their rents from their tenants, their suite appeared in new clothes, and the burgomasters made their appearance dressed in the full regalia of their dignity. More or less costly presents were exchanged, and the cities gave dinners to their magistrates and nobles; while the burghers entertained their friends and blood relations. The evening passed in revelry.

One of the Shrove Tuesday customs was a children's

masquerade. They walked through the streets with the *rommel-pot*, a pot covered with a tightly stretched bladder, in the centre of which was a hole in which a stick was tightly jammed. When this stick was moved up and down, it made a dull, rumbling noise. The children went from door to door rattling the pot and singing the following verse:

> 'k Heb zoo lang met de foekepot geloopen,
> Nog geen geld om brood te koopen,
>   Haringpakkerij, haringpakkerij!
> Geef me een oortje, dan ga ik voorbij!
>
> I've run so long with the rumbling-pot
> And have as yet got no money to buy bread,
>   Herring-packery, herring-packery,
> Give me a penny and I'll go by!

They wore masks and false faces and sometimes "a devil's suit of clothes." This masking, dressing up, and begging for pennies still survives in New York at Thanksgiving Day. Another favorite Shrove Tuesday amusement was "Riding the Goose" (see page 296).

A petition to restrict the Shrovetide festivities from the Consistory of Wildwyck on Feb. 12, 1664, reads as follows:

The Consistory here, moved by their consciences and their duty as officers, petition the Magistrates of this place with all proper humility, that the public, sinful and scandalous Baccanalian days of Shrovetide (descended from the Heathen from their idol Bacchus, the God of wine and drunkenness: being also a leaven of Papacy, which the Apostle, 1 Cor. 5, has warned us to cast off), which are near at hand, may be prohibited in this place by proper Placards from you, that we, by its publication and reproof may eradicate this abomination, and thereby through the Grace and Blessings of God, we, each of us,

From an old print

THREE KINGS' EVENING
(TWELFTH NIGHT)

SPORTS, FESTIVALS, AND PASTIMES

may do the good which will come of it to this place, and the souls and bodies of its inhabitants, the more as we live in such sorrowful days of God's wrath upon us in this place for our sins. If people will still indulge in the pleasures of such scandalous sins as those of Shrovetide, they will more and more provoke God and bring his wrath on us again, for His rod is yet over us, and his punishment of war yet afflicts us; yea, and will thus yet further oppress this land and its inhabitants. Shall they then rolick in their sins while the whole land weeps and make merry when we are every month called to sorrow, wailing and lamentation?

Waffles, rice-pudding, and pancakes were the special dishes enjoyed on this day.

The ancient celebration of the awakening of spring was held on May Day. This was the time when lovers' vows were made and floral festivals were held. Early in the morning, young people went out to gather boughs and blossoms with which they decorated their houses and the tall May-pole, which was also wreathed with ribbons. Around this they danced on the green and drank the spiced May-wine. The May-pole was in some towns in Holland and England felled by the youths and brought to the village green drawn by oxen; in others a permanent May-pole stood on the village green. There was a permanent May-pole on the Merry Mount in the Fort, as we learn from the following record of June 10, 1645, when " William Gerritson pleaded guilty to singing a defamatory song against the Rev. Francis Douty and his daughter." He was sentenced " to stand bound to the Maypole in the Fort with two rods around his neck, and the libel over his head until conclusion of the sermon; and should he ever sing the song again to be flogged and banished." May-poles, however, were planted for every season, and were the occasion of so much hilarity that in December, 1655, the following ordinance was passed:

Whereas experience has shown and taught us that on New Year's Days and on May-days, from the firing of guns and planting May-poles and drunken drinking, there have resulted unnecessary waste of powder, much drunkenness, and other insolent practices, together with other lamentable accidents and bruises that generally arise therefrom. Therefore, in order to prevent these, it is hereby expressly ordered by the Director-General and the Councillors, that, from this time forth, within this Province of New Netherland, on the New-Year and May-days, there shall be no firing, nor May-poles planted; nor shall there be any beating of the drum; nor shall there be on the occasion, any Wines, Brandywines, or Beer dealt out.

May-Day jollity continued, however; and the Maypole continued to be a gathering point for the merrymakers, for, five years later, on Dec. 31, 1660, we read:

This date is renewed the Placard against firing on New Year's Day, or planting Maypoles on May day, or making a present of any drink to any person for that purpose.

One of the customs was to send little cards decorated with green sprays to friends, and gifts of flowers and knick-knacks were also exchanged. Dances often took place in the evening, and there was much drinking in the taverns. Those in New Amsterdam who came from some parts of Holland rose early on May Day, and, climbing the roofs of houses in which young girls dwelt, would place green boughs or dead twigs there, and sometimes, as a joke, a straw man. Not unfrequently they would go into the fields and procure all the scarecrows they could find and put them on the roofs of the old maids' homes. A May-pole decorated with rags was sometimes used to insult a bride and groom (see page 234). Some people planted a May-tree, and took great care of it and hung it with garlands, flowers, and other devices and ribbons, and also fastened verses on the tree for particular persons.

Pinkster, or Whitsuntide, was also a time of pleasure. During the period before the Reformation, on Whitsuntide, white pigeons, emblems of the Holy Spirit, were let loose in the church. The next day was given up to revelry. White and gilt pigeons were the aim of the archers, and priests and scholars gave scriptural plays in the market-places and churchyards, in which the "white dove" always had a prominent part. Later these religious plays were followed by a farce. The Reformation prohibited a great many of these abuses; but these holidays had become so entirely a part of the life of the people that neither Luther nor Calvin, neither church nor civic threatenings, could put a stop to them. It is true that no consecrated doves nor pigeons were brought to the church in New Amsterdam, but processions, bird-shooting, and the Whitsuntide dances, singing and general merry-making were in vogue. One of the processions was that of the "Whitsuntide Flower." With wreaths of green and flowers woven in their flowing hair, dressed in white and each carrying in her hand a May-branch twined with leaves and flowers and decorated with gold or silver bows, the young maidens walked through the streets, escorting the Whitsuntide bride or "Flower bride," the queen of the feast, dressed and ornamented at the public expense. One of the group went around the various doors and collected the gifts which were spent in excesses in the evening. These excesses were so great, and the songs were of so light a character, that eventually government was compelled to stop the processions of the Whitsuntide bride, at a fine of a golden florin for every child that carried the May-branch on that day.

The great autumn festival was Saint Martin's Eve. Saint Martin enjoyed great popularity. Numerous churches, chapels, altars, and villages bore his name in Holland, and an oath taken on his name was as sacred as " by God's Faith," " by my father's soul," " by the Emperor's head," etc. His day, November 11, became a day of peculiar veneration, extravagance, and excess. No one could be induced to stay near a crossroad on Saint Martin's Eve. Terrible things were heard and seen there, for it was as if Hell had let loose its occupants. Evil spirits roamed around in company of those who had sold their souls to Satan for money or other gifts, on condition of wearing a werewolf shirt on Saint John's or Saint Martin's Eve. Then sounded the horn blasts of wild hunters. No cloister was so strict, no hovel so poor, but had its feast. One Dutch dish on this festival was pancakes; another, served for a second course, was a dish of medlars; but the principal dish was the world-renowned " Saint Martin's goose," which was found on every table. He who had not eaten goose had not celebrated the day, and the goose graced the board of the aristocrat and was found on the dimly lighted table of the laborer. Surrounded with burning candles, it was the centre of attraction in the middle of the table, and after partaking of the toothsome roast, then — the old superstitions were observed with a heathenish custom — the breastbone was examined to see whether the softness or hardness of it gave signs of a mild or severe winter, and if much snow could be expected. Much has been written about the origin of the Saint Martin's goose; but the most acceptable explanation is

SPORTS ON THE ICE

From an old print

that Saint Martin, as the probable representative of the God Ullr, to whom a goose was sacrificed, was remembered by slaughtering one in his memory, and from this the prophetic qualities of the bird may be derived. The goose was accompanied by the " must " (new wine), which was drunk on the evening of the 11th of November to the singing of the verse

> Saint Martin, Saint Martin;
> To-day the Must, To-morrow Wine.

Verses were prepared by the schoolmasters, and translated from the Latin to be sung by their pupils.

In the evening Saint Martin's fires were burned. The day on which this happened was also called " Saint-Martin-shake-the-basket-day." This comes from the custom of shaking a basket of chestnuts and other nuts slowly in the bonfire, and grabbing them at the risk of burning the hands.

In addition to the merry-making and ceremonies belonging to stated festivals, the Dutch burghers and their families, particularly the youths and maidens, had many simple pleasures.

The Dutch, like the English, were great lovers of out-of-door life and games; and many excuses were made for trips to the country and for excursions and picnics of all kinds by both boat and wagon. In a sailboat, rowboat, or wagon the merry party would travel in the bright days of spring and summer to some pleasure resort on the Hudson or the East River, Harlem, Long Island, or Staten Island. Sunday was the favorite day for these excursions in New Amsterdam, as it was in Holland, but many persons disapproved of spending the Lord's Day in holiday-making.

As a rule the merry-makers started early in the morning and took breakfast at some wayside tavern or country-seat. This consisted of delicious bread and butter, crisp biscuits, luscious strawberries or cherries, sweet and sour cream, old and new cheese, and wine. After breakfast the company again entered the wagon or boat, and drove or sailed farther. Sometimes they would stop in the fields or woods and make wreaths of the long grasses and flowers they plucked, or gather wild-flowers to carry home. They sang, they danced, they played games, and they ate heartily. If the noonday meal was not eaten in a tavern, baskets of provisions were carried along for an *al fresco* lunch. If the merry-makers went to the shore, they amused themselves with the game of sea-carrying (*zee-dragen*). There was no more dangerous game than this " Carrying into the Sea." The young man took a girl in his arms and walked with her into the sea until the water came over his high boots, and then he carried her back again into the dunes, where he rolled her over and " salted her with sand." This, according to some writers, was done with the idea of the young man finding out what kind of a temper his sweetheart had; and if she did not lose it or become angry, he was sure of having a good and patient wife. How much truth there is in this can be guessed when many times the girls would walk along the sands of the seashore and ask of their escorts "if there was no water in the sea." Many a tear was shed on account of this *zee-dragen*, and many a sad accident resulted from it.

Sometimes, particularly when the party went by boat, a fish dinner or supper was ordered at a tavern some distance from town. In this case a large fish surrounded with parsley and accompanied by a fine Dutch sauce of melted butter and vinegar occupied the center of the table. After this, fruit, tastefully decorated with vine leaves, was served.

SPORTS, FESTIVALS, AND PASTIMES

No matter where they went or what they did, kissing formed no small part of the day's pleasure and entertainment. The Dutch were as fond of love-making as any other nation; and historians admit that the Dutchman deserves his nickname of the " kissing Dutchman." Kissing is constantly referred to in the poems of the period, and the song-books are full of allusions to it. Kissing shepherds and shepherdesses appear in all the Arcadias, and even the most serious poets liked to write about it. When rising in the morning, retiring at night, leaving the house to go to work and returning from it, people used to salute with a kiss. A family or state visit began and ended with kissing. If a young man took his girl from her home to go out, he greeted her with a kiss; did he take her home after the outing, a kiss was given at parting. A kiss was the greeting of honest friendship; a kiss with honor would harm nobody; a little kiss was no sin!

There were few games in which kissing did not have a part, and many were the excuses invented during the country excursions. When the pleasure-wagon crossed a bridge and the horse walked slowly, not needing the attention of the driver, a kiss was quickly given and never resented. This custom was greatly in vogue in New Amsterdam, and very often parties drove towards Hellgate, because in this neighborhood and over a little stream called the Tamkill, emptying into the East River nearly opposite Blackwell's Island, was the famous " Kissing Bridge," in driving over which every one was at liberty to salute the lady.

In the winter sleighs took the place of wagons, and many were the excursions both by night and day. Winter pleasures were greatly enjoyed in New Amsterdam. The Dutch brought with them their love of skating and sleighing and games that were played upon the ice, such as hockey and golf. Not only were the Hudson and the East Rivers often alive with skaters, who went from shore to shore or from settlement to settlement on business errands, but the ponds and canals of New Amsterdam were filled with busy or merry people. The Collect was a favorite spot for the joyous crowds of young and old. When the ice was thick enough, everybody put on skates — men, women, and children, young and old — and were soon skimming over the shining surface like birds, or flying like the sails of a windmill. The best skates came from Volendam, but there were many varieties. Generally speaking, they were made of iron and wood, some longer than the foot and some exactly its length. Some people screwed their skates to their boots; others fastened them with leather straps (see facing page 308).

When once these were on, the heavy and somewhat clumsy Dutch were swift, light, agile, and graceful. Many were the ways, however, of skating. Those from South Holland skated " leg over," and could make innumerable curls and figures on the ice, performing all kinds of antics and fancy skating as they pleased, skating backwards and making the alphabet as they whirled about gracefully; those from Friesland traveled like the wind, and generally won the silver or pewter cups, plates, and spoons that were offered for prizes. Women also took part in the skating-matches, and at such times the ice was as gay as a *kermis*. From far and near people came to the gathering-place, and everything was prepared for their reception. Booths were erected on the ice, and also the *Kraampje,* or tent, in which there were wooden stools and a wooden table on which stood two large bottles of Brandewyn, sugar, and tumblers, while a kettle filled with a decoction of aniseseed and milk simmered on top of a fire.

SPORTS, FESTIVALS, AND PASTIMES

Many young couples were introduced on the ice, and many were the engagements that followed a long winter. Woolley noted in his "Journal":

The diversion especially in the winter season used by the Dutch is aurigation, i. e. riding about in wagons, which is allowed by physicians to be a very healthful exercise by land. And upon the ice it's admirable to see men and women as it were flying upon their skates from place to place with markets upon their Heads and Backs.

Skaters also pushed along the sleighs that contributed no little to the brightness of the scene. Here an old lady bundled up in furs sped by in a swan, here a young girl with rosy cheeks flashed by in a blue and gilded dolphin, and here some merry children were flying over the ice in a bright boat, for the sleighs of this period were often made into fantastic shapes, such as animals, ships, fabulous monsters, or shells, carved, gilded, and brightly painted. Sometimes the sleighs were also drawn by horses. We are indebted to Madam Knight for a little glimpse of this Dutch pastime. She says:

Their Diversions in the Winter is Riding Sleys about three or four miles out of Town where they have Houses of entertainment at a place called the Bouwery, and some go to friend's houses who handsomely treat them. Mr. Burroughs carry'd his Spouse and Daughter and myself out to one Madame Dowes, a Gentlewoman that lived at a farm House, who gave us a handsome Entertainment of five or six Dishes and Choice Beer and Metheglin, Ceyder, etc., all which she said was the produce of her farm. I believe we mett 50 or 60 slays that day — they fly with great swiftness and some are so furious that they'le turn out of the path for none except a Loaden Cart. Nor do they spare for any diversion the place affords, and sociable to a degree, theyr Tables being as free to their Naybours as to themselves.

In the long winter evenings the young people of New Amsterdam frequently met and played simple games or amused themselves with music and dancing. Another pleasure was that of writing verses and painting pictures in the albums, or *juffer-bockjes* (literally, girl-books). Sometimes these were printed and illustrated, the contents being a collection of verses from famous poets, and were bound in leather or velvet with silver mounts. As a general rule, they were the gifts of young men to their sweethearts.

We know by the dancing that there must have been musical instruments, but, strange to say, they do not appear in the inventories. It would be very singular if the various forms of the lute and guitar, clavichord and spinet, violin and violoncello, that so constantly appear in the Dutch pictures of the period, did not cross the water. "Thirty knots of fiddle strings" in Lawrence Deldyke's shop, however, show that the fiddle certainly was known.

Merry-makers danced around the May-pole to the sound of the drum and horn, and without doubt the wandering fiddler played at all village festivals and before taverns, as he does in the pictures of Teniers and Ostade.

What astonishes a student is the great number of Jew's-harps found in the shops of many merchants. For instance, Dr. Jacob De Lange had seventy-two Jew's-harps, while Mr. Coesart had forty-eight dozen iron Jew's-harps and twenty-four dozen copper Jew's-harps. In 1705, Joseph Nunes had forty-two dozen at twelve pence a dozen. They were probably chiefly used by negroes.

Another indoor pleasure was the "sausage-making evening." Every citizen who could possibly afford it bought a cow and a pig in the autumn, or, if his family were too small, he shared one with a neighbor. A few days later, the animals were slaughtered — sometimes in the backyard — and hung. Guests were then bidden to come and help make the sausages, head cheese, and *rolpens* (tripe cut small and made into bags and then filled with chopped beef). While the servants were doing the roughest part of the work, the housewife and her friends stuffed and flavored the sausages and forcemeat. There was no thought of dinner that day, a slice of bread and cheese and a glass of beer were quickly taken; but in the evening, when the work was done, the table was spread with sausages and blood-puddings, and the bottle and glass circulated freely.

These animals were purchased at the market, and on market days there was always more or less excitement in the town. As soon as the gates were opened, the farmers drove their cattle to the market place, where tables with refreshments had been prepared, and in fact a miniature *kermis* was held. Some hours later the citizens came, both rich and poor, — the first accompanied by a licensed butcher to examine the cattle. He generally brought a fat bullock and a fat pig. The animals were then brought to the dwelling of the purchaser, fastened to a post in front of his house, and praised by the neighbors. A few days later the beast was slaughtered in the backyard and hung up. Guests flocked to the house and partook freely of the good cheer offered by the host.

The great event of the year was the annual cattle fair, or *kermis*, instituted, in 1641, by Director Kieft as follows:

Be it known hereby to all persons that the Director and Council of New Netherland have ordained that henceforth there shall be held annually at Fort Amsterdam a

Cattle Fair on the 15th of October and a fair for Hogs on the 1st of November. Whosoever hath anything to sell, or to buy, can regulate himself accordingly.

This, however, became of more importance under Stuyvesant's rule, for in 1648 the stranger and inhabitant were

given and granted a Weekly Market-day, to wit Monday, and annually a Free Market for ten consecutive days, which shall begin on the first Monday after Bartholomew's day, New style, corresponding to the legal Amsterdam Fair, on which weekly and annual days the Neighbour and Stranger, as well as the Inhabitant, are allowed and permitted to supply the purchaser from a Booth, by the ell, weight and measure, wholesale and retail, according to the demand and circumstances of each, in conformity to the weight, ell and measure as aforesaid, and no other.

Eleven years later (1659), special privileges were granted in order to attract a large attendance.

The Schout Burgomasters and Schepens make known that they establish for the accommodation of the public, a market for store and fat cattle, sheep, goats, hogs, bucks and such like, and to that end they mean to erect stalls and other conveniences for those who bring such animals to market. This market will be opened the 20th day of October and close the last day of November precisely in each year; during such time it shall remain a free cattle-market and no stranger shall during that time be liable to arrest or citation, but shall be permitted to attend to his business without molestation or hindrance.

It will be observed that the New Amsterdam Fair was modeled on the Fair or *Kermis* of Amsterdam. Whenever the red cross — the sign of liberty and law-

KERMIS
TENIERS

SPORTS, FESTIVALS, AND PASTIMES

lessness — was set up outside the towns of the Low Countries, every one knew that the *kermis* had begun and that he might "keep *kermis*." The decorated town-gates opened earlier than usual, and crowds passed through to give themselves up to the general joy.

Whence comes the word *kermis?* Some say it is derived from the German word *messen*, to measure, because the merchandise bought at these yearly markets was to a very great extent measured by length or sold by measure. Others declare that the word must not be read *kermis*, but *market mis*, consisting of two Latin words of the Middle Ages, *mercada*, merchandise, and *missabicum*, a part of the country where a potentiary was sent to have it under his domain or supervision; so that the word *markt*, or *merkt mis*, would mean nothing else than a solemn yearly trading. A third, and perhaps the right, explanation is that *kermis*, also called *kermesse* and *year messe*, means yearly, free, or simple Mass, — in other words, the church Mass. The deity, however, some writers object, was not God, but one's stomach. It was remembered with great pleasure that while milk pap was eaten, wine was drunk like water. The *kermis* dish, a cake or pasty cased with mustard and sugar, surrounded with large piles of biscuits, capers, and raisins, was eaten in nearly every family. In some villages the *kermis* ox was led around, decorated with wreaths of flowers. Every villager would buy his part when the ox passed his door. After all the parts had been sold, the animal was slaughtered and divided. There also were many booths where cakes were baked, and where the young people regaled themselves with hot cakes smeared with treacle or molasses, and with spiced cakes, *speculation* (a small batter cake in various designs), tea-cakes, and saffron cakes. The waffle booth was also a special feature, and at every *kermis* there was an old woman with oil-fritters. In the inns the favorite tipple was wine with sugar or white brandy with sugar, which was ladled out of a cup with a spoon, and passed around in the company. A typical *kermis* scene faces page 316.

Both church and government complained:

"The taverns, inns streets roads were witnesses of lawlessness and the committing of punishable illdeeds. There is no class in society which is not under the evil influences of the Kermis. It looks as if the Kermis causes a general change in everybody. Before and after it people are entirely different from what they appear to be while it lasts. Curiosity is the general motive power. Everybody goes about. All houses are open. Everybody is welcome. It is as if the olden time hospitality is reviving. The days are short, and the nights are for amusements. The highest classes lower themselves, severity unbinds itself, modesty blushes less, and the tenderest ears, without being hurt, listen to the grossest equivocal expressions.

Another wrote:

In the evening there are play houses open for the lowest class of people. Sometimes quite a respectable class of people will go to these houses to see how the lower classes behave, and sit and watch them, dance, with an even face, pipe in mouth, and a look of general respectability, that one would rather think they were sitting in a church instead of running after the lowest pleasures.

Under the Puritanical rule of Stuyvesant, when the *kermis* reached its height as a yearly market and festival, there was naturally not quite the same lawlessness. The mountebanks, the quack doctors, and the vagabonds were doubtless absent; but nevertheless the

SPORTS, FESTIVALS, AND PASTIMES 319

little town was gay enough. The *kermis* took place during the most delightful season of the year, when Manhattan Island enjoyed, as now, its most golden days of sunshine and its invigorating sea-breezes. Market-boats and boats of all kinds were riding at anchor and sailing or being rowed from shore to shore, while the Strand from Whitehall to Broad Street was filled with booths and tents gayly decorated with flowers, greenery, and flags. The clatter of the *rommel-pot,* the beat of the drum, the sound of the trumpet, and the cry of the vender were heard on every side. The prize cattle were greatly in evidence; but the stalls offered many other attractions to the citizens and visitors from both shores of the Hudson, from Staten Island, Long Island, New Jersey, and Connecticut. Some of them displayed clothing, cloth, linen, silk, velvets, braids, buttons, furs, laces, ribbons, gloves, neckcloths, and caps; others, watches, necklaces, and other trinkets; others, razors, scents, pomatums, and all toilet articles. There were also toy booths to attract the children; gingerbread booths, cake and pastry booths, booths for waffles and oil-fritters; booths where all the native and imported cheeses were displayed. Here too could be seen capons, quails, pigeons, ducks, chickens, wild and tame, turkeys, oysters, lobsters, crabs, and fresh and dried fish. Then there were all the vegetables in season, and dried grains for man and beast.

Puppet shows, peep shows, masqueraders, fools, and jesters were not lacking to contribute to the general merriment. The strong man, the juggler, and the conjurer gave exhibitions of their skill, and the trained bear and his leader were also in evidence. In two respects the New Amsterdam *kermis* differed from that of the old country, — the presence of the negro and the Indian. The one gave exhibitions of his proficiency in song and dance; the other brought his native wares — beads, birch-bark, baskets, blankets, and other wares — and showed his skill as acrobat, juggler, or fortune-teller.

CHAPTER XIV

MERCHANTS AND TRADE

THE Atlantic voyage of that day was an arduous undertaking. The early colonists had to endure many and often unnecessary hardships. The author of Wassenaer's *Historie van Europa* (1621–1632) says that New Netherlands is usually reached in seven or eight weeks from Amsterdam. The course lies towards the Canary Islands, thence to the Indian Islands, then towards the mainland of Virginia, steering right across, leaving in fourteen days the Bahamas on the left, and the Bermudas on the right hand.

The livestock received better treatment than the human cattle, as we learn from a description (1625) of Pieter Hulst's transport of one hundred and three head of cattle, horses, hogs, and sheep

in two ships of one hundred and forty lasts, in such a manner that they should be well foddered and attended to. Each animal had its own stall with a floor of three feet of sand; fixed as comfortably as any stall here. Each animal had its respective servant who attended to it and knew its wants so as to preserve its health, together with all suitable forage, such as oats, hay and straw, etc. What is most remarkable is, that nobody in the two ships can discover where the water is stowed for these cattle. As it was necessary to have another [ship] on that account, the above parties caused a deck to be constructed on board. Beneath this were stowed in each ship three hundred tons of fresh water which was pumped up and thus distributed among the cattle. On this deck lay the ballast and thereupon stood the horses and steers, and thus there was no waste. He added the third ship, so that, should the voyage continue longer, nothing may be wanting to the success of the expedition.

People might take passage in the Company's ships by swearing to the Articles and paying six stivers *per diem* for provisions and passage; and such as desired to eat in the cabin, twelve stivers, and had to give assistance like others in cases offensive and defensive.

The price of the passage naturally varied in accordance with the character of the accommodation. In 1638, we find the following account:

Michiel Jansen, wife and two children	fl. 140	16
Tonis Dirksen, wife, child and two servants	141	14
Jan Michiels and little boy	50	0

Many disputes over passage money had to be settled by the court. In 1656, Captain Jansen of the *St. Jacob* sued to recover board and passage money from Martin Arentsen, but the latter proved that he worked as a carpenter and seaman for his passage. The captain also sued Adam Roelantsen for payment for passage of himself and son; but lost again, as it was proved that the father was promised his passage on condition of working as a seaman; and the son was allowed his board because he said prayers. On May 16, 1668, Johannes Luyck sued Gabriel Thomsen for the balance of the passage money of himself and sister from Holland. The defendant replied that he paid for freight of himself and sister one hundred and twenty florins in silver, and agreed to pay forty guilders more in case they should be entertained in the cabin, which he had not enjoyed, and therefore the said one hundred and twenty was full payment. It was finally mutually agreed that Thomsen should pay one hundred and sixty florins in beavers, and receive the one hundred and twenty florins in silver coin back.

The names given by the Dutch to their trading-vessels are significant of their tastes, reverences, beliefs, occupations, and trades. The farm, garden, and forest are remembered in the *Milkmaid, Oak Tree, Cedar, Rose Bush, Blossom, Brindled Cow, Spotted Cow, Sparrow Hawk, Black Eagle, Falconer, Huntsman, White Raven, Otter, Water Dog, Cat, Bear, White Horse, Blue Cock, Sunflower, Pear Tree, Rose of Guelderland, Sieve, Woodyard,* and *Mill*. The sea and its denizens and dangers prompt the *Golden Shark, Mermaid, Neptune, Whale, Sea Mew, Sea Bear, Mackerel, Herring, Sea Horse, Brown Fish, Shark, Sea Flower, Gilded Shell, Pearl, Fortune, Supply, Expedition, Farewell, Hope, Providence, Glad Tidings, Broken Heart, Welcome, Happy Return, Morning Star, Seven Stars,* and *Watchful Buoy*. The Bible and religion are manifest in *Peace, Love, Contentment, Amity, Concord, Justice, Faith, Hope of a Better Life, Abraham's Sacrifice, Gideon, Angel Gabriel, Flying Angel, King David, King Solomon, Star of Bethlehem, Three Kings, Virgin, St. Peter, St. James, St. Martin, Purmerland Church,* and *Quaker*. Trade and civic pride are honored with the *Bourse of Amsterdam, Nevis Factor, Netherland Indian, Balance, Good Beer, New Netherland Fortune, Arms of Norway, Arms of New Netherland, Arms of Amsterdam, Arms of Rensselaerswyck* and *Real*. Home affections give us the *Bride* and *Bachelor's Delight*. Rulers and national heroes and politics appear in the *Princess, Prince Maurice, Lady Maria, Prince William, Young Prince of Denmark, Ruyter, Society,* and *Union*.

Then we have the *Flying Deer, Blind Ass, Golden Hind, Ostrich, Gilded Fox, Diamond, Cat and Parrot, Canary, Unicorn, Fire of Troy, White Horseman, Harlequin, Orange Tree, Sphera Mundi,* and many other quaint names.

The Dutch had scarcely got rid of their sea legs here before beginning to build vessels for the coast trade. Seventeen ships had already been built in New Netherland by 1639.

After escaping the dangers of the seas, including tempests, famine caused by calms and contrary winds, and capture by Barbary corsairs or pirates, fervent indeed were the thanksgivings offered up on arrival in Godyn's Bay (Sandy Hook). The Labadists give us a lively impression of the scenes on arrival. After anchoring inside Sandy Hook, they tell us that in the morning the anchor was raised and they sailed between Staten Island and Long Island through the *Hoofden* (Narrows). The woods, hills, dales, green fields and plantations, houses and dwellings struck them as cheerful and sweet. "As soon as you pass through the *Hoofden* the city presents a pretty sight. The fort lies on a point between the two rivers; and, as soon as they see a ship coming, they raise a flag on the high flag-staff." It was about three o'clock when they arrived; and people came from shore in all sorts of craft, "each inquiring and searching after his own and his own profit."

Various ordinances were passed regulating shipping. In 1638, it was ordered that no sailors should remain on shore at night without permission, and there was to be no intercourse between shore and ship between sunset and sunrise. The anchorage ground was the roadstead between Capske Point (South Ferry and the guideboard near the City Tavern (head of Coenties

MERCHANTS AND TRADE

Slip); ships anchoring elsewhere were to be fined fifty guilders. They were not allowed to be discharged between sunset and sunrise, and had to give twelve hours' notice of sailing (1647). They were not allowed to be boarded before they had anchored or had been entered. Goods might be sold on board by wholesale or retail (1648). They had to be inspected on arrival and departure. Goods were to be discharged on shore and received on board during sunshine (1656). In 1653, the Farmer of the Customs was empowered to visit departing ships. The following typical bill of lading was

> Recorded from Capt. William Morris ye 19th day of February, 1696:
> shipped by the Peace of God in good order and well conditioned by Mr. William Morris in and upon ye good ship called the *Beaver*, wherof is Master under God for this Present Voyage Robert Sinclair and now riding att anchor in the River of New Yorke and by God's Peace bound for London
> to say two hogsheads of sugar, one bundle of whale bone containing one hundred pounds on the Draper account & Resque of William Morris being marked and Numbered. God send the good ship to her desired Porte in safety. Amen.

At first the Company had a monopoly of all trade. In 1626, we read:

> People work there as in Holland, one trades, another builds houses, a third farms. Each farmer has his farm and the cows on the land purchased by the Company; but the milk remains to the profit of the Boor; he sells it to those of the people who receive their wages for work every week.

The volume of the trade of the West India Company from 1624 to 1635 appears in the following "list of returns from the New Netherlands":

Date	Beavers	Otters	Guilders
1624	4,000	700	27,125
1625	5,295	463	35,825
1626	7,258	857	45,050
1627	7,529	370	56,420
1628	6,951	734	61,075
1629	5,913	681	62,185
1630	6,041	1,085	68,012
1632	8,569	546	94,925
....	4,944	1,115	48,200
1633	8,800	1,383	91,375
1635	14,891	1,413	134,925
			725,117

In 1670, Denton says the inhabitants have a considerable trade with the Indians, for beavers, otter, raccoon skins, with other furs; and also for deer and elk skins; and are supplied with venison and fowl in the winter, and fish in the summer by the Indians, which they buy at an "easie" rate.

The most profitable trade being with the Indians, the Dutch had to adopt the Indian currency. In 1626, De Rasières says:

As an employment in winter they make sewan, which is an oblong bead that they make from cockle shells, which they find on the seashore, and they consider it as valuable as we do money here, so much so that one can buy everything they have for it; they string it and wear it round the neck and hands; they also make bands of it which the women wear on the head in front of the hair, and the men about the body; and they are as particular about the stringing and sorting as we can be about pearls.

MERCHANTS AND TRADE

John Josselyn says:

Their beads are their money; of these there are two sorts, blue and white; the first is their gold, the last their silver. These they work out of shells so cunningly, that neither Jew nor devil can counterfeit them.

Sewan, seawant, or *zewant,* was the name of the native currency; it was also known as wampum. The white beads were made from the stem of the periwinkle, and Suckanhock, or black beads, of the heart of the clam shell. The black was double the value of the white. Three black, or six white, beads were equivalent to an English penny. Wampum was sometimes measured by the fathom. A string one fathom long varied from five shillings among the New Englanders to four guilders of Dutch money ($1.66).

Sewan was jewelry as well as money, and distinguished the rich Indians from the poor ones. Of great importance was the belt of *sewan*. This was a sort of wide sash upon which the white, purple, and black beads were arranged in rows and tied with little leather strings. The length, width, and color were regulated by the importance of the matter to be negotiated. Ordinary belts consisted of twelve rows, each containing one hundred and eighty beads. If a message was sent without the belt, it was considered unworthy of serious consideration: if the belt was returned, the offer was rejected; if kept, it was a token that the offer was accepted, or the offense forgiven.

These shells, indeed, had more virtue among the Indians than pearls, gold and silver had among Europeans. Seawant was the seal of a contract, the oath of fidelity. It satisfied murders, and all other injuries, purchased peace and entered into the religious as well as civil ceremonies. A string of seawant was delivered by the orator in public council, at the close of every distinct proposition made to others, as a ratification of the truth and sincerity of what he said, and the white and black strings of seawant were tied by the pagan priest around the neck of the white dog suspended to a pole and offered as a sacrifice to Thaloughyawaagon, the upholder of the skies, the god of the Five Nations.

Sewan was chiefly made on Long Island, which was called by the Indians *sewan-hacky* (the place where sewan was made), and this Indian mint at their doors gave the Dutch an immense advantage over the other colonists.

The Dutch naturally wanted to keep control of the wampum traffic in the Narragansett country. "The seeking after sewan by the Puritans," said De Rasières, is prejudicial to us, inasmuch as they would, by so doing, discover the trade in furs, which, if they were to find out, it would be a great trouble for us to maintain; for they already dare to threaten that, if we will not leave off dealing with that people, they will be obliged to use other means. De Rasières sold a large amount of it to the Puritans. Hubbard said:

Whatever were the honey in the mouth of that beast of trade there was a deadly sting in the tail. For it is said they [the Dutch] first brought our people to the knowledge of *wampum-peag;* and the acquaintance therewith occasioned the Indians of these parts to learn the skill to make it, by which, as by the exchange of money, they purchased store of artillery, both from the English, Dutch and French, which proved a fatal business to those that were concerned in it.

In Kieft's time (1641) four beads of "good splendid sewan, usually called Manhattan's sewan," were reckoned equal to one stiver. Gradually inferior wampum, rough, loose, and unstrung, began to threaten

MERCHANTS AND TRADE

"the ruin of the country"; an order was soon made regulating that six loose beads should pass for a stiver, because "there was no coin in circulation and the labourers, boors and other common people having no other money, would be great losers."

In Stuyvesant's time (1650), the currency was again regulated. Wampum was made lawfully current, six white and three black beads of commercial sewan or eight white and four black of the "base strung" for one stiver.

The Governor and Council in the city of New York in 1673 made an order declaring that on account of the scarcity of wampum what had passed at the rate of eight white and four black pairs for a stiver or a penny should pass at the rate of six white and three black pairs for a stiver, and three times so much the value of silver. There was very little "certain coin" in the colony at this period.

There is no doubt that the Indians were originally peaceably disposed towards the Dutch, and that the Indian wars and massacres were reprisals for outrage and oppression. Many laws were made regulating the trade with the Indians, restricting barter to the trading-posts. In 1647, people were forbidden to go into the interior to trade with the Indians. Woolley tells us the Indians have

> swift canoes in which they bring oysters and other fish for the market; they are so light and portable that a man and his squaw will take them upon their shoulders and carry them by land from one river to another with a wonderful expedition; they will venture with them in a dangerous current, even through Hell gate itself, which lies in an arm of the sea, about ten miles from New York eastward to New England, as dangerous and as accountable as the Norway whirlpool, or maelstrom.

In September, 1648, it was complained that some people put the natives to work and employ them in their service and then dismiss them without pay. The Indians threatening to pay themselves or revenge themselves, the authorities order all employers to pay the Indians "without contradiction" under penalty of a fine.

In 1654, it was forbidden to sell liquor to Indians under a penalty of five hundred guilders. Drunken Indians were to be imprisoned until they told who sold them the liquor. The authorities complain that many Indians are daily seen intoxicated, and being drunk and fuddled, commit many grave acts of violence. Two years later, the penalty was increased by corporal punishment and banishment.

In 1645, it was prohibited to supply Indians with munitions of war on pain of death.

In 1656, it was ordered that nobody was to harbour an Indian overnight below the Fresh Water under a penalty of twenty-five guilders. In 1666, Abram Carpyn lodged nine Indians. It was notorious that he resided in Paulus vander Grift's rear building only for the purpose of selling brandy to the Indians; so he was ordered to leave "or the said little house shall be pulled down."

In 1663, drunken Indians are to be imprisoned until they have paid a fine of £1 Flemish.

The constant complaint of the West India Company was that its own officials as well as the colonists seemed to care nothing for the Company's interests, but assiduously devoted their energies to lining their own pockets; and many efforts were made to stop illicit trade. The laws, however, were shamelessly broken and defied. In 1638, it is complained that indentured servants as well

WINTER SCENE
OSTADE

From an old print

as freemen are pursuing a private trade in furs and other irregular courses.

In November, 1640, the price of goods in the Company's store was fixed at fifty per cent advance, and people were notified to report if overcharged. In the following February, Commissary Lupold acknowledged having charged too much for the goods sold in the public store, and was fined, dismissed, and declared unfit to hold any public office. In 1651, an ordinance was issued to prevent smuggling.

The Company's proclamation of free competition in trade in 1638 resulted in a rapid increase of colonization and prosperity. Internal trade and commerce being made free for all, colonists were immediately attracted from New England and Virginia. In 1640, the commercial privileges, which the first charter had restricted to the Patroons, were extended to all free colonists, but the Company maintained onerous imposts for its own benefit. The prohibition of manufactures within the province was abolished. In 1645, the Company "resolved to open to private persons the trade which it has exclusively carried on with New Netherland," and to permit all the inhabitants of the United Provinces to sail with their own ships to New Netherland, the Virginias, the Swedish, English, and French colonies, but all colonial trade was concentrated in the custom house of Fort Amsterdam.

Although the colonists welcomed permanent settlers, they had a great antipathy for itinerant traders; and a law had been made to the effect that whoever wished to engage in trade in New Netherland must keep "fire and light," — in other words, he must have a dwelling. By charter, Manhattan was made the emporium and had been invested with "staple right." The residents were, however, greatly annoyed by the constantly increasing "Scotchmen," or peddlers, who on arrival hastened to the interior and procured their furs and other commodities and returned home. The burgomasters and schepens, therefore, in 1657, petitioned the Director that no persons but city burghers should be allowed to trade in the capital, and none but "settled residents to trade in any quarter hereabout, without this place."

The provincial government, considering the petition a just one, established the Great and Small Burgher right "in conformity to the laudable custom of the city of Amsterdam in Europe." Those who wished to belong to the Great Burgher class had to pay fifty guilders, and "all such and such only shall hereafter be qualified to fill all the city offices and dignities." They were also exempt for one year and six weeks from watches and expeditions and were "free in their proper persons from arrest by any subaltern court or judicial benches of this province." This class included the present and future burgomasters and schepens and the Director, councilors, clergymen, and military officers with their male descendants. The class of Small Burghers included all natives and all who had lived in this city a year and six weeks, all who had married or should marry the daughters of burghers, all who kept stores and shops, or did business within the city, and all salaried officers of the Company. "Arriving traders" were ordered before selling their goods "to set up and keep an open store within the gates and walls of New Amsterdam," for which they had to obtain from the burgomasters and schepens the Small Burgher right, for the sum of twenty guilders, which went to the support of the city.

In March, 1648, the nine elected Selectmen verify

the daily decline and violation of Trade and Navigation, proceeding for the most part from the underselling, frauds, smuggling, perpetrated by the one against the other, principally by such as take little or no interest in this new growing Province and feel little concern and care for its prosperity and welfare, and, therefore, do not benefit it either by Bouweries or Buildings, but solely applying themselves with small capital and cargoes (for which they hire for a brief period only one large room or house) to the Beaver and Fur Trade, and having traded and trucked said peltries from the good Inhabitants, or the Natives sufficiently high beyond their value, have recourse to all sorts of means, by night and at unseasonable hours, to convey them secretly out of the Country, or to the North, without paying the proper duty thereon; and having enriched themselves by these and other illicit practices and means, they take their departure and go back home without conferring or bestowing any benefit on this Province or the Inhabitants thereof. By this underselling and fraudulent trade, the Wares and Merchandizes of others who, by means of Bouweries or with handsome Buildings in regard to this place, interest themselves in the Country, are depreciated and remain unsold to their great loss and damage.

In 1657, it was found more every day that great frauds and smuggling were committed by the importation of merchandise under the name and cloak of sailors' freight, and measures were taken to stop it.

Smuggling and piracy were popular and profitable activities of the honest burghers. In 1654, an ordinance was passed against harboring robbers and pirates, but the most pious were not above illicit traffic. In July, 1659, Stuyvesant writes to the Directors in Holland:

All possible care shall be continually taken to prevent smuggling, in pursuance of the placats, heretofore passed and now sent us by you in print. In the meantime, we await anxiously the further and stricter orders, to be issued at your request by their High: Might:; after having received these, we shall vigorously carry them out to the best of our ability. Your recommendations to the Fischal on this subject have been communicated to him by reading your Honors' letter, which we further impressed upon his mind by some earnest words. The order, to place some faithful soldiers on board while the freight is discharged and the Fiscal makes his search, is and always has been observed. In order to prevent corruption, they are often relieved every day and we have promised and paid not only to these soldiers, but also to everybody else, whatever position he may have, free man and Company's servant, who discovers and reports an attempt at smuggling one full third share, as shown by our Resolution and the placat publishing the same of the 23d of April, 1658.

In 1659, the Company consented to the

experiment of a foreign commerce with France, Spain, Italy, the Carribean Islands, and elsewhere, upon condition that the vessels should return with their cargoes either to New Netherland, or to Amsterdam, and that furs should be exported to Holland alone.

Elizabethan ethics, of the school of Drake, Hawkins, Cumberland, Raleigh, and Frobisher, still prevailed. If the Spaniard was shy and prizes were scarce, a vessel belonging to a brother trader of your own port was regarded as fair quarry. Thus, in September, 1644, John Wilcox charged Mr. Clercq with fitting out a privateer to capture and make prize of plaintiff's ship, asking that the defendant's vessel might be detained in port. In July, 1648, Jacob Reynsen and Jacob Schermerhorn for smuggling were banished for five years and their property confiscated. This sentence was too severe for the popular taste, and was recalled three weeks later.

In May, 1648, Hans Hansen, for fourteen years a respectable resident of New Amsterdam, was pardoned for smuggling on condition that he beg pardon of God and of the court.

In 1654, the Director-General and Council are informed that "pirates and vagabonds are countenanced, favoured, harboured, entertained, and supported by subjects and inhabitants having fixed domicile, and are so encouraged and incited that some have dared to spy into even this city under the colour and guise of travellers." Therefore a fine of twenty-four guilders was ordered for neglect to report strangers.

Pirates infested the shores of the East River and committed ravages around New Amsterdam and on Long Island. They were chiefly English, and many of the English settlers were accused of communication with them. Sir Henry Moody at Gravesend joined in accusing Captain John Manning of carrying on an unlawful trade. The Governor raised troops and commissioned several yachts to act against the pirates. Manning was arrested and tried in New Haven in April, 1654; his vessel was condemned and sold "by inch of candle" as a lawful prize. In 1653, Thomas Baxter, a resident of New Amsterdam, turned pirate and committed outrages on Long Island. He seized in Heemstede harbor a vessel belonging to New Plymouth and captured a Dutch boat. Stuyvesant sent out two boats with a hundred men to blockade Baxter in Fairfield Roads. Baxter was finally arrested by the authorities of New Haven and Hartford. He was surrendered by Stuyvesant's requisition, but escaped from jail. His house and ship at New Amsterdam were sold.

The "constant and profitable correspondence with foreigners and pirates" had been "diligently obstructed" by Andros, by order of James II, "which was very disagreeable to many persons who had even grown old in that way of trade."

Piratical trade had attained vast proportions under the Dutch rule, but under the early English governors of New York the evil grew to an almost incredible extent. The chief task allotted to the Earl of Bellomont, who arrived in 1698, was the suppression of piracy. By his efforts William Kidd, highly respected in this community, was brought to justice; and his letters to the Lords of Trade reveal conditions of shameless corruption and open defiance of the law. He encountered bitter opposition from the merchants here. In an early report he says:

This city hath been a nest of Pirates, and I already find that several of their ships have their owners and were fitted from this Port, and have Commissions to act as privateers, from the late Governor here. There is a great trade between this port and Madagascar, from whence great quantities of East India goods are brought, which are certainly purchased from Pirates. I find that this practice is set up in order that the spoils taken by the Pirates (set out from this Citty) may be brought in hither in merchant ships, whose owners are likewise owners and interested in the Pirate ships, and I particularly find that one Captain Moston, Commander of the ship *Fortune* (now under seizure) altho' an unfree bottom had a Commission from Coll. Fletcher to be a privateer, and as if protected by that did publickly load here for Madagascar and came back laden with East India goods supposed to be partly the produce of the cargo and partly the Pirates goods, which were landed and concealed, all but the last boat and it was so contrived that this ship was sent from hence to Madagascar at the same time that Hore and Glover's ship (two most notorious pirates) were there, both of which had Commissions from Coll: Fletcher at New Yorke. Piracy does and will prevail in the

MERCHANTS AND TRADE

Province of New Yorke in spite of all my endeavours unless three things be done out of hand, viz: good Judges and an honest and able Attorney-General from England, a man of war commanded by an honest stout Captain, and pay and recruits for the four companies. Captain Giles Shelly, who came lately from Madagascar with 50 or 60 Pirates has so flushed them at New Yorke with Arabian Gold and East India goods, that they set the government at defiance. . . . Your Lordships orders to me to trouble and prosecute Pirates and suppress unlawful Trade can never be complied with, if you will not afford me the means. Had there been a man of war at Yorke, Shelly and his Pirates in all probability had been taken and £50,000 in money belonging to them: and for want of a Man-of-War I could not attempt anything against a great ship that hovered off this coast 5 or 6 days together about the time I secured Captain Kidd, supposed to be one Maze, a pirate, who is said to have brought £300,000 from the Red Sea, and who 't is believed here would have come into this place could he have hoped to make his terms; but hearing how it fared with Kidd, he bore away and 't is said he is gone to Providence.

The Governors of Pennsylvania, New Jersey, and Maryland also seized a number of pirates, all of whom were brought by Shelly from Madagascar, and a good many of them had forsaken Kidd. One of Kidd's deserters was Edward Buckmaster, who was taken prisoner by Bellomont, and another was Otto van Toyle. In another letter Bellomont says:

When any seizure is made here the merchants are ready to rise in rebellion, and so little have they been used to that in Colonel Fletcher's government that they look on it as a violence done them when we seize unlawful goods in their warehouses and shops. 'Tis almost incredible what a vast quantity of East India goods would have been brought into this port had there not been a change in the

Government. Two men in this town had for their share £12000 each, which were brought from Madagascar and got there with the barter with pirates. Besides there came home to the mouth of this port 8 or 9 pirate ships since my coming to this government, which would have brought in a vast quantity of those goods, and by the confession of the merchants in the town they would have brought in a £100,000 in gold and silver, and this inrages them to the last degree that they have missed of all this treasure and rich pennyworths of East India goods and now they drink Colonel Fletcher's health with the greatest devotion imaginable, upon the remembrance of his kind concessions to them and the dispensing power he gave himself and them against the laws of trade and piracy.

I formerly acquainted your Lordships that Nassaw Island alias Long Island was become a great Receptacle for Pirates; I am since more confirmed that 'tis so. Gillam, a notorious pirate, was suffered to escape thither from Rhode Island, and 'tis believed he is still there, notwithstanding the Lieutenant-Governor of New Yorke published by my direction a reward of £30 for his apprehension, and at the same time £10 a piece for two of Kidd's men that escaped from this town to Nassaw Island. I take that Island, especially the East End of it, to exceed Rhode Island. The people there have been many of them pirates themselves, and to be sure are well affected to the trade; but besides that they are so lawlesse and desperate a people that I can get no honest man that will venture to goe and collect the Excise among them and watch their Trade. There are four towns that make it their daily practice to receive ships and sloops with all sorts of Merchandize, tho' they be not allowed ports.

The most prominent and opulent merchants in the city — De Lancey and Philipse among them — accumulated much of their wealth by piracy.

Shelly is one of the Masters of Ships that I formerly informed your Lordships went last Summer from New

York to Madagascar; he is a dweller at New Yorke, and Mr. Hackshaw one of the Merchants in London that petitioned your Lordships against me is one of his owners, and Mr de Lancey a Frenchman at New Yorke is another. I hear too that Captain Kidd dropped some pirates in that Island. They write from New Yorke that Arabian Gold is in great plenty there. When Frederick Phillipp's ship and the other two come from Madagascar (which are expected every day) New York will abound with gold. 'Tis the most beneficiall trade that to Madagascar with the pirates that was ever heard of, and I believe there's more got that way than by turning pirates and robbing. I am told this Shelly sold rum which cost but 2 shillings per gallon at New Yorke for 50 shillings and £3 per gallon at Madagascar, and a pipe of Madera Wine which cost him £19 he sold there for £300. Strong liquors and gun powder and ball are the commodities that go off there, to the best advantage, and those four ships last summer carried thither great quantities of those things.

The carelessness and corruption of the officers of the revenue and customes have been so great for some years past that althogh the Trade of this place hath been four times as much as formerly and the City greatly enlarged, and inriched, yet His Majesty's revenue arising from the Customes, hath decreased the one half from what it was ten years since; and the Merchants here have been so used to unlawful trade that they were almost ready to mutiny on some seizures I caused to be made (a few days after I landed) on Goods imported in an unfree bottom in the ship *Fortune*, commanded by Captain Moston, and it was with the greatest unwillingness and backwardness that his Majesty's Collector, Mr. Chidley Brooks did make the seizure, who told me it was none of his business, but belonged to a Man of Warr; that he had no boat, and other excuses; and when I gave him positive commands to do it, which he could not avoid, yet his delay of four days time gave opportunity to the ship wholly to unlade a rich cargo of East India goods, believed to be worth twenty thousand pounds; and only the last boats laden from her were seized to the value of about one thousand pounds, and I am informed that several other ships have since my landing here, transgressed the acts of trade which I could not prevent.

Continuing his investigations, the Earl found that the pirates that had caused the greatest havoc in the East Indies and the Red Sea had been either fitted out in New York or Rhode Island, and manned from New York. The ships commanded by Mason, Tew, Glover, and Hore had their commissions from the Governor of New York, the last three from Fletcher, and although these commissions appeared to be given only against the King's enemies, yet it was known to all the inhabitants of this city that they were bound to the Indies and the Red Sea, it being openly declared by the said commanders, whereby they raised men and were quickly able to proceed so notoriously publicly that it was generally believed that they had assurance from Colonel Fletcher that they might return and be protected. Bellomont says further:

Capt. Tew, that had been before a most notorious Pirate (complained of by the East India Company) on his return from the Indies with great riches made a visit to New York, where (although a man of most mean and infamous character) he was received and caressed by Coll: Fletcher, dined and supped often with him, and appeared publickly in his coach with him, and they exchanged presents, as gold watches, etc. with one another, all this is known to most of the City.

Fletcher also received private presents for his wife and daughter. Mason's ship returned under the command of one Coats about 1693, and was protected by Fletcher.

Bellomont found the officers of the Customs at New York most corrupt and negligent, and his removal of Mr. William Nicolls (chief broker in the matter of protection of pirates) from the Council made an enemy of him; and he and the merchants formed a cabal against the Earl. He also removed Brooks. His enemies charged that he had ruined the town by discouraging "privateering," as they euphemistically termed piracy, and preventing goods to the value of £100,000 from being landed.

The obstacles thrown in the Governor's path were many, and the opposition was exceedingly bold.

Having intelligence where some uncustomed goods were, I sent Mr. Monsey and Mr. Evats, a Searcher, to seize them, who went, found and seized them at Mr. Van Sweeten's house, but before they could convey them again to the Custome house, called together a number of the Merchants and by their advice locked up all the windows and doors, and made the said officers prisoners in a Close Garret, where they made the seizure and put them in danger of being stifled. News of this was brought to me about three hours after being nine of the clock at night with notice that the Officers were in danger of being murthered. I was therefore forced immediately to send my Lieutenant-Governor with three files of Soldiers and my own Servants from the Fort, who went and forthwith broke open the doors of Van Sweethen's house (which were denied to be opened to them) and rescued the King's Officers, and assisted in carrying the Goods seized to the Custom House. The Merchants of the Town were in such an uproar at this seizure (not being used to such things) that they exclaimed against me, as if all the English Laws and Rights were violated, and had the insolence to present to me, a most reproachful scandalous Petition.

There is thus no mystery about the origin of the lacquer, porcelain, silks, brocades, embroideries, and other rich Oriental wares and fabrics found in such quantities in the New York inventories.

Let us now follow from the breakfast-table the "master" of the house to his business.

The model Seventeenth Century house in the Utrecht Museum contains a small office, or counting-house, correctly furnished. On the right are two bookshelves full of books (also on the left wall), below which are a wooden bench and five rolls of tobacco. Against the wall, beneath the shelves, hang two shears, one saw, one chopper, and two strings of bills. Farther back in the room stands a bookcase in which are five packets of white paper tied with red tape and thirty-six bound books of white paper. Above the desk hangs a wooden shelf on which are twenty packs of paper tied with red tape. Under the bookshelf at the back stands a money-chest on carved legs, in which are packets of blue and of white paper tied with red tape and files of bills and receipted bills. In the front part of the room is a desk on which are a silver inkstand and an ivory seal with a monogram, a black *étui* case of silver work and a knife, three quill pens, a sand-shaker for drying the ink, a wooden paper-cutter, a wooden ruler, and a pile of letters.

In front of the desk stands a high stool, on which a doll, representing the merchant, is seated. He wears an indoor jacket of brown silk with an orange silk scarf, white silk breeches, and red slippers. On the floor stands a basket containing long Gouda pipes and two bootjacks, and also a wooden cellaret with nine green glass bottles.

The office usually contained also a clock, or an hour-glass, especially if clerks were employed. It was customary for both master and clerks to keep their caps or hats on while at work.

The counting-house was entered either directly from the street or side passage, or else through the shop, for on no account would the strict housewife allow customers or business callers to walk through the hallways of their homes and soil the clean tiling. An Amsterdam Xantippe of the Seventeenth Century is heard to say:

As soon as my husband's feet reach the threshold off come his boots, and either leather or felt slippers which always stand near the entrance are put on. Then the servant hands him his dressing-gown and cap, while he takes off his street clothes; and, quiet as a lamb, he steps into his office, and is buried in his books. If anybody ever comes to visit him, he never comes farther than the office. The rest of the house is mine, from front to rear, from top to bottom. Sometimes but very rarely, and when it is a special friend, he is allowed to bring him into the small front room to take a glass, but that is on special occasions only, and not a regular habit. Everything referring to his trade he knows; and his room is full of bills of lading, insurance policies, ledgers, day-books, etc.

The industries of New Netherland were very trifling. The temptations and profits of trade and barter, legitimate and illicit, were too strong to induce the cobbler to stick to his last. Very little merchandise was manufactured, — some furniture, brick, beer, fur garments, homespun linen, and woollen stuffs, shoes, and, of course, cereal and dairy products were made, but for their wealth the inhabitants of the colony depended on domestic and foreign exchange of commodities. Miller (1695) writes:

The industry that now is used is but little; the few inhabitants, having a large country before them, care not for more than from hand to mouth, and therefore they take but little pains, and yet that little produces very good beer, bread, cider, wine of peaches, cloth stuffs and beaver hats, a certain and sufficient sign how plentiful and beneficial a country it would be did but industrious art second nature's bounty, and were but the inhabitants more in number than at present they are.

Merchandizing in this country is a good employment, English goods yielding in New York generally 100 per cent. advance above the first cost, and some of them 200, 300, yea, sometimes 400: this makes so many in the city follow it, that whosoever looks on their shops would wonder, where there are so many to sell, there should be any to buy.

This, joined to the healthfulness, pleasantness, and fruitfulness thereof, are great encouragements to people rather to seek the bettering of their fortunes here than elsewhere; so that it may be hoped that a little time will render the inhabitants more numerous than at present they are.

In 1670, Denton says:

they sow store of flax which they make every one cloth of for their own weaving, as also woollen cloth and linsey-woolsey, and had they more tradesmen amongst them, they would in a little time live without the help of any other country for their clothing. Here you need not trouble the shambles for meat, nor bakers and brewers for beer and bread, nor run to a linen-draper for a supply, every one making their own linen and a great part of their woollen cloth.

With regard to the trades, the only ones that corresponded to some degree with the Dutch guilds were those of the butcher, baker, and brewer. The houses with the verandas under which goods were displayed in

From an old print

OLD DUTCH HOUSE IN BROAD STREET
NEW AMSTERDAM, 1698

Holland existed here; but, as a rule, the shop-goods consisted of a heterogeneous conglomeration in which the purchaser might find anything from a prayer-book to a pack of cards, a Jew's-harp to an anchor. The bakers, of course, confined their wares to the favorite Dutch confectioneries. Thus, in 1661, Hendrick Jansen was sued for exhibiting gingerbread in his window without offering large bread for sale.

It may be noticed, in passing, that authorities whose duties corresponded to a modern board of health deprived the owner of perishable goods when they became sufficiently malodorous to create a nuisance and sold them for the benefit of unnamed parties — perhaps for negro or Indian consumption. Thus, in May, 1660, some Dutch imported cheeses were seized and sold by auction because they created a great stench both in Van der Vin's cellar as thereabout.

Very few merchants made a specialty of any commodity; the average inventory gives only the jumble of a country store. To take only one (and a very small one) of the innumerable shops as an example, we find among the goods of Peter Marius: 140 small Dutch books of several sorts; 25 pieces blue tape; $17\frac{1}{2}$ ells of calico painted; 29 white washes and one hand-brush; 6 scrubbing-brushes and 5 hand-brushes; 5 pieces and 3 remnants of blue linen; two small pictures, one church chair, a small Dutch hamper, a cask of sugar, a white wood chest, 4 small pewter salts, 50 Indian stools, 41 "dustails," one dozen small butter ladles, one sugar loaf, 15 "old-fashioned Dutch childrens bodyes," $22\frac{1}{4}$ lbs. of "suggar candy in a tin box"; $31\frac{1}{4}$ pounds of fine hooks and eyes; one large nickers and 60 dozen of other ties," $1\frac{1}{2}$ lb. long Indian beads, one Dutch sea-card or draft, and "19 lbs. of swan shott."

We have seen that the ordinary currency was wampum and beaver, Carolus guilders and other florins and dollars. In a port resorted to by pirates and all the traders of the earth, however, it is only natural that the merchant's money-box should contain coins of every ancient and modern mint. Arabian gold, which seems to have been the principal currency among the Madagascan pirates, frequently appears (see page 337). Lewis Morris (1691) had one hundred and eighty guineas, one double guinea, six half guineas, four quarter guineas, one pistole, and two double doubloons. For the relative value of Dutch, New York, and English money at the end of the century, we may quote the following from the inventory of John Coesart (1700):

11181 guilders 10 stivers at ¼ prime cost Dutch money the prime cost in Dutch money amounts in the whole 11189–10–4 15095–10–11 to which at 50% advance amounts to £2830–8–9 New York money.

The differences in Holland and New Amsterdam values frequently gave rise to disputes which had to be settled by the courts here.

The arithmetical troubles, however, that required expert accounting in consequence of the multitudinous coins, tokens, and values were fewer than might be supposed. The reason for this is that the bulk of the domestic trade was transacted in kind. One man would supply another with dairy produce or build a house for him or give professional, or other, services, and be credited in return with shop-goods or labor. Countless instances of this practice appear in the records. For example, in May, 1654, when Matewis de Vos sues Beeltie Jacobsen for 9.4 florins for stockings, shoes, and a clothes-line, Beeltie says she has paid him 3.10 florins in peaches and washing.

One striking point in New Netherland trade is the

MERCHANTS AND TRADE

extent to which women were independent participants, thus rendering them very desirable widows. It is also noticeable that many of the opulent matrons had two or three husbands. Among the rich widows may be mentioned Anneke Jans; Mrs. Drisius, the latter's daughter; Mrs. Cornelis Steenwyck; Margaret Philipse, who traded directly with Fatherland, travelling in her own ships; and many others. Lysbet Greveraet, first married to Mr. De Reimer, a young merchant of New Amsterdam, became the wife of Dominie Samuel Drisius. She owned much real estate and the mercantile effects of her late husband. Her shop was in Pearl Street between Whitehall and Broad Streets. When she died, she owned, among other property, four houses in New York worth £371, £300, £300, and £275, respectively. Many of the wealthy wives and widows made their money in tavern-keeping.

A short survey of the conditions of commerce in New Amsterdam would not be complete without an inquiry as to the standings of the Jews here. When Portugal monopolized the trade of the Eastern seas, the bulk of the trade was in the hands of the Portuguese Jews, and to the Dutch who then transshipped Oriental goods from the Tagus to the Texel the name Portuguese was synonymous with Jews. When Philip II, the oppressor of the Low Countries, took possession of Portugal and the Jews were subjected to the tortures of the Inquisition, they found a welcome asylum in Amsterdam, where they were allowed the free exercise of their religion and where they still have many synagogues. They were not only tolerated, but they stood high in the councils of the nation and in art, and, particularly, in commerce. The ultra-sectarians of the Protestant religion, like Stuyvesant, hated the Jew, and, like Cromwell in England, would gladly have excluded and banished him; but to the level-headed Directors of a trading-company such a policy was naturally distasteful. However, for a long time the West India Company refrained from granting Jews Patroon rights, and frowned upon all attempts of members of that race to found colonies. In 1651, however, as a result of "continual coming," the Jews had evidently wearied the Directors, for they informed Stuyvesant that they had licensed Jan de Illau to settle with some of his co-religionists at Curaçao as an experiment, although the Company shrewdly suspected that the real project of the "colony" was to trade thence to the West Indies and the Main. Three years later, a company of Jews headed by Asser Levy arrived in New Amsterdam from the West Indies, and the popular prejudice against them, which was fully shared by Stuyvesant, immediately showed itself in published disabilities.

They were forbidden to train and mount guard with the trainbands for two reasons: — first, the disgust and unwillingness of these trainbands to be fellow-soldiers with the aforesaid nation and to be on guard with them in the same guardhouse and on the other side, that the said nation was not admitted or counted among the citizens, as regards trainbands, or common citizens' guards neither in the illustrious City of Amsterdam nor (to our knowledge) in any City in Netherland.

On Nov. 5, 1655, Jacob Barsimon and Asser Levy's petition to stand guard like other burghers of New Amsterdam, or to be relieved of the tax paid by other Jews, was refused, and the petitioners were told they might go elsewhere if they liked. On Dec. 23, 1655, Salvador Dandradi, a Jewish merchant, prayed for a deed of a house he had purchased at public auction, being ready to pay the money. His petition was refused.

Instead of going elsewhere, they stayed; but, in view of their problematical ultimate destination, they asked to have a place allotted to them where they might bury their dead out of their sight. This request was refused on the ground that it was not yet necessary; but one of their members, having obligingly removed the objection, on Feb. 22, 1656, the Jews were granted a burying-place outside the city.

The ostracizing of the Jews by Stuyvesant and his subordinates naturally aroused the indignation of the Directors in Holland, who, on June 14, 1656, wrote to Stuyvesant:

We have seen and heard with displeasure that against our orders of the 15th of February, 1655, issued at the request of the Jewish or Portuguese nation, you have forbidden them to trade to Fort Orange and the South River, also the purchase of real estate, which is granted to them without difficulty here in this country, and we wish it had not been done and that you had obeyed our orders which you must always execute punctually and with more respect: Jews or Portuguese people, however, shall not be employed in any public service (to which they are neither admitted in this city), nor allowed to have open retail shops, but they may quietly and peacefully carry on their business as before said and exercise in all quietness their religion within their houses, for which end they must without doubt endeavour to build their houses close together in a convenient place on one or the other side of New Amsterdam — at their own choice — as they have done here.

They add:

The permission given to the Jews to go to New Netherland and enjoy there the same privileges, as they have here, has been granted only as far as civil and political rights are concerned, without giving the said Jews a claim to the privilege of exercising their religion in a synagogue or at a gathering; as long therefore, as you receive no request for granting them this liberty of religious exercise, your considerations and anxiety about this matter are premature and when later something shall be said about it, you can do no better than to refer them to us and await the necessary order.

On March 14, 1656, Abraham de Lucena, Jacob Cohen Henricque, Salvador Dandrada, Joseph Dacosta, and David Frera, petition that as they are taxed as other citizens they should have same rights in trading and acquiring real estate according to grant, Feb. 15, 1655.

On April 11, 1657, Asser Levy, a Jew, appears in Court requests to be admitted a Burgher; claims that such ought not be refused him as he keeps watch and ward (*tocht en wacht*) like other Burghers, shewing a Burgher certificate from the city of Amsterdam, that the Jew is burgher there. Which being deliberated on, 'tis decreed as before that it cannot be allowed and he shall apply to the Director-General and Council.

In the end, the local authorities had to give way, and the Jews were admitted to the right of citizenship in 1657.

INDEX

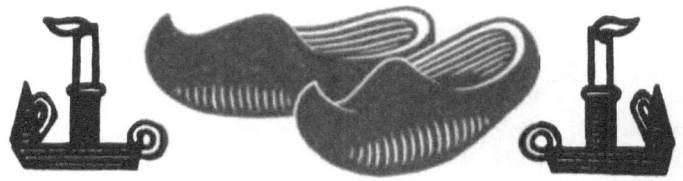

INDEX

AELST, W. van, 32, 102
Albums, 314
Anabaptists, 186, 189, 199
Anchorage ground, 324-325
Andros, Gov., 53, 192, 199
Apron, 61
Arabian gold, 337, 346
Arak, 268
Archery, 296
Arms of Amsterdam, The, 2, 3, 5
Assault with a glass, 270

BACKERUS, Johannes, 187
Backgammon, 297
Bakers, 126-127
Ball, 299
Bann dinners, 221
Banns, laws regarding marriage, 209-210
Banns, marriage, 209-213
Baptism, 248
Baptisms, irregular, 249
Baptists, 189, 199, 200
Barber surgeons, 237-239
Barbers, ships', 238-239
Barentsen, Peter, 2
Barter, 346
Baxter, .. (pirate), 335
Beaker, 110
Beaver, The, 196
Beds, 83
Beeck, Johannes van, 212-214
Beer, 121, 229
Beers drunk in Holland, 267
Bellomont, Earl of, 225
Bells, hand, 129
Betrothal, 210, 217-220

Betrothal gifts, 217-218
Betrothal, infant, 207
Beverninck, 29
Bibles, 181
Bigamy, punishment for, 216
Bill of lading, 325
Billiards, 297
Birch-beaker, 270
Bird cutting, 296
Biscuit, lying-in, 247
Bitters, 268
Bleachery, 160
Block, Adriaen, 1
Blom, Hendricus, 194-195
Bogardus, Dominie, 6, 17, 60, 159, 183, 185, 186
Books, 180-181
Borsum (or Borssum), Egbert van, 44-45
Bouwerys, the Company's, 16-17
Bowery, Stuyvesant's, 42, 195-196
Bowne, John, 156, 191, 192
Boys, mischievous, 23
Brandy, 268
Brandy distillery, Kieft's, 276
Breach of promise, suits regarding, 210-211
Bread, 121
Breads, festival, 300
Breakfast, 121
Bressani, Father, 186
Breweries, early, in New Amsterdam, 276
Brewer's street, 48, 165
Brickman, quoted, 104, 136-137
Bricks, 39, 40, 41, 45, 54
Bride, 218, 220, 223-232

INDEX

Bride and groom, insult to, 227, 233-234
Bride's bouquet, 226
Bride's crown, 222, 226
Bride's dress, 220-221, 222, 223-224
Bridesmaids, 218-219, 223
Bride's reception, 221-222
"Bride's Tears," 219, 226
Bride's veil, 224, 226
Bridegroom, 220
Bridegroom, dress of, 225
Bridegroom, gifts to, 226
Broad Street, 30, 319
Bundling, 207-208
Burgomasters, suit of, 72
Burial customs, 256-262
Burial of suicides, 260
Bush-burning, 12-14
Buttons, 71-72
Byrd, William, quoted, 54, 199

CAKE-PASTING, 298
Cakes, 125-126
Cakes festival, 301, 302
Cappoens, Cristina, 65, 67, 68, 104, 106, 110, 112, 114-115, 129, 181
Caps, 63
Cards, 297
Carrying into the Sea, 310
Carter, Capt. C., 74, 75, 76, 78, 79
Carters, 53, 296
Carts, 53, 296
Casket, 87
Castle Philipse, 47
Cattle, 15, 16, 17, 18, 19, 22, 23, 40, 160
Cattle fair, 315-316
Cattle, slaughter of, 315
Chairs, 87-88
Châtelaines, 56, 64, 217-218
Cheese, 125
Chess, 297
Children, clothes of, 69-70
Children, wills concerning, 147-149
Chocolate, 133
Chocolate-pot, 133

Christening-customs, 248-251
Christening-dinner, 250
Christening-gifts, 251
Christening-robes, 249-250
Christmas, 301
Church, 7, 41, 183-185
Church seat, 135-136
Churching feast, 248
Churching of women, 248
City improvements, 24
City Taverns, 271-272
Clarkson, Matthew, 74, 78, 80, 141
Clarkson, Mrs. M., 59, 61, 62, 63
Classis of Amsterdam, 182, 194, 198
Cleaning, 122, 136-138
Cleef, Hendrick Christiaensen van, 1.
Clergy, Dutch, 235
Cloaks, 79
Clothes, men's, 71-80
Clover leaf, 230, 269-271
Clubbing the Cat, 292-293
Coffee, 121, 133
Collect, The, 312
Comforters of the Sick, 4, 164
Company's counting-house, 4
Confections, 125-126, 229
Confections, festival, 300
Consolers of the Sick, 182, 252
Conventicles, 189-190, 200
Coronets, bridal, 222-223
Corpse dressers, 255
Corrupt revenue officers, 339, 341
Cortlandt, Catharine van, 46, 47
Cortlandt, Olaff Stevensz van, 45, 46, 82, 111
Cortlandt, Stephanus van, 46
Cortlandt, van, house, 46
Counting-house, 342
Courtship, 208-209
Cox, Sarah, 98-99
Cox, William, 98
Crundall, Thomas, house of, 97
Cupboard. *See Kast*
Currency, 327, 346
Curtains, 88
Curtius, Alexander Carolus, 174-175
Cushions, 88

INDEX

DAMEN, Jan, lots of, 15–16
Dancing, 177–179, 230–231
Death customs, 252–255
Death robes, 253
Death "wade," 253
Deldyke, L., 61, 68, 73, 74, 75, 76, 77, 78, 79, 132, 297, 314
Delft ware, 113
De Vry, quoted, 220–221
Diamonds, 67–68
Dice-throwing, 297
Dinners at City Tavern, 273
Dinners, civic, 272
Dinners, complimentary, 273
Directors, the first, 3
Disc-throwing, 292
Divorce, 214–216
Doctors, Dutch, 235–237
Doctor's fees, 241–245
Dogs, 19–21, 134
Dolls' houses, 118
Donck, A. van der, quoted, 10–11, 12–14, 29, 32–34, 124
Dongan, Gov., 46, 54, 199
Dress, rich, of Dutch women, 56
Drink measures regulated, 276
Drinking, immoderate, laws against, 275
Drinking-vessels, 269
Drinks, Dutch, 219, 267, 312, 318
Drinks, favorite, in New Netherland, 268
Drisius, Samuel, 187, 188, 190, 194, 196, 197, 198, 200
Drunkenness an excuse for forgetfulness, 265
Drunkenness, Dutch, 326
Drunkenness no crime, 265
Dutch service, 192–193
Dyck, Cornelis van, 90, 110

EAST INDIA goods, 83, 336, 337, 340, 342
East India pictures, 107
Ebony, 81–82
English colonists, 7
Entombment, 256, 258

Excise cases in court, 285, 286
Excise laws, 276–284
Excursions, 309

FANS, 57
Farm, the Company's, 16
Farmers, clothes of, 80
Farm-houses, 14
Farms, 4, 14–15
Farral, Joseph, 73–74, 77, 78
Fast Days, 203, 204
Fences, 19, 21–22, 40
Fencing, 178
Fiddlers, 314
Fire, danger from, 50–51
Fire-wardens, 50
Fish, 124–125
Fish suppers, 310
Fletcher Gov., 83, 336, 338, 340
Flowers, 27–30, 192
Food, 130
Foot-warmer, 135
Forks, 107, 108, 109, 110, 129
Fort, 6
Fort Amsterdam, 4, 5
Fort Orange, 2, 9, 40, 41
Fort Wilhelmus, 2
Fortune-telling, 204
Frederijcke, Krijn, 4
Free trade, 331
French, 177
Fresh Water, the, 18, 19, 38
Fruits, 27–38
Funeral expenses, 261–263
Funeral feasts, 259, 260
Funeral pomp, 258
Furniture, 81–101
Fur trade, 2, 3

GALLOWS, 10
Game, 17–18, 124
Games, 290–297
Games, winter, 311–314
Gaming-houses, 297
Garden, the Company's, 15, 30
Gardens, 14, 27–34
Gate City, 52, 53

INDEX

Gate, East River, 47
Gate, the Water, 47
Gideon, The, 156
Gin, 268
Glass, 117
Glass, window, 42-43
Glaziers, 42-43
Glover (pirate), 340
Gloves, 64, 77
Goats, 18, 19, 23, 26
Gold, Arabian, 337, 346
Gold headdress, case regarding, 65, 66-67
Golf, 290-291, 312
Governor's Island, 6
Graveraet, Mrs. E., 64, 65, 69, 77
Great Burgher right, 332

HARD drinking, 233, 271
Hardenbrook, Margaret, 46
Hats, 78-79
Head ornaments, 64-65
Heem, De, 32, 102
Heere Graght, 48
Hell Gate, 6, 311
Herb garden, 33
Herring, The, 6
Hobbema, 103
Hockey, 312
Hogs, 18, 25-26
Hondius, 28, 31
Hoods, 63
Hoorn, Cornelis, 3
Hore (pirate), 340
Horses, 15, 17
Houses, 40-41, 42, 46, 47, 89-101
Houses, furnishing of, 97
Hudson, 1
Huges, Dr. J., 240, 243
Hulst, Willem van, 3
Hutchinson, Anne, 186
Huych, Jan, 4

ICE, games on the, 292, 311-313
Illiteracy, 172
Independents, 199
Indian convert, 187

Indian labor, 330
Indians, drunken, 330
Indians, harboring, 330
Indians, illicit trade with, 330
Industries of New Netherland, 343-344
Injury, compensation for, 238
Inn, 44
Interiors, paintings of, 102-103
Irving, W., 58

JANS, Annetje, 60, 183
Jew burghers, 350
Jewels, 64-69, 222, 224-225
Jews, 127, 199, 347
Jews, disabilities of, 348-350
Jews, Stuyvesant's intolerance of, reproved, 349
Jew's-harps, 314
Jogues, Father, quoted, 8-9, 186
Jokes, practical, 233-234
Josselyn, John, quoted, 45
Justice, administration of, 3

KAETZEN, 290
Kas, kast, kasten, 83, 84-87, 93, 99
Kermis, 209, 315, 320
Kermis, Amsterdam, 316-317
Kidd, Capt., 98, 337, 338, 339
Kieft, Willem, 6, 7-8, 15, 16, 46, 184-186, 203, 315
Kierstede, surgeon, 183, 239, 241, 242
Kint in 't Water, 51-52
Kip, Jacob, house of, 45
Kissing, 311
Kissing Bridge, 311
Klootbaan, 291
Klos, 291
Knight, Madam, quoted, 54-55, 200, 313
Krol, S. J., 4

LABARDIST Fathers, 36, 43
Lange, Dr. De, 57, 67, 68, 73, 74, 75, 76, 77, 78, 79, 83, 88, 90-93, 104, 105-106, 107, 114, 116, 132, 180-181, 314

INDEX

Lange, Mrs. De, 59, 60, 61, 62, 63, 65, 67, 138
Latin, 174
Laws of trade, violation of, 332
Lawson, John, quoted, 56
Laying out the corpse, 253
Leisler, Jacob, 198
Le Nôtre, 28
Levy, Asser, 62, 68, 73, 74, 77, 78, 79, 108, 129
Levy, Mrs. Asser, 57, 59, 61
Libraries, 180
Life, daily, 120
Linen, household, 138–142
Linen, table, 127–128
Liqueurs, 268
Live-stock, care in transporting, 321
Long Island (pirate resort), 337
Long Island, religious services on, 188, 196
Lutherans, 199
Luyck, Ægidius, 175
Lying-in, 247

Mackerel, The, 2
Madagascar, a pirate clearing-house, 336, 337, 338, 339
Mahogany, 82
Maize, 14, 34
Manhattan Island, population of, 4
Manhattes, Island of, purchased, 3
Marchpane, 125, 126, 227, 300
Marius, Peter J., 65, 67, 68, 109, 129, 141, 262
Marius, Peter J., house of, 93–95
Market days, 316
Marketing, 123–125
Marriage, ceremony of, 21, 226–227
Marriage of poor people, 232
Marsepein. *See* Marchpane
Marshes, 18
Mason (pirate), 340
Masquerading, 304
Mauritius River, 1, 2, 3
May Day, 301–302, 305–306
May-pole decorated with rags, 234
May-poles, 301, 302, 305, 306

May-tree, 307
Meal, noonday, 130
Medals, funeral, 263
Medals, wedding, 230
Medicinal plants, 245–246
Megapolensis, 187, 189, 194, 197, 198
Megapolensis, Samuel, 197–198
Melons, 32
Merchant, subservient to wife, 343
Merry Mount in the Fort, 305
Michaëlius, 182
Mignon, 32, 102
Miller, John, quoted, 18, 200
Milt, A. De, 101
Minister, regulations regarding, 186–187
Minuit, Peter, 2, 4, 5, 6, 182, 183
Mirrors, 88–89
Montagne River, 1, 2
Montanus, quoted, 9–10, 11–12, 37
Moody, Lady Deborah, 186
Morris, Lewis, 156, 157, 193
Mourning, 235–236
Mourning-gloves, 261
Mourning-hatbands, 261
Mourning-rings, 261
Mourning-scarfs, 261
Muff, 57
Murderer's Island, 2

NECKWEAR, men's, 74–75
Neer, Aert van der, 103
Negro Quarter, 155
Negroes, 26, 82, 153–157, 196
Negroes, the Company's, 156–157, 160
New Amsterdam, city, 24
New Amsterdam, streets of, 47–53
New Amsterdam, view of, from bay, 324
New Netherland, The, 1, 2
New Year's Day, 203, 301–302, 306
Nicholas, Saint. *See* Saint Nicholas.
Nieuwenhuys, William, 198
Nut Island, 6
Nutwood, 3, 82, 86

INDEX

ORCHARDS, 36-38
Oriental goods, 83, 107, 108
Orphans, 136-152
Ort, Sarah, 110, 116

PALISADES, the, 47, 48
Palms, wedding, 227
Parival, De, quoted, 105, 136-137
Parrot, 134-135
Partridge, Elizabeth, 59, 61, 62, 63, 128, 129, 141
Passage money, 322
Patroons, 4
Peaches, 36-37
Pearl necklace, 225
Pearl pins, case regarding, 69
Pearl Street, 6, 39
Peasants, costume of, 70-71
Penn, Wm., 156
Perfumes, 64
Petticoat, 58-60
Pets, 134
Pewter, 112-113
Philipse, Frederick, 46
Pictures, 103-107
Pigs, 23, 24
Pinkster, 307
Pipe, bridegroom's, 218-219
Piracy, 333-341
Pirates, harboring, 335
Piratical New York merchants, 336-341
Plak, the, 166, 168-169
Playmates, 218, 219, 226, 228, 235
Play-youths, 218, 219
Plucking the Goose. *See* Pulling the Goose
Polhemus, J. T., 188
Porcelain, 113-117
Presbyterians, 199
Prince's Island, 2
Princess, The, 8, 186
Privateering, 341
Pulling the Goose, 293-296
Pumpkin, 33
Punishments, 108-109

QUAKERS, 189, 191, 192, 193-194, 199, 200
Queester, 208

RACING with carts, 296
Rain dress, the, 60
Rapelje, Sara de, 111
Rasieres, De, 4
Religion, 8, 179-180, 199-200
"Remonstrance," quotations from, 155, 162
Rensselaer, Dominie N. van, 106, 115, 142, 180
Rensselaer, Patroon van, 6, 9, 225
Rensselaerswyck, Colony of, 7, 9
Riding the Goose, 304. *See* Pulling the Goose
Rijks Museum, 117
Rings, finger, 222, 224, 225
Roelantsen, Adam, 6, 159-161
Roelofs, Sara, 172
Roman Catholics, 199
Rombouts, F., 73, 74, 76, 77, 78, 79, 99-100, 110, 115
Romeyn, The, 162
Rommel-pot, 304
Rosa Solis, 268
Ruffs, 62-63
Ruisdael, 103
Ruysch, Rachel, 32, 102

SABBATH-BREAKING, 285-288
Sacredaan, 87, 88
Sailors' freight, 333
Saint Martin's Eve, 308-309
Saint Martin's fires, 309
Saint Martin's goose, 308-309
Saint-Martin-shake-the-basket-day, 309
Saint Nicholas, 125, 126, 297-299
Saint Nicholas bread, 298, 300
Saint Nicholas cake, 298, 300
Saint Nicholas Church, 297
Saint Nicholas Eve, 297, 300
Saint Nicholas rhymes, 298, 299
Salisbury, Capt. Sylvester, 77, 148
Samare, 60-61

INDEX 359

Sausage-making evening, 314-315
Sauzeau, Mme., 129
Schœyinge, the, 47
Schoolmaster, the, 167-168
Schoolmaster, the first, 6
Schoolmasters, 159-165
Schools, 158, 159, 166, 169, 172-173
Schools, girls', 170
Schools, Latin, 174-177
Scotchmen, 332
Sea Mew, The, 2
Seawan, 327-329
Selyns, Henricus, 195-196, 198
Senneca, 297
Servants, 143-157
Sheep, 18, 23
Shelly, G. (pirate), 83, 338
Shipbuilding in New Netherland, 324
Shipping regulations, 324-325
Ships, names of, 323-324
Shoes, 64, 77
Shoes, Saint Nicholas supposed to fill, 299
Shop goods, 57-58, 345, 346
Shops, 344
Shrove-tide, 294, 304-305
Shrove Tuesday, 293, 296, 303-304
Sick, Comforters of the, 4. See Consolers of the Sick
Silver, 107-112
Skates, 312
Skating, 311-313
Skittles, 291-292
Sleepy Hollow Church, 47
Sleeve, 62
Sleighing, 311-313
Small Burgher right, 332
Smith, Col. William, 74, 79, 110
Smuggling, 24, 278, 333-334
Soldiers, first, 6
Spoons, 107, 108, 109, 110
Sport, 296
Squash, 33
Stadt Huys, 40
Staple right, 331
Staten Island, 5

States-General, 3
Steen, Jan, *Parrot Cage*, 102, 103, 126, 300
Steenwyck, C., 48, 57, 68, 69, 72-73, 74, 76, 79, 86, 106, 109, 122, 128, 130, 134, 138, 141, 156
Steenwyck, C., house of, 93-95
Stockings, 70, 76-77
Stomacher, the, 63
Storehouse, the Company's, 331
Strand, the, 39, 47, 319
Streets, 47-53
Streets, filth in the, 25-26
Streets, lighting of, 53
Stuyvesant, 24, 47, 135, 147, 150, 161, 162, 187, 190, 191, 192, 194, 195, 197, 200, 206, 293, 302, 318
Stuyvesant Bouwery, 164
Stuyvesant, dinner to, 273
Stuyvesant, garden of, 42
Stuyvesant, house of, 42
Succotash, 34
Suicides, 260
Sunday closing, 275, 279, 283
Sunday, holiday making on, 309
Sunday, keeping of, 200-203
Sunday, laws regarding, 200-203
Sunday, profanation of, 185-186
Superstition, 204-206
Supper, 134
Surgeons in New Netherland, 239-241
Swords, 79-80
Sylvester, N., 99, 116, 142

TABLES, 87
Table-ware, 128
Tankards, 110, 111
Tap-houses, grades of, 274
Tavern, 10
Tavern brawling, 272, 288
Tavern dinners, 272
Tavern games, 291, 297
Tavern keepers, women, 347
Tavern life in Holland, 265
Taverns, civic importance of, 265-266

INDEX

Taverns, Dutch, good and bad, 266
Taylor, Dr. H., 244
Taylor, Matthew, 57
Tea, 132-133
Tea, afternoon, 132
Teaching, 170
Tew (pirate), 340
Thanksgiving Day, 203
Three Kings, The, 5
Three Kings' Night, 302-303
Tienhoven, quoted, 14
Tiles, 42, 54-55
Tobacco, 37
Tobacco house, 17
Toys, 119
Toys, silver, 108
Trade, 346
Trade commodities, 325-326
Trade, Indian, 327-329
Trade, volume of (1624-35), 326
Traders, women, 347
Treating, 269
Trees, 12
Trousseau, 232-233
Twelfth Night, 302-303
Twelfth Night Cake, 302
Twiller, Wouter van, 6, 16, 159, 183
Tulip mania, 28, 30

Union, The, 6
Utrecht Museum, miniature house in, 118

VARICK, Mrs. Margarita Visboom van, 65, 67-68, 72, 83, 88, 104, 106, 108, 119, 122, 129, 130, 132, 134, 135, 139, 180, 199, 301
Varick, Rudolphus van, 198, 199
Varleth, Judith. *See* Verleth
Vasten avond, 303
Vegetables, 14, 27, 33
Velde, Adriaen van de, 103
Verleth, Casper, 212-214
Verleth, Judith, 21-22, 206, 214
Verleth, Maria, 212-214
Voorhuis, 89-91

Voyage, Atlantic, 321
Vries, De, quoted, 183-184
Vries, P. R. de, 46

WADE, 253
Walking-sticks, 79-80
Wall Street, 47
Walloons, 1, 182
Wampum, 327-329
Wassenaer, quoted, 17-18
Watch, Burgher, 52
Watch, Citizen's, 52
Watch, Rattle, 52
Watkins, Ann, 61, 62, 63
Wedding, 221
Wedding-dinner, 228-230
Wedding-entertainments, 233
Wedding-gifts, 222, 231-232
Wessels, Dr. H., 240, 244, 245
West India Company, 1, 2, 5, 6, 15, 40, 150, 153, 158, 182, 186, 194, 197
Westerbaen, 29
Whipping-post, 10
Whitehall, 39, 42, 319
Whitsuntide, 307-308
Whitsuntide bride, 307-308
Wigs, 78
Williams, Roger, 33
Winder, John, house of, 98
Windmill, 4, 39
Wine, 37
Wines drunk in Holland, 229, 267
Wines, wedding, 229
Witchcraft, 204-206
Witchcraft, trials for, 206
Witches, 204-205
Witch-finders, 205
Wittepaert, The, 156
Wolves, 19
Woods, 12, 81-83
Woolley, quoted, 313
Wounded, care of, 238

Zee-dragen. *See* Carrying into the Sea
Zoutberg, De, 6

www.ingramcontent.com/pod-product-compliance
Lightning Source LLC
Chambersburg PA
CBHW021813300426
44114CB00009BA/155